HELLENIC STUDIES 24

CONCORDIA DISCORS
Eros and Dialogue in Classical Athenian Literature

Other Titles in the Hellenic Studies Series

Plato's Rhapsody and Homer's Music
The Poetics of the Panathenaic Festival in Classical Athens

Labored in Papyrus Leaves
Perspectives on an Epigram Collection Attributed to Posidippus
(P.Mil.Vogl. VIII 309)

Helots and Their Masters in Laconia and Messenia
Histories, Ideologies, Structures

Archilochos Heros
The Cult of Poets in the Greek Polis

Master of the Game
Competition and Performance in Greek Poetry

Greek Ritual Poetics

Black Doves Speak
Herodotus and the Languages of Barbarians

Pointing at the Past
From Formula to Performance in Homeric Poetics

Homeric Conversation

The Life and Miracles of Thekla
Victim of the Muses: Poet as Scapegoat, Warrior and Hero
in Greco-Roman and Indo-European Myth and History

Amphoterōglossia
A Poetics of the Twelfth Century Medieval Greek Novel

Priene (second edition)

Plato's Symposium
Issues in Interpretation and Reception

http://chs.harvard.edu

CONCORDIA DISCORS
Eros and Dialogue in Classical Athenian Literature

Andrew Scholtz

CENTER FOR HELLENIC STUDIES
Trustees for Harvard University
Washington, D.C.
Distributed by Harvard University Press
Cambridge, Massachusetts, and London, England
2007

Concordia Discors: Eros and Dialogue in Classical Athenian Literature
    by Andrew Scholtz
Copyright © 2007 Center for Hellenic Studies, Trustees for Harvard University
All Rights Reserved.
Published by Center for Hellenic Studies, Trustees for Harvard University, Washington, D.C.
Distributed by Harvard University Press, Cambridge, Massachusetts and London, England
Production: Kristin Murphy Romano
Printed in Ann Arbor, MI by Edwards Brothers, Inc.

LIBRARY OF CONGRESS CATALOGING-IN-PUBLICATION DATA:
Scholtz, Andrew.
    Concordia discors : eros and dialogue in classical Athenian literature / by Andrew
    Scholtz.
        p. cm. — (Hellenic studies ; 24)
    Includes bibliographical references.
    ISBN 0-674-02598-9
    1. Harmony (Aesthetics) in literature. 2. Greek literature—History and criticism.
    3. Sex in literature. I. Title. II. Series.
    PA3014.H37S36 2007
    880'.9—dc22

                                                                        2007017715

For Addie
ἐγὼ δέ κέ τοι ἰδέω χάριν ἤματα πάντα.

PREFACE

THE PRESENT VOLUME ARGUES FOR "DISCORDANT HARMONY" (*concordia discors*) as an aesthetic principle where classical Athenian literature addresses politics in the idiom of sexual desire. Its approach is an untried one for such a topic. Drawing on theorists of the sociality of language, it examines various ways in which *erôs*, consuming, destabilizing desire, became a vehicle for exploring and exploiting dissonance within the songs Athenians sang about themselves. Thus it shows how societal tension and instability could register as an ideologically charged polyphony in works like the Periclean Funeral Oration, Aristophanes' *Knights* and *Assemblywomen*, and Xenophon's *Symposium*.

This book began life as a dissertation submitted in 1997 to the Department of Classics, Yale University. One chapter has appeared as an article (Scholtz 2004); various parts of it have been delivered as talks at the APA and elsewhere. Thanks go first of all to my dissertation advisor, Victor Bers, who originally steered me toward the topic, and whose friendship, advice, benevolent prodding, unstinting vetting, and constant encouragement did more than get me through when the going got rough. It offered and continues to offer an inspiring example of what dedicated mentoring is all about. Thanks go also to Gregory Nagy, Leonard Muellner, the anonymous reader for the Center for Hellenic Studies, and the editorial staff of the Center for their comments, patience, support, and expert editing and production. Readers of and/or responders to various parts of the manuscript and ideas contained therein include Binghamton University colleagues Saul Levin, Gerald Kadish (who provided invaluable comments on chapter 4), Daniel Williman, Zoja Pavlovskis-Petit, Tony Preus, and Kevin Lacy; David Konstan, whose comments on my dissertation were crucial to its development into a book; and Kurt Raaflaub and Deborah Boedeker, former directors of the Center for Hellenic Studies, where parts of the book were researched and written on a Summer Scholars fellowship in 1999. I also wish to thank Harpur College at Binghamton University for a Dean's Research Semester Award for spring 2003; without that, this book could not have been completed. Thanks, too, to colleagues from Wabash College for their advice and support: Leslie and Joe Day, John Fischer, and David Kubiak. Chief thanks go, however, to my wife and children, in particular to Addie, my wife, whose loving support and epic patience I can never repay. To her I dedicate this volume: *kharin oida*.

ABBREVIATIONS

D-K   Diels, H., and W. Krantz, eds. 1952, repr. Dublin, 1966.
      Die Fragmente der Vorsokratiker, ed. 6. Berlin.

FGrH Jacoby, F. 1957–. *Die Fragmente der griechischen Historiker*. Leiden.

PCG   Kassel, R., and C. Austin, eds. 1983–. *Poetae comici graeci*. Berlin.

PMG   Page, D. L. 1962. *Poetae melici graeci*. Oxford.

SSR   Giannantoni, G. 1990. *Socratis et Socraticorum reliquiae*. Naples.

GHI   Meiggs, R. and D. Lewis, eds. 1988. *Greek Historical Inscriptions to the End of the Fifth Century B.C.* rev. ed. Oxford.

SEG   *Supplementum epigraphicum graecum.*

TABLE OF CONTENTS

Preface vii

Abbreviations viii

CHAPTER ONE Introduction 1

CHAPTER TWO "Lovers of It":
Erotic Ambiguity in the Periclean Funeral Oration. 21

CHAPTER THREE He Loves You, He Loves You Not:
Demophilic Courtship in Aristophanes' *Knights*. 43

CHAPTER FOUR Forgive and Forget:
Concordia discors in Aristophanes' *Assemblywomen* and *Lysistrata* 71

CHAPTER FIVE Satyr, Lover, Teacher, Pimp:
Socrates and His Many Masks 111

CHAPTER SIX Conclusions. 145

Bibliography 147

Index 165

1

INTRODUCTION

Problem

WRITING TO A FRIEND, Horace describes the man as fascinated by "the discordant harmony of the cosmos, its purpose and power" (*Epistles* 1.12.19). Horace refers to Empedocles' doctrine of a world order in constant flux between cohesion and fragmentation, Love and Strife, harmony and discord. Compressed into a single concept, this flux represents, in Horace's phrase, *concordia discors*, a dynamic tension whose meaning offers something for Horace's friend to ponder.

I mention Horace's concept of *concordia discors* because, as I argue in this book, it will help us understand the fit between text and context, representation and reality, in literature produced under the classical Athenian democracy. For that fit is, by its very nature, susceptible to destabilization in ways described by David Konstan:

> Where society is riven by tensions and inequalities of class, gender, and status, its ideology will be complex and unstable, and literary texts will betray signs of the strain involved in forging such refractory materials into a unified composition.[1]

Texts will always bear the stamp of their social-cultural-political matrix. But when they actively engage tensions within that matrix, when they reflect on what throws their world off balance, then we often find "lapses in unity at the level of plot and characterization"[2] — ambient dissonance, one might call it, marring the harmonious unity of the literary *Kunstwerk*.

---

[1] Konstan 1995:5.
[2] Konstan 1995:6.

1

An example will help. Produced in 424 BCE, Aristophanes' comedy the *Knights* could be described as a play with not one but two plots.[3] Of course, those are not really separate plots but different ways of "spinning" one, basic story line, the unlikely tale of a Sausage-Seller's rise from humble street-vendor to democratic leader. But that one plot seems to end up in different places: on the one hand, with the ouster of the play's demagogic villain and the restoration of the ancestral democracy; on the other, with all three main characters, comic stand-ins for politicians and the Athenian body politic, pursuing self-interest at its most unenlightened and narrowly defined. Again, those are not separate sub-plots, but discrepancies in the development of a single, master plot — discrepancies projecting ambivalence about democracy as a system in which the collectivity, the *dêmos*, has succeeded to the powers, perks, and vulnerabilities of an absolute monarch,[4] a system freeing individuals and groups to compete in a zero-sum game destabilizing the system.[5]

And through it all runs the theme of *erôs*, desire to possess and dominate love-objects — pleasure, power, honor, wealth — that in their turn possess and dominate the desiring subject. But what about the playwright's ambition — his *erôs* — to win a favorable hearing for his play?[6] Is it not ironic that Aristophanes, to make his critique stick, avails himself of a *rhêtôr*'s trick in attacking tricky rhetoric, and goes in for some audience-bonding of his own when satirizing the audience-bonding of politicians? We see, then, our playwright fighting rhetoric with rhetoric and doubtless enjoying himself in the process. But to the extent that his play mirrors what its satire targets, does it not at some level bite its own tail? Does not any work that goes in for social or political commentary, yet voices its critique from within the frame of its focus?

---

[3] So Brock 1986.

[4] "Tyranny"-despotism of the people, "slavery" of tyranny: Aristophanes *Knights* 1111–1114, 1330; *Wasps* 518, 548–549; Thucydides 2.63.2; Plato *Republic* 572e–573b; Aristotle *Politics* 1292a11–17; Wohl 2002:105–123, 215–269; McGlew 1993:183–212.

[5] Cf. Darius on the instabilities of oligarchy and democracy: Herodotus 3.82. Thucydides on the shape of Athenian democracy after the death of Pericles: 2.65.10, with Rusten's note, 1989:211–212. Thucydides on *stasis*: 3.81–84. See also Rosenbloom 2004b; Rosenbloom 2004a on the stasiastic atmosphere at Athens in the post-Periclean period; chapter 3 below for Aristophanes' *Knights*.

[6] Aristophanes compares the challenges of comedy producing to "having a go at," and seeking "gratification" from, a sexual love object: *Knights* 517, for which LSJ s.v. πειράω A.II.2 citing the scholiast *ad loc.*

Symptomatic Reading

Let me stress that those are not rhetorical questions, but genuine problems. How, then, to proceed? If our aim will be to take the pulse of attitudes and assumptions in the classical city, then "symptomatic reading" like that pursued by Konstan and others has much to offer.[7] What is symptomatic reading? We can think of it as interpretation sensitive to the symptoms of a text's blind-spot to social, political, or other forces at work in its production — reading, in other words, that "palpates" texts for surface anomalies and deeper instabilities, for lapses in ideological coherence. This approach owes much to post-structural and psychoanalytic theory,[8] but its chief debt will be to philosopher Louis Althusser, who coined the term "symptomatic reading,"[9] and whose concept of ideology as "a system . . . of representations" with a "role" to play "within a given society" more or less describes what symptomatic reading is all about.[10]

Being a Marxist, Althusser understood that role chiefly within a modern, capitalist context, one very different from classical Athens. Yet Athens, a developed society reliant on a sizable citizenry's acquiescence and participation in its institutions, ought to offer a proving ground as suitable as any for Althusser's view that "ideology represents the imaginary relationship of individuals to their real conditions of existence."[11] Ideology supplies us, one might say, with a "backstory" to explain who we are and why we do what we do, a script for how we are to visualize ourselves as autonomous subjects. In so doing, it "interpellates" us; it beckons us to assume ready-made identities, and to fulfill pre-set roles, within the social matrix.[12] To illustrate, Althusser offers the image of a grand music lesson teaching us society's songs, a score harmonizing our relationship to our "real conditions of existence." With these themes swimming in our ears, we imagine that we are in control of our destinies, whereas the song actually controls us[13] — such is the music that finds its way into the texts we read, study, and teach. The symptomatic critic's task will then be to help "listeners" — readers — snap out of it, to hear off-key notes, to

---

[7] Wohl 2002; Monoson 2000:21–50; Konstan 1995.

[8] See Wohl 2002:20–29; Konstan 1995:3–11.

[9] Althusser and symptomatic reading: Montag 2003:82–84; Payne 1997:74–75; Althusser 1977:28–30.

[10] Quoting Althusser 1979:231.

[11] Althusser 1972:162; also 127–186; Montag 2003:77–80; Althusser 1979:231–236.

[12] Interpellation: Althusser 1972:170–186.

[13] Althusser 1972:154–155.

become attuned to the feedback generated when texts try to encompass the social forces conditioning their production and reception.

What insights has symptomatic reading to offer? Important ones, I would suggest. For it shows just how much we can learn from writings whose "music," though originally meant for ears very different from ours, still resonates with just that sort of feedback. So, for instance, Victoria Wohl brilliantly psychoanalyzes the mindset of an Athens "hopelessly smitten with far-off things," as Thucydides' Nicias puts it (6.13.1). In the process, she brings to light lapses in the historian's telling of the tale, lapses that bespeak a kind of *hubris* on Thucydides' part. Just as Athens would find itself tripped up by *erôs* to dominate other lands and peoples, so the historian's ambition to produce a master narrative, a "possession for all time" (1.22.4), ultimately masters his efforts to capture city-*erôs*, that quintessentially irrational emotion, in rational discourse.[14]

Dialogical Reading

But I would still ask how *rounded* a view of the fit between text and context will come from stressing the latter as destabilizing in relation to the former. Even granting such instabilities, what can we learn by viewing them *a*symptomatically, as somehow integral to the structure of texts manifesting them? To find out, I follow an aesthetic approach — "aesthetic" not in the commonly understood sense of "beauty-related" nor in any purely formalist sense, but as Mikhail Bakhtin, the twentieth-century Russian theorist, uses the term. In "Author and Hero in Aesthetic Activity," Bakhtin lays out a highly original phenomenology of authorship as the perceiving subject's encounter with objects and subjects (fictitious, factual, in between) populating his or her purview, and of texts as records of that "seeing" — or one might say "hearing."[15] Building on that, I argue that texts, as aesthetic artifacts, can register contextual instability as *concordia discors*, by which I mean an ideologically charged polyphony constitutive of a text's *Sturm und Drang* on the analogy of musical dissonance in tonal harmony.

---

[14] Instabilities in Thucydides' Sicilian and herm-mutilation narrative: Wohl 2002:21–25, 152–158, 203–214. Cf. Parry's and Dover's comments quoted p. 212n80 and p. 213.

[15] Bakhtin 1990:4–256, where the term "aesthetics" (Russian *estetika*) draws close to Greek *aisthêtika*, "things pertaining to perception." In an intertextual model of authorship, that "seeing" additionally involves an author's confrontation with, and assimilation of, other texts; see Edmunds 2001.

That way of thinking about polyphony, though it leans heavily on Bakhtin, will not have found favor with the critic who famously hailed Dostoevsky as the first truly "polyphonic" author.[16] But I do not mean by "polyphony" exactly what Bakhtin does, namely, a counter-hierarchical leveling of speaking voices, including the author's.[17] Closer to what I mean is Bakhtin's "heteroglossia," the "socio-ideological contradictions" authors give "bodily form" to in their texts.[18] Closer still is Edith Hall's notion of tragic dialogue as a polyphony of voices rising up to challenge assumptions cherished by tragedy's target audience, yet constituting a discourse — that of tragedy — celebrating the very values tragedy put on trial.[19] Extending that idea to a whole range of genres and discourses, I ask whether dissonance like that described by Hall does not deserve to be included within a text's aesthetic horizon.

I should, at this point, stress the dialogical dimension of the question I pose, one concerned with how voices — ideological perspectives — embodied in texts "address" (in more than one sense of the term) the worlds they observe, one another, and the audiences they speak to. For help, I turn to the work of Bakhtin and his circle, thinkers who laid the groundwork for dialogical theory almost a century ago.[20] What is dialogical theory? Premised on the notion that utterance does not simply express but responds, dialogical theory asks *how* utterance responds, among other things, to the objects and subjects within the field of a speaker's or writer's seeing. Texts provide, then, a record of that seeing, a record of authorial response. Here, the distinction between inner and outer seeing, imagination and reality, matters less than the process itself: how an author's seeing supplies raw material for symbolic representation, for a narrative, a *text*. And it is in the process of individuating and identifying the elements

---

[16] Bakhtin 1981:178.

[17] Polyphony: Morson and Emerson 1990:231–268.

[18] Bakhtin 1981:291, describing language generally. Cf. ibid. on prose fiction, where today's and yesterday's ideological languages are often given "embodied representation . . . in unresolvable dialogues." The preceding, from Bakhtin's "Discourse in the Novel" (1934–1935), does not square with the same critic's 1961 notes for the second edition of his Dostoevsky study: "Discord is poor and unproductive. Heteroglossia is more essential, in effect, it gravitates towards concord, where the voices are always preserved as different and unmerged" (trans. Plaza 2005:220). Bakhtin's own dialogue with discord produced no satisfying resolution.

[19] Hall 1997:118. Bakhtin himself was careful to distinguish polyphony from heteroglossia (*raznorecie*, literally "multi-speechedness"): Morson and Emerson 1990:232. In Hall's "polyphonic tragic form," the two ideas operate simultaneously yet independently.

[20] Bakhtin 1990; Vološinov 1986; Bakhtin and Medvedev 1985; Vološinov 1983; Bakhtin 1981. The Bakhtin circle: Brandist 2002a; Brandist and Tikhanov 2000.

populating one's seeing, of making connections and of finding ways to communicate those connections, that texts take shape.[21]

But authors do not just respond to their seeing; they respond as well to audiences and readers. For all utterance, literary and otherwise, anticipates response, which shapes utterance already at its point of origin. Think of it this way: If thought can somehow affect other thought, influence it somehow, by whatever means, through whatever channels, then we can think of the word as the articulation of that interaction, as the shaping and reshaping of that interface — as thought in conversation with thought. But what if we allow ourselves to imagine the unimaginable: that all thought is locked up within itself, unable to make contact with its outside? For our purposes, what matters is not the reality of external consciousness, but its effect on internal consciousness, even at the purely imaginary level, where merely to imagine another is to be affected by that other. Thus when I express myself, that is, "push" thought "outward" (Latin *exprimere*), my effort, through its outward directedness, posits an outside and, in so doing, anticipates response. Whether or not anyone is actually listening or reading or ever will do so at whatever remove is not the point. It is, rather, that utterance, even if we view it as hermetically sealed within its own act, still feels around the edges of its act, still presses outward toward the world. For the word exists at the edge between the speaking/writing subject and that world.[22] And it is that kind of intentionality, the word as social gesture, a verbal "reaching forth" (Latin *intendere*) as if to shake hands, on which notions of the utterance as dialogical are founded.

Which is not to deny words semantic force. It is, rather, to assert the importance of social considerations along with semantics. Vološinov illustrates with the interjection "well!" — in Russian, *tak*. "Taken in isolation," Vološinov writes, "the utterance 'well!' is void and quite meaningless."[23] In context, though, it becomes something else: a potential point of contact and shared understanding between individuals, as when someone turns to a companion and, with his or her "well!," conveys an attitudinal stance toward something within the purview of both.[24] Does that mean that words at their moment of use achieve a fixed, determinate meaning? It means that through

---

[21] Dialogue and architectonics (the structuring of authorial seeing): Holquist 1990; Morson and Emerson 1990 passim.

[22] All speech-acts, including monologue and "inner speech," presume a respondent, notional or actual: Vološinov 1986:38, 95.

[23] Vološinov 1983:10.

[24] Brandist 2004:108–111; Brandist 2002a:62–66; Vološinov 1983:10–13.

communication, we negotiate our relationships with others, with our world, and, not least, with the meanings and values carried by the words we use.

Important here is the notion of the speech-act, a concept mostly associated with J. L. Austin,[25] but with a history going back to the work of Karl Bühler, whose Sprechakt consists of three stages, distinct only in the abstract: notification, representation, and triggering. To that correspond three positions of the utterance: speaker, state of affairs (i.e. subject matter), and hearer or responder.[26] Vološinov, influenced by Bühler, extends that schema in the direction of the social. Through dialogue, we set up between ourselves what Vološinov terms an "ideological chain": we enact social bonds by sharing information, ideas, values, mindsets.[27] Meaning here is not illusory or evanescent, but neither is it stationary or absolute. Rather, it is continually re-transacted socially: it *evolves*. Through multiple speech-acts, a speech-community takes shape, and with that a shared consciousness grounding further dialogue.[28] Key to the process is evaluation, the attitudinal stance one takes to what one sees, hears, experiences, reads. Evaluation registered in speech Vološinov calls "evaluative accent." Through these accents, whether expressed intonationally, lexically, or otherwise, speakers convey their response to — whether they "connect" or fail to connect with — something someone else has said or done. Evaluation thus underpins the sociality of language. And ideology is, at base, social evaluation expressed through signs: "*Without signs there is no ideology*."[29]

This view of ideology is not so very different from Althusser's. As Michael Gardiner notes, Bakhtin (but this applies as well to Vološinov and Medvedev) resembles Althusser and Gramsci because he "conceives of ideology not as epiphenomena, or as a distorted representation of the 'real', but as a material force in its own right."[30] Even so, in the writings of Bakhtin and his circle, ideology presents us with a distinctively complex dimensionality, a force

---

[25] Austin 1975.

[26] Here I closely paraphrase the summary provided by Brandist 2002a:63–64.

[27] "Ideological chain": Vološinov 1986:11.

[28] Edmunds 2001:23–34 questions whether literature generally, and poetry in particular "does things" in the Austinian sense (e.g. the marriage formula "I do!"). Dialogical theory holds that, at the *social* level, all speech does something: it reaches out. For speech-community, cf. "discourse community" in Schiappa 1992; Lakoff and Johnson describing the socio-linguistic maneuvering involved in bridging cultural divides, 1980:231–232.

[29] Vološinov 1986:9 (author's emphasis). See generally Neuman and Tabak 2003:266; Bakhtin 1990:15–16, 41, 103–104; Bakhtin 1986:69; Vološinov 1986; Bakhtin and Medvedev 1985. Language as social was Saussure's breakthrough insight; meaning as social evaluation, that of the Bakhtin circle.

[30] Gardiner 1992:7. Bakhtin and Gramsci: Brandist 1996.

exerting itself along multiple vectors: top-down (monological discourse, "the word of the fathers"), down-up (carnival, popular culture), and across (dialogue). These multiple evaluative accents reflect multiple worldviews; they can crisscross through one and the same utterance, even a single word.[31] Conversely, that word can become the site for multiple practices to be sized-up against each other and treated as ideologically commensurable.

Dialogical and Deconstructive Reading

We have, then, this notion of an ideological chain that both enables and enacts dialogue. But one still wonders what it might mean if these connections were to prove more imaginary than real — whether, in other words, Vološinov's ideological chain represents just another instance of what Derrida calls the "metaphysics of presence," the habit of privileging certain modes of discourse as inherently more "true" than others, as better equipped to connect discursive subjects with one another and with their objects of thought.[32] Do, then, dialogical approaches fail to account for fissures that, according to Derrida's way of thinking, accompany all communicative acts?

For Bakhtin and others of his circle, dialogue clearly represents a privileged discursive mode, a step up from the monological, normative discourses Bakhtin decried in life and art. But I am not sure it instantiates a metaphysics of presence. For when we reach out to forge a discursive connection, we necessarily gesture to the many gaps between us,[33] to the ruptures between verbal intention and verbal effect — to meaning as irreducibly differential.[34] Just as Derrida made it his mission to expose the flawed thinking behind what he also termed logocentrism, so, too, dialogue rejects the authority of the word as transparent, final, unambiguous. Yet whereas Derrida critiques notions of communication as unmediated transmission, Bakhtin celebrates *mediated* communication as "re-accentuation": the reception, evaluation, and transformational diffusion of another's word.[35] At no point does the word stay the same; at each link in the chain, words and texts pick up new spin, and from

---

[31] ". . . each living ideological sign has two faces, like Janus. Any current curse word can become a word of praise, any current truth must inevitably sound to many other people as the greatest lie," Vološinov 1986:23. Cf. revalorization of "bad," "ill," and "sick" in popular usage.

[32] For an overview, Derrida 1991:3–139.

[33] Absence as necessary precondition for communication: Derrida 1982:314–318.

[34] See Derrida 1982:1–27.

[35] Dentith 1995:98–99; Bakhtin 1981:417–422.

that, new life. Thus if Derrida indispensably reveals tears in the discursive fabric, Bakhtin and his circle no less indispensably remind us of forces holding it taught and responsive. Let me, then, propose for dialogue not a metaphysics but an *erotics* of presence: our longing to span the spaces between us through our signaling.[36]

So rather than contest the insights of an Althusser or Derrida, I hope to engage them dialogically: to explore the chemistry between discursive subjects without ignoring ruptures in the discursive continuum, to understand authorship as a process simultaneously structured and subverted by the *concordia discors* of social reality — as itself *concordia discors*. At times I shall focus on rhetoric, especially, its ideological grounding, at times, on substance. But one needs to be careful not to draw too strict a distinction; at best, rhetoric and substance are only different ways of looking at the same thing. So, too, the distinction between an author's depiction of the world and that world's intrusions into his or her text, between dissonance represented and dissonance reproduced, will not always hold, not if texts do neither more nor less than record an author's struggle to grasp and convey what he or she sees.

Contextual Considerations: *Erôs* and *polis*

Politics and *erôs* have come up in the preceding and will figure prominently in what follows. It is, therefore, important to convey a basic sense of what *erôs* meant to classical Athenians, and how for them it could overlap or connect with politics. Let us begin, then, with *erôs* — what is it? It is desire, potentially, for anything: wealth, power, pleasures of all sorts. But its default association was with sexual lust.[37] That was not always the case. Early Greek seems to have distinguished between, on the one hand, *erôs/erŏs*, an "all-purpose" appetite of varying levels of intensity, for instance, for food and drink (Homer *Iliad* 1.468), and, on the other hand, *himeros*, "compulsive desire of external origin," among other things, for sex.[38] Later, that distinction seems to have waned. *Himeros* could still refer to overpowering desire, but classical Greek (ca. 500–ca. 300 BCE), especially Attic prose, will prefer to call it *erôs*. Hence *erôs* as desire

---

[36] Dialogue versus deconstruction, de Man's deconstruction of dialogue: Morson and Emerson 1990:324–325.

[37] Cf. LSJ s.v. ἔρως; Dover 1989:43.

[38] Weiss 1998:49–50; see also Ben 1986:10–11. Cf. *himeros* in the "Nestor's Cup" inscription: *SEG* xiv 604; *GHI* #1, on which Weiss 1998:50–51; Faraone 1996.

that seizes control of one from the outside, that afflicts one like a madness or disease — desire undiminished by fulfillment or frustration.[39]

What, then, to make of *erôs* as a specifically *political* emotion? Arguing that "eros is not merely a metaphor for politics but also its object and arena and part of the mechanism of its operation,"[40] Victoria Wohl aptly borrows from Lacan the term "quilting point" to describe how both *erôs* and politics cut across the same psychic territory, a plane on which dominance, subjection, and desire all come into play.[41] But I would return to a point to which Wohl alludes: that *erôs* provided Greeks with metaphors through which to talk *about* politics. I would expand that point as follows: *erôs*, sexual *erôs* especially, provided a shared consciousness upon which to ground political discourse, if not always the discourse of politics itself (we shall see that *erôs*-language shows up but little in assembly rhetoric and related evidence), then discourse *about* politics. Take, for instance, Socrates in Plato's *Gorgias*. Commenting on shared emotion as a dialogical bridge, a point of recognition between speaker and listener, Socrates might as well be describing the forging of that first link in Vološinov's ideological chain. As it turns out, Socrates is not just offering a random observation. For he uses *erôs* to open a channel to a skeptical Callicles. Both he and Callicles have loved, so Callicles must know what Socrates means. But Socrates also uses those commonalities as a way to accentuate areas of difference, to size up his — Socrates' — own love for philosophy against Callicles' for politics (481c–d).

Of course, Socrates' point is not just that he and Callicles love differently, but that Socrates, because he loves wisdom, not the Athenian body politic (the *dêmos*), loves *better*. Thus he uses *erôs* as an evaluative grid to show that Callicles' conduct does not, in fact, measure up. But *erôs* here represents more than an instrument by which to gauge same and different, better and worse. Through *erôs*, Socrates taps into the Athenian imaginary, that great sea of

---

[39] *Erôs* overcoming one from the outside: Sappho 47 L-P; Ibycus 286 *PMG*; Aeschylus *Agamemnon* 341; Euripides' *Iphigenia at Aulis* 808; Thucydides 6.24.3. *Erôs* = madness (*mania*): Plato *Phaedrus* 241a, 244a–245c, etc.; cf. Archilochus 191 West; Theognis 1231, for which Müller 1980:163, 149–199; Euripides *Iphigenia at Aulis* 1264–1265. *Erôs* (sexual and non-sexual) as pathological, incapacitating: Hippocrates *De mulierum affectibus* i–iii 177; *De virginum morbis* i; *De humoribus* 9; Thucydides 3.45.5; Erasistratus 25–27 Garofalo; Winkler 1991:222–223. *Erôs* as fortified *epithumia* ("desire"): Xenophon *Memorabilia* 3.9.7; Prodicus fr. 7 D-K; cf. Isocrates 10.55. *Erôs* sharpened by separation: Thucydides 6.13.1; Carson 1986:30. Satisfaction leads to intensification: Foucault 1990:49–50, 66. See generally Ludwig 2002:121–157; Wohl 2002; Thornton 1997; Dover 1989:42–49; Carson 1986.

[40] Wohl 2002:26–27.

[41] Wohl 2002:2.

images and feelings swimming within the Athenian unconscious. In so doing, Socrates exteriorizes and reifies feeling; he seeks to create a sense that all who share certain basic notions of masculine dignity and civic autonomy have their eye on Callicles and do not like what they see.

In this book, we shall view *erôs* as just such a grid, a way to charge the evaluative accents of political discourse with intense feeling — a touchstone, in other words, for a shared ideology. Have we, though, evidence for *erôs* as an image widely circulated in the social and political discourses of the classical city? We cannot, of course, go back and listen in on conversations in the agora. I would, however, suggest that we know enough to piece together a rudimentary sort of context. True, the texts we use to frame our target texts need their own framing, their own context.[42] But that larger framing comes from the whole into which all these parts fit. And it is that fit that interests us, the relationality of parts to whole and *vice versa*.

Allowing, then, relevant features of ancient culture to fill in needed background, we shall find what we are looking for in, among other places, the Tyrannicide legend: the story of how a pederastic couple murdered a tyrant and, through that violent act, founded the Athenian democracy in 514 BCE. Of course, no democracy was, in fact, founded that year. Nor did the historical "tyrant-slayers" in fact slay the reigning tyrant; they killed his brother. Indeed, revenge, not regime change, appears to have been foremost on their minds.[43] But that did not prevent the Athenian public from celebrating the killing as the single most important and symbolically resonant event in Athens' march to democracy.[44]

Of interest to us will be the bond between the two friends, how it could connote two dynamics with wide resonance in the evidence: "self-assertive *erôs*," the desire for personal autonomy, power, and self-actualization, and "communal *erôs*," the collective desire to come together as one. But before discussing that, I would emphasize the pederastic, that is, sexual, nature of

---

[42] The problem is well articulated in Dougherty and Kurke 1998:1–6; Derrida 1982:322–327.

[43] Hipparchus, brother of the reigning tyrant Hippias, had courted, but was rebuffed by, Harmodius, already the beloved of Aristogeiton. The jilted lover insulted Harmodius and his family; Harmodius and Aristogeiton plotted against Hipparchus and (of necessity) Hippias. Hipparchus, Harmodius, and Aristogeiton were killed; Hippias and his tyranny survived. But there is no single, canonical version: Herodotus 5.55, 6.109.3, 123; Thucydides 1.20.2, 6.54.1–59.1; Aristotle *Constitution of the Athenians* 18; Plato *Hipparchus* 229b–d; Wohl 2002:3–10, 210–213; Monoson 2000:21–50; McGlew 1993:150–156; Pomeroy 1975:75–76.

[44] E.g. 893–896 *PMG*; cf. Plato *Symposium* 182c. For these commemorations, including hero cult, a famous sculpture group in the Agora, and a grand tomb in the Ceramicus, Monoson 2000:22–28 with notes, citations, and bibliography.

the bond obtaining between our two Tyrannicides. Thus Aristogeiton, the older of the two, was the *erastês*, which is to say, the desiring partner. He, not Harmodius, felt *erôs* — or at least, that was how pederasty was supposed to work. Along with that went a kind of senior rank in the relationship, and, under the protocols of pederasty in its more respectable, quasi-institutional aspect, the expectation that the senior partner would mentor the junior.[45] But there was a side to pederasty besides the pedagogical or sexual: the *competitive* side. A handsome youth like Harmodius could expect multiple admirers, all vying for the honor of the "conquest." Rival lovers fought;[46] losers clearly felt the sting of defeat and might spitefully try to sabotage the boy's reputation.[47]

Clearly, something like that occurs in the Tyrannicide narrative, in which Aristogeiton, a "middling citizen" and a "man of the people" (*anêr tôn astôn, mesos politês*), "held" Harmodius as a kind of possession (*eikhen*) — that in contrast to Hipparchus' failure (Thucydides 6.54.2–3), symbolically, at least, a blow to tyranny itself.[48] Or, as Plato's Socrates puts it, Aristogeiton, regarding Hipparchus as his "competitor" (*antagonistên*), prided himself in being the one to have "educated" the lad (*Hipparchus* 229c). Thus to ordinary Athenian men, themselves conventionally figured as *mesoi politai*, "middling citizens" like Aristogeiton, Harmodius' lover would have represented a role model, an example of what the non-aristocrat could achieve against the forces of tyranny and in competition with aristocracy.[49] Politically, that would have meant a lot, to judge from a passage suggesting a close link between democratic freedom, self-determination, and individual motivation. According to Herodotus, Athenians, when they finally found themselves freed of their tyrants, fought better for the city because each man felt that he was fighting for himself. And it was "equality of speech" (*isêgoria*) that made them feel that way, the sense that each and every voting citizen, because empowered to speak his mind in the assembly, had a say in the city's destiny.[50]

---

[45] Dover 1989 remains the chief source.

[46] See passages collected and discussed in Dover 1989:54–57.

[47] Aristophanes *Wasps* 1025–1027; Cohen 1991:196–197.

[48] Herodotus states that both Aristogeiton and Harmodius came from the same aristocratic clan of *Gephuraioi* (5.55, 57.1, 62.1), but Thucydides' version, in which only Harmodius appears to be aristocratic, arguably reflects popular tradition.

[49] Wohl 2002:7–8. The *mesos*, the "middle-class" peasant farmer, from about the 420s on, seems to have been adopted as poster-child by moderate democrats and oligarchs: Euripides' *Suppliants* 244–245; cf. the Herald's abuse (implicitly suspect) targeting democratic bumpkins at Athens, 417–422; see Carter 1986:88–98.

[50] Herodotus 5.78; cf. Eupolis fr. 316 *PCG*; Pseudo-Xenophon 1.6–7; Demosthenes 15.18; 60.28; Monoson 2000:56–60; Ober 1989:296–298.

Self-Assertive *erôs*

We have seen that, for Athenian citizen-men, Aristogeiton's victory over his rival could carry political resonance. But what if we reverse the terms? Does, in other words, this narrative and its reception suggest a *sexual* side to the average citizen's sense of his autonomy, privileges, and powers? Since others have already argued as much (p. 11n43 above), I shall leave it at that. But I would still like to elaborate on the erotics of civic empowerment and self-actualization, though in contexts outside the Tyrannicide legend.

This idea that civic self-assertion could find erotic expression owes much to David Halperin, who detects in a variety of sources a sexually empowered Everyman, a "penetrator" of sexual, social, and political inferiors: women, slaves, foreigners.[51] But that schema's varied articulations also reveal shifting evaluations: the closer to "home," politically or socially, the object of domination, the more problematic. Nowhere do we see that more clearly than in the case of the tyrant's *erôs*[52] — vividly, in fact, when aspiring tyrants and conquerors dream the Oedipal dream, where "mother" equals the land that gives one birth, and sex with her, conquest and rule.[53] On the one hand, that suggests connections between war, politics, and sex, as if they could in similar ways fulfill male fantasies of domination. But evidence seems also to transfer the transgressive character of incest ("unlawful" in Plutarch, a "violation" [*stuprum*] in Suetonius) to the inordinate power wielded by despots over their compatriots, their political "kin."[54]

Put simply, tyranny posed a threat to the *polis* and to the citizen's franchise — a threat from within. That schema, tyranny as systemic dysfunction, finds expression in one Presocratic thinker's metaphor for bodily health. We are told that Alcmaeon described physical illness as "monarchy" (*monarkhia*, "rule by one"), where just one of the body's elements or "powers" (the hot, the cold, etc.) rules

---

[51] Halperin 1990:88–112. Cf. the Eurymedon vase, ethnic-military dominance expressed sexually: Smith 1999; Davidson 1997:180–182; Cohen 1991:184; Dover 1989:105; Pinney 1984; Schauenberg 1975. Also Eupolis' *Poleis*, where subject states figure as desirable women: Rosen 1997. Debate over the (a)symmetries and symbolics of ancient Greek sexuality, p. 54n41 below.

[52] Erotics of tyranny: Archilochus 19.3 West; Sophocles *Oedipus the King* 587–8; Herodotus 1.96.2, 3.53.4; 5.32; Isocrates 8.65, 113; Plato *Republic* 572e–573c; Wohl 2002:215–269; McGlew 1993:183–212; Rothwell 1990:39.

[53] Herodotus 6.107.1–2; Plutarch *Caesar* 32.9; Suetonius *Julius* 7.2. Cf. Artemidorus 1.78, where the dreamer *arkhei* ("rules") over a "willing" partner in incest, just as he "will stand at the head of the affairs of his city."

[54] In Suetonius, Caesar's mother — Mother Earth — is *subiectam* in his dream. *subigere* in sexual contexts ordinarily refers to the male-active role: Adams 1982:4, 155–156; cf. *subegit* in Suetonius *Julius* 49.4.

over the others. Health, by contrast, he explained in terms of equality or *isonomia*, a balanced mixture of those same powers (fr. 4 D-K). Again, Alcmaeon will have been addressing bodily health, not politics. But his language — *dunameis* ("powers"), *isonomia, monarkhia* — suggests he was working from a political analogy.

What counts for us is that a similar schema structured how Athenians viewed tyranny as both a foil and a model for their democracy. As we have seen, the killing of a supposed tyrant marked for Athenians the beginnings of democracy, what they in their drinking songs called *isonomia*, "equality," a balanced distribution of prerogatives once held by the city's tyrant-rulers.[55] Thus democracy could in the popular imagination equate with a kind of collective tyranny. So long as *everyone* was tyrant, then *no one* was, and all was well.[56]

Yet even with democracy firmly in place, people could still fear that the process might turn back on itself, that powers, passions, and license might revert to a few or one.[57] That fear found plenty to feed it in Alcibiades, a charismatic orator and general who, at the height of his influence, was widely suspected of aiming at tyranny.[58] And, of course, that fear found fulfillment in the bloody revolutions of 411 and 404. But it also found expression in satire targeting leaders like Pericles, whose quasi-monarchial authority the comic poet Cratinus lampooned as the despotism of a Zeus-like tyrant.[59]

Tyranny could, then, figure as individualism run amuck, a threat to the *polis* from within. But so could excessive competition between political rivals. Thucydides writes about the post-Periclean democracy as a system beset by *stasis*, "factionalism" or "discord," with one leader as bad as the next trying to claw his way to the top.[60] In a similar vein, Plato's Socrates compares competition for office to the brawling of rival lovers (*anterastai, Republic* 521b), a comparison growing out of his characterization of politics-as-usual as shadowboxing and *stasis* (520c). Those views, Thucydides' and Plato's, arguably reflect bias against radical democracy as *polupragmosunê*, the meddling of men unworthy to lead. But that sort of bias will not account for every such view, as when Thucydides presents ambition and greed as motivation for individuals and groups, oligarchs as well as democrats, to gamble the city's wellbeing on

---

[55] The catchphrase for the early democracy seems to have been *isonomia*, "equality": frr. 893, 896 *PMG*; Herodotus 3.80.6; Ober 1989:74–75.

[56] Tyranny and democratic sovereignty, tyrannical surfeit and lack: p. 2n4 above.

[57] See pp. 73–74, 78 below.

[58] See Wohl 2002:124–170.

[59] Cratinus fr. 258 *PCG*; cf. Telecleides fr. 45 *PCG*; Thucydides 2.65.9; Plutarch *Pericles* 16.1–3; see Schwartze 1971:11n13.

[60] Thucydides 2.65.10. For the post-Periclean *stasis*, Rosenbloom 2004a; Rosenbloom 2004b.

the single-minded pursuit of personal or factional interests (3.82). Hence *stasis* as a manifestation of *erôs* — the *erôs* of those whose ambition (their "fierce *erôs* for renown") threatens to plunge the city in *stasis* if it cannot find foreign enemies to keep it busy (Aeschylus *Eumenides* 861–866). No surprise, then, that *erôs* could itself be seen as inherently stasiastic.[61]

To sum-up, Aristogeiton, lover and supposed tyrant-slayer, became a touchstone for a civically and sexually empowered masculinity, a cynosure for social dialogue expressing male-Athenian desire. Still, desire as one might, to actualize empowerment in self-interested ways, to be seen using one's right of free speech to push policy benefiting not the many but just a few or even one — *that* prospect summoned misgivings lest ambition develop into a rapacious kind of *erôs*. For individualism, once it entered the public sphere, found itself face to face with a rival value: communitarianism.

Communal *erôs*

It is, therefore, curious that communitarianism could likewise figure as *erôs*. Again, Harmodius and Aristogeiton will illustrate. Earlier, we examined Aristogeiton as model for democratic self-actualization, a socially and politically approved pattern so long as the well-being of the group was not threatened. But his collaboration with Harmodius, and its basis in *erôs*, for Athenians could also model the kind of unity that held the city's enemies at bay, whether at home or abroad. It is important to keep in mind that this is not some new sort of *erôs*, different from the preceding. In distinguishing between "self-assertive" and "communal *erôs*," I am distinguishing between different ways of inflecting the same thing. Self-interest persists, as does a sense of phallic victory. Only now, these reside in team effort, in the bond formed by lover and beloved fighting for the city[62] — in the desire to become part of a larger and stronger collective self.[63]

Crucial here is the power of love to draw people together, a power poets liken to a cosmic force. In Hesiod's *Theogony*, Eros, one of the first-born, makes possible all the couplings whence come the gods, humans, everything.[64] So, too, Empedocles identifies a sexually inflected Love, variously labeled Philotes, Philia, Harmonia, Gethosyne ("Joy"), and Aphrodite, as the force drawing

---

[61] See pp. 65–66 below.

[62] See especially Wohl 2002:5; Monoson 2000:25–26, 31–32 on the elements of erotic male bonding and democratic-phallic threat embodied in the fifth-century statuary group of the Tyrannicides.

[63] As e.g. in Aristophanes' famous myth in Plato's *Symposium* (189c–193e), on which Ludwig 2002:27–118.

[64] See West 1966:195 on Hesiod *Theogony* 120. Cf. Acusilaus 2 F 6 *FGrH*; Parmenides fr. 13 D-K; Plato *Symposium* 178a–180b.

the universe into a harmonious whole out of the strife or *neikos* into which it periodically descends.[65] Aristotle remarks that "*erôs* seems to resemble *philia*" — affection or love — since the lover "hungers" for the pleasures of sharing his life with his beloved (*Eudemian Ethics* 1245a24–25). Hence *erôs* as a form of *philia* — "*philia* in the extreme."[66]

This power of *erôs* to cement bonds — to promote *philia* — could prove useful militarily. At Thebes and Elis, entire detachments were formed of what can only be described as Harmodius-Aristogeiton pairings — that on the theory, one reportedly borne out in battle, that lover and beloved, if stationed side-by-side, would fight at their bravest, each to earn the other's admiration and avoid disgrace.[67] Phaedrus in Plato's *Symposium* speculates that not just armies but cities — collections of citizens — could benefit from that sort of camaraderie (178e). Sosicrates reports that Spartan and Cretan warriors forming ranks would sacrifice to Eros, the Spartans "in the belief that safety (*sôtêria*) and victory (*nikê*) depend on friendly feeling (*philia*)" (*FGrH* 462 F 7). Thus Zeno the Stoic made Eros god of friendly-feeling (*philia*), freedom (*eleutheria*), and concord (*homonoia*). For Eros, said Zeno, "is a god fundamentally concerned with helping to promote the safety (*sôtêria*) of the city" (Athenaeus 561c).

At Athens, an erotic side to civic cohesion seems to have found expression not just in commemorations of the Tyrannicides but in cult to Aphrodite. Late for our purposes is evidence for cult to Aphrodite as "Guide of the People";[68] similar may have been cult to Aphrodite Pandemos in partnership with Peitho, "Persuasion" personified. Many have, in fact, argued that an Aphrodite "Of All the People" (*pan + dêmos*) must have played some role in safe-guarding the body politic or in promoting civic cohesion.[69] While etymology offers no decisive evidence,[70] the fact that Peitho was honored with public cult in the fourth century suggests that she, perhaps in association with Pandemos, held special meaning for Athenians in promoting civic *homonoia* (consensus) and

---

[65] Empedocles frr. 17–36, 59 D-K. Cf. the "bridal of Heaven and Earth": Aeschylus fr. 44 Nauck; Euripides fr. 898 Nauck.

[66] Aristotle *Nichomachean Ethics* 1171a11–12; cf. Euripides fr. 358 Nauck; *Suppliants* 1088.

[67] Xenophon *Symposium* 8.32–34; cf. Plato *Symposium* 178e–179a. See Leitao 2002 (Theban Band's erotic character as philosophical fiction); DeVoto 1992; Dover 1989:190–192.

[68] "To Aphrodite *Hêgemonê tou dêmou* and to the Graces," late third-century BCE dedication from an altar found near Aphrodite Ourania's sacred area in the Athenian Agora: *IG* II^2 2798; Pirenne-Delforge 1994:39.

[69] See Rosenzweig 2004:13–28 with bibliography; also political, Pirenne-Delforge 1994:26–40. (Possibly) political Pandemos at Ionian Erythrae: Merkelbach 1986. On Cos: Dillon 1999.

[70] See Scholtz 2002/3.

persuasion-based government, especially after the nightmare of oligarchic *stasis* in 404/3.[71]

Prior to that, did Aphrodite or Peitho play a similarly political role? Whatever the official status of such cult in earlier times, by the early fifth century, Peitho was bridging the political and the sexual-matrimonial spheres in the city's public poetry, which is to say, in its drama. Thus in Aeschylus' *Suppliants*, the goddess makes two appearances: once as sponsor of persuasive speaking in the Argive assembly, once in the company of deities — Pothos ("Yearning"), Peitho, Harmonia ("joinery," "harmony"), the Erotes ("Loves") — assisting Aphrodite in her sponsorship of marriage. That dual appearance, suggests Froma Zeitlin, draws attention to parallel roles for persuasion, along with compromise and consent, in both marriage and politics.[72] In the same playwright's *Eumenides*, a sexy sort of *peithô* helps Athena conciliate a disgruntled group of Furies threatening to inflict blight and discord on her favorite city.[73] So effective does Athena's *peithô* prove that those same Furies, far from blighting Athens, pray instead for blessings on the city's behalf — the blessings of civic harmony founded on mutual love and, interestingly, shared hate:

> May faction (*stasis*), insatiate of ill, ne're raise her loud voice within
> this city. . . . Rather may they return joy for joy in a spirit of common
> love and may they hate with one accord; for therein lieth the cure of
> many an evil in the world.

Aeschylus *Eumenides* 977–987, trans. Smyth

Mutual love, shared hate for a common foe, "therein lieth the cure of many an evil" — or so Aeschylus' Furies would have us believe. For when we think and feel alike, then are we liable to feel empowered to defeat our enemies and achieve our desires. Let us not, then, mistake this "spirit of common love" for some sort of philanthropic compassion. Again, it is just as aggressive as its self-assertive *erôs* counterpart. Only now, "team spirit," consensus and cooperation, outweigh individualism.

But to place so high a premium on same-thinking, what the Greeks called *homonoia*, does that not amount to a self-imposed check on *isêgoria*,

---

[71] Peitho cult at Athens: Isocrates 15.249; Demosthenes *Exordia* 54. Peitho as goddess: Buxton 1982:31–48. *Peithô* and democracy: Lysias 2.18–19.

[72] Aeschylus *Suppliants* 523 (goddess or quasi-personification?), 1040, on which Zeitlin 1988.

[73] Aeschylus *Eumenides* 885–891, 970–972, on which Kambitsis 1973 (Athena's love for Peitho's eyes). Persuasion in Greek culture, politics, literature: Worthington 1994; Buxton 1982.

the "freedom of speech" that symbolized the citizen's stake in his government (Herodotus 5.78)? Lysias writes, "The greatest consensus (*homonoian*) is the freedom of all" (2.18). Consensus, he means, is strongest when achieved without coercion. And democracy survives through consensus, specifically, collective acquiescence to the will of the many. But what about consensus as a political imperative, an end in itself? If everyone thinks, speaks, and votes alike as a matter of principle, where are free speech, dissent, and debate, the "reality check" enabling democracy to avoid or correct misguided groupthink (cf. Thucydides 2.40.2, 3.36.4)? "Paradoxically," remarks Ober, " 'same-mindedness' on a political plane threatened to tear society apart."[74]

This tension between free speech and consensus, each treasured by the Athenian democracy,[75] seems mostly to have been ignored by Athenians, though not by *every* Athenian. In their respective accounts of the Sicilian Debate, deliberations leading to the invasion of the island in 415 BCE, Aristophanes and Thucydides address the power of a passionately felt consensus to control the discourse. In Thucydides' version (6.8–26), as in Aristophanes' (*Lysistrata* 387–398), an individual speaker plays a key role in swaying opinion. Yet that speaker ultimately proves no more than a conduit for something else: Aristophanes' Demostratus, for an ecstatic mania that had assemblymen voting unreflectively for an unwise proposal;[76] Thucydides' Alcibiades, for an "*erôs* to sail" that, like a hostile force or a fit of laughter, "fell upon (*enepese*)" its victims "all alike" (6.24.3). This *erôs* left Athenians feeling empowered and confident, but it also exercised power *over* them, a power so forceful that nothing Nicias could say would deter support for the invasion. On the contrary, his attempts at reverse psychology only reinforced the city's resolve (Thucydides 6.24.2). Nor were those opposed to the motion willing to vote their convictions, since to do so would have involved appearing hostile to the city's interests (*kakonous . . . têi polei*, 6.24.4; cf. 6.13.1). Thucydides' point? Among other things, that consensus, when it gains the kind of momentum this "*erôs* to sail" did, can create a social-discursive atmosphere hostile to the free exchange of ideas, to *dialogue*.

This coercive side to consensus shows clear affinities with a dynamic Bakhtin terms "centripetal discourse," speech that literally "seeks the center," that tries to force the whole conversation onto one track — normative

---

[74] Ober 1989:298.

[75] See Ober 1989:299 on *homonoia* and *isêgoria* as "good, valuable to state and society, and attainable" in popular ideology.

[76] See Henderson 1987:117–120 on the passage from Aristophanes' *Lysistrata*.

discourse intolerant of a plurality of views. Its opposite is "centrifugal" (center-fleeing) or pluralistic discourse,[77] a dynamic evident in the democratic exercise of free speech. Hence paradox underlying democratic consensus, where the discourse of the many effectively suppresses all discourses but one. Part of that has to do with the ideological environment, how it provides common ground necessary to dialogue, yet in so doing, *limits* dialogue, too. But we need also to keep in mind specifically *political* factors: politicians jockeying for power and influence over the *dêmos*. In such a setting, the whole idea is to win assent to one's views, to create *consensus*. Thus in the moment of the persuasive act, to foster consensus and impose one's will become objects of a single desire. But no democracy can allow every citizen to have his or her way all the time. In the end, individual voices and desires have to yield to a single voice like the one proclaiming, "The people have resolved" (*edoxe tôi dêmôi*) in Athenian decrees. That voice we may understand as notional or actual, however we please.[78] Either way, it shows how consensus, that indefinable point at which the many seem, *but only seem*, to coalesce into one, represents no fixed state but a dynamic process, a *concordia discors*.

Overview of Book

In what follows, we shall look at that process and its reflection in the literature of classical Athens. Our focus: the dissonance between communitarianism and individualism, consensus and conflict, in the works of authors for whom *erôs*, passionate, destabilizing desire, symbolized that dissonance with a powerful expressiveness. Thus in chapter two, we explore the Periclean Funeral Oration as response to a crisis in persuasion, a way to unite a fractious and fragmented citizenry behind a controversial war policy. To that end, Pericles bids listeners "gaze upon the city's power and become lovers — *erastai* — of it." But does he mean lovers of the city or of its power? That, I suggest, Pericles leaves unclear. And so this image of the citizen as lover, while it encourages patriotic self-sacrifice, also appeals to the self-centered motivations of citizens. But that dissonance works in the orator's favor. In telling listeners to become lovers of the city (or of its power), Pericles calls on them to abandon the logic of day-to-day for the "logic" of *erôs*. That logic lifts them up and out from routine

[77] Bakhtin 1981:275–288.

[78] *Dêmos* could mean "the voting collectivity as a whole," "the assembly," "the poor" (this implied by Aristotle *Politics* 1279b21–22). As cited in decrees, *dêmos* designated the collectivity as a whole, though that collectivity would not typically come together in its entirety for assembly meetings. See Ober 1994:109–110.

deliberation and puts them in touch with a higher discourse-community, the heroic dead, whose self-sacrifice becomes not just commendable but positively irresistible, the fulfillment of a citizen's deepest desires.

Turning from funeral oratory to comedy, I argue in chapter three that the politician-as-lover conceit in Aristophanes' *Knights* presents us with a comic twist on the "demophilia topos," the charge that one's opponent in court or assembly is trying to seduce listeners with specious claims of affection. Staging demophilic politics as sexual courtship, Aristophanes foregrounds tensions between benevolence and its "evil twin," flattery, in the leadership-styles of the city's politicians. But Aristophanes does not stop there. Demos, the Athenian people personified and a virtual prostitute complicit in his leaders' efforts to con and "bugger" him, pursues self-interest no less passive-aggressively, cynically, or covertly than they do. Hence value-reversals suggesting *stasis*, "strife" or "discord," in relations between leaders and led.

In chapter four, we consider how the "music" of democratic consensus, antidote to *stasis*, plays against that of civic-phallic autonomy, bulwark against antidemocratic *hubris*, in Aristophanes' *Assemblywomen*. That counterpoint, I suggest, builds on similar themes in the same playwright's *Lysistrata*, likewise a drama in which women take on the male establishment. Both comedies play the ideal of *homonoia* and *koinônia*, concord and fellowship, off against fears of civil strife and socio-political emasculation. And both press the dissonant implications of civic *erôs* — its integrative aspects versus its divisive aspects — to their illogical extreme.

In chapter five, we turn to Socrates' literary portrait, how it models the dialogical self as a sort of boundary phenomenon, a negotiation between speaker and listener, teacher and pupil, leader and led. That view may come across as counterintuitive. Socrates' apologists pay tribute to the sage as one-of-a-kind, a man so uncompromising in his morality and habits, a lover so resistant to the temptations of love, as to seem utterly apart, what the Greeks called *atopos* ("place-less," "strange"), in relation to his fellow human being. Yet Alcibiades' image of the man as god in a satyr's skin (*Symposium* 215a–222b) suggests a more complex creature, one whose outer layers express connection with, as well as disconnection from, the outside world. That complexity, I argue, finds expression in works manifesting tension between the simple, singular Socrates privileged by Plato, Xenophon, and Aeschines Socraticus, and a more multi-faceted and ambivalent Socrates deviously working his way into Socratic apologetic.

In closing, I consider the methodological and ethical implications of my findings, and their relevance for today's world.

2

"LOVERS OF IT"
EROTIC AMBIGUITY IN THE
PERICLEAN FUNERAL ORATION

And so it is that these men have proved themselves worthy of their
city. As for you, the living, pray that your resolve will be no less
unshakable, yet resolve to be no less bold against the enemy. And
don't just calculate the benefits of beating him back — benefits that
it would take too long for someone to recount, nor do any of you
need reminding. No, you must actually gaze daily upon the city's
power and become lovers of it. And when all this magnificence has
impressed itself upon you, reflect on the kind of men who made it
possible, men whose deeds told of bravery, duty, and honor. For if
some mishap were to trip them up, rather than deny the city the
benefit of their courage, they would contribute to the common
enterprise in the most glorious fashion imaginable.

Thucydides 2.43.1

"**P**ERICLES SON OF XANTHIPPUS WAS CHOSEN TO SPEAK." And so he did in the
epitaphios logos of 431 BCE, the "speech at the grave" to honor the past
year's war dead.[1] The written text of Pericles' speech, if it ever existed,
has not survived. What has is Thucydides' version (2.35–46), which reaches
its climax when the orator, having just expounded the rationale behind the
heroes' choice to die, proceeds to advise his listeners that rational calculation — *logos* — will not suffice if they, the living, are to live up to the standard
set by the fallen. "No, you must actually fix your gaze daily upon the city's

---

[1] Thucydides 2.34.8. For the custom of the annual public funeral for the war dead, and the
funeral oration (*epitaphios logos*) that went along with it, Rusten 1989:135–136; Loraux 1986;
Ziolkowski 1981.

power, and become lovers of it," he declares. But why the sudden inadequacy of *logos* in this *epitaphios logos*? And what is this "it" (*autês*) that the orator expects his listeners to fall in love with? Is it the city or — more unsettling — its *power*?

In what follows, we shall explore the Periclean Funeral Oration as the orator's response to a crisis in persuasion, a moment when Pericles, faced with the uncertainty of rational deliberation as a means of uniting the *polis*, resorts to an image, that of the *erastês*, designed to accommodate — and thus conquer — a divided audience. For it is an image that through its paradoxical and dissonant implications will unite an audience deeply divided over how to fight the war that Pericles has got them into.

Erôs and Oratory

Let us begin with a truism: objects of desire must either be persons, whether divine or human, or things, whether concrete or abstract. In classical Greek, the verb *eran* and words derived from it (henceforth, "*erôs*-vocabulary"), where they denote desire for persons, refer in nearly all cases to desire of a *sexual* nature.[2] Could, then, an *erôs* for *things* — as we have seen, not the default association for *erôs*[3] — have occupied a special category? That it did for the orators I argue in what follows. To summarize, the orators appear to have treated an *erôs* for things, especially a commendable one, as something out of the ordinary, a sentiment evoking complicated, even risky, associations. Later, we shall see Isocrates glossing his own use of *erôs*-vocabulary as boldly paradoxical, even transgressive, when he commends *erôs* for renown or eloquence. So, too, when Thucydides' Pericles, deprecating the logic of day-to-day, urges listeners to feast their eyes on the city's power and thereby fall in love,[4] he sets in motion a dynamic putting listeners in touch with a higher discourse-community and a higher logic, the logic of *erôs* — a logic, as we shall see, of paradox and revalorization.

How, though, can we be sure that city-*erôs* (as opposed to *erôs* for sex itself) would have occupied so special a category? Here is where the orators come in. When we examine their use of *erôs*-vocabulary, we notice a curious fact. Outside the corpus of Attic oratory (the "ten Attic orators," Demades), *erôs* could express desire for all manner of love-objects, sexual and otherwise. But *within* that corpus, certain patterns emerge. Thus no surviving text of a speech delivered in

---

[2] Exceptions: p. 16 above.

[3] P. 9n37 above.

[4] For the role of the gaze in kindling *erôs*, Calame 1999:20–21.

either a political or a judicial setting, or plausibly meant to model such speech-making to any degree, shows confirmable instances of *erôs*-vocabulary in non-sexual contexts.[5] Judicial oratory will, of course, have had occasion to address the issue of sexual desire, and did in fact make use of *erôs*-vocabulary to that end.[6] But non-sexual instances are confined to Isocrates, and those only in writings never intended for delivery before a jury or assembly.

To be sure, we find exceptions — not many — to this pattern when we move beyond the strict confines of the corpus. Yet the "epideictic" (i.e. non-judicial, non-political) cast of the passage in which Pseudo-Demades' speaker proclaims himself an "*erastês* of peace" is difficult to miss, and, I would suggest, explains the author's choice of noun (fr. 78 de Falco; see below on *erôs* and epideictic). Different is the use made by a pair of Thucydidean assembly speakers and a courtroom defendant in Gorgias. Both appear to echo medical notions of *erôs* as a psychologically incapacitating condition, a usage that could have enjoyed a certain currency in the later fifth century, though it must have quickly died out, to judge from the evidence.[7] But what about Aristophanes' *Knights*, a comedy shot-through with parody of demagogic speechifying? Do we not find there assembly politicians, or their comic surrogates, proclaiming *erôs* for the body politic of the city of Athens? Indeed we do, a fact that, along with the parallel offered by the Periclean Funeral Oration, has led some to argue for *erôs*-language in the real-life audience-bonding of late fifth-century assembly-speakers.[8] Yet in comparing *Knights* with usage patterns in the orators, we discover that the latter avoid not just *erôs*-vocabulary outside sexual contexts. They avoid all sorts of warmly patriotic, first-person affirmations of a type much in evidence in Aristophanes' play.[9]

Of course, I cannot rule out the possibility that a play like *Knights* opens a window into oratorical fashions, those of 420s Athens, otherwise poorly

[5] I acknowledge that few ancient texts or none will mirror verbatim an orally delivered speech. I do, though, recognize a category of speech-texts purporting to record "real" speeches (e.g. Lysias 1, 3 etc.) or to model same (Antiphon *Tetralogies*). These, I assume, negotiate, or try to, the challenges of real-world speaking. I do not mean to gloss over problems raised by privileging a subset of the evidence this way. But our texts cannot be well served if treated uniformly as de-historicized fictions. I further acknowledge the problem posed by speeches in Thucydides. Are they "realistic"? Are they dramatizations conditioned by thematic or intellectual preoccupations? I am not sure the two conflict. Linguistically difficult, they nevertheless explore the production and reception of speeches in relation to occasion, situation, setting (cf. Thucydides 1.21.1). See further Garrity 1998; Badian 1992; Rusten 1989:7–17; Kagan 1975; Stadter 1973.

[6] E.g. Lysias 3, 4; Aeschines 1; Demosthenes 21.38; 47.19; 59.

[7] Thucydides 3.45.5; 6.13.1; Gorgias fr. 11a15 D-K. Pathological *erôs* in Hippocratic writers: p. 10n39 above. Thucydides and the medical-psychological dimension: Rechenauer 1991:351–361. A later fifth-century vogue for arguments from human nature, psychology: Dover 1968:74–76.

[8] For that view, p. 45 below.

[9] Chapter 3 below.

documented in surviving evidence.[10] Still, it matters that our earliest preserved speeches, the courtroom and assembly orations of Antiphon, Lysias, Andocides, and Isocrates, like later political and judicial oratory, avoid speaking of *erôs* for this or that constitution, for city or *dêmos*, for success, whether honestly won or not, in the field, courts, or assembly, even where such an *erôs* arguably would have made sense.[11] Why, then, that pattern of lost opportunities, opportunities that an Isocrates writing not for oral delivery in courts or assembly readily avails himself of?[12] I suggest we are dealing with what Bakhtin would term "speech genre"[13] and Aristotle, *to prepon*, "appropriateness." Dionysius remarks that juries and assemblies "are more easily pleased by a simpler and more ordinary manner of speech" (*Demosthenes* 15). With that contrast what Dionysius has to say about Isocrates' "sprawling and rich abundance" and "emotive element," features of a style more congenial to ceremonial recitation than to the courts (*Isocrates* 2). Isocrates himself doubtless would have agreed. In the Antidosis, where the author assumes the persona of a court pleader, we learn all about Isocrates' preferred discursive mode: how it is more poetic and more varied, strives after loftier and more inventive thought, and employs compositional features of a more striking character than one associates with the courts (15.46–50). Indeed, the philistines who lump petty court-case speeches with orations of loftier aims do not realize that the former should be composed *asphalôs* ("taking no risks") and *haplôs* ("simply"), the latter *epideiktikôs* ("in showy fashion") and *akribôs* ("elegantly").[14] Isocrates, in short, feels a special affinity for display oratory — for *epideictic*.[15]

[10] So Ludwig 2002:151; see generally 141–153.

[11] Revenge-lust as *epithumia*: Antiphon *First Tetralogy* 1.7 (probably 430s BCE). Patriotism, partisanship, ambition, disreputable proclivities as *epithumia*: Antiphon fr. 1.1a; Lysias 20.3–4; 25.8; Isocrates 16.14, 37, 41–42; 18.29, 48; 20.1; 21.8, 10, 16; Aeschines 3.249. Greed as *epithumia* in Aeschines 3.218, *eran* in Euripides *Suppliants* 239. Philathenian *epithumein* and *spoudazein* in Demosthenes 23.126, *erôs* (*erastês, eran*) in Aristophanes *Acharnians* 142–146.

[12] Apart from speeches ghost-written for use in the courts (orations 16–21), Isocrates wrote pamphlets and other works. Some of these pose as judicial or political rhetoric (*Antidosis, On the Peace, Areopagiticus*), though directed to a reading public. For his use of *erôs*-vocabulary in those speeches, see further below.

[13] I.e. features of style, intonation, etc. organized around particular contexts, communities, occasions: Bakhtin 1986:60–102.

[14] Isocrates 4.11. O'Sullivan 1992:56n189 points out in Demosthenes 61.2 a similar contrast between persuasion-speeches written for oral delivery and "showy" (*epideiktikous*) speeches composed for posterity.

[15] Dionysius *Isocrates* 2 prefers to view Isocratean oratory in terms of ceremonial epideictic rather than judicial or courtroom oratory. According to Michelini, "Isocrates imperialistically attempts to occupy all generic positions at once" (1998a:126 citing Too 1995:7, 13–21). Note that an Isocratean pamphlet, though meant to be read, is a performance also meant to impress its (reading) audience.

Extrapolating, then, from usage patterns noted earlier, *erôs*-vocabulary would seem a feature of Isocrates' distinctively "showy" style. But a feature distinctive to "show" rhetoric generally? That is, I admit, a lot to hang on the stylistic habits of just one writer. Yet Thucydidean and Gorgianic usage seems to follow a similar pattern. Both Thucydides and Gorgias blame misguided decisions on *erôs* (Thucydides, 3.45.5, 6.13.1, 6.24.2; Gorgias frr. 11.15–19, 11a.15 D-K); that accords with our sources' widespread approval for reasoned deliberation as essential to any kind of prudent decision-making (e.g. dicast's oath, Aristotle *Rhetoric* 1375a29; *Politics* 1287a25–27; Thucydides 3.42.1; Sophocles *Oedipus the King* 524). Yet Thucydides in the Periclean Funeral Oration, and Gorgias in his own *Funeral Oration*, commend the *erôs* of the self-sacrificing citizen-soldier: an irrational city-*erôs* in Thucydides ("don't just calculate" etc., 2.43.1), a safely "legitimate" sort of *erôs* (*nomimôn erôtôn*) in Gorgias (fr. 6 D-K). Focusing now on Thucydides, why this turn to the erotic? What Pericles *must* do is praise the dead as they deserve. What he *can* do is turn that into an opportunity to exhort the living in ways problematic for any but the epideictic orator.

Festival and Ceremony

What is epideictic? According to Aristotle, it is oratory to be read (*Rhetoric* 1414a18–19). Yet Aristotle's examples suggest connections between epideictic as he conceives of it and speeches delivered at ceremonial occasions (1414b27–35, 1415b31, 1418a33–38). At such occasions, what would have been expected? Something out of the ordinary, an impressive performance. For, as Aristotle points out, what sets audiences for epideictic apart is that they are "beholders" of a speaker's "power."[16] The epideictic orator will, then, have had to speak in a fashion that Isocrates describes as *epideiktikôs*, "showy," and anyone who does so must, as we have seen, take risks.

---

[16] Aristotle divides rhetoric into judicial, political, and epideictic, or *epideiktikon*, from *epideiknusthai*, "to show." The topics proper to epideictic are praise and blame; its hearers are to be regarded as spectators (*theatai*) of an orator's skill (*Rhetoric* 1358a36–b8). Schiappa 1999:185–206 rightly points out that "epideictic" as a technical term and developed concept seems not to precede Aristotle. In retaining "epideictic" as catch-all for various sorts of non-judicial, non-political oratory, I merely highlight the often "showy" character of such oratory; I do not suggest that earlier practice was conditioned by later theory. I do, however, rely on Aristotle for insights into earlier practice.

Likening epideictic to the dithyramb,[17] Aristotle provides us with a clue to the character of this risk-taking. For it is distinctive of epideictic to use bold figures of speech and thought, conceits that seem to test the limits of oratory itself by tracing out the fault lines between ceremonial decorum and a kind of festive license. One occasion for what we are terming "epideictic" was the public funeral, and it is the oratory of such funerals that provides the most extensive record of ceremonial oratory in the classical period.[18] Funerals were, of course, solemn events, but in ancient Greece they could take on a carnivalesque character: feasting and athletic competition along with grieving. Even lamentation itself could represent a release of inhibition. Thus Homer describes the grieving Achilles as indulging a "lust" (*himeros*) for the "pleasure" (*tetarpato*) of tears during his meeting with Priam (*Iliad* 24.513–514). Expressions of grief, and the funeral generally, could even turn into a frenzied display threatening the public order. That, at least, was one of the reasons why funerals often came under regulation by the *polis*.[19]

This tricky negotiation between license and restraint will doubtless have raised the stakes for funeral orators like Pericles.[20] But funeral oratory called for more than a delicate touch; speakers were expected, among other things, to induce in listeners an ecstatic thrill.[21] To be sure, the imagistic and linguistic extravagance of funeral oratory could fall flat — such at least is the reaction of Pseudo-Longinus to expressions like "Xerxes, Zeus of the Persians," or "vultures, living tombs" in the *Funeral Oration* of Gorgias (Pseudo-Longinus 3.2 = Gorgias fr. 5a D-K). As for the Demosthenic *Funeral Oration*, a risky venture from the start, since the orator must negotiate the delicate task of praising the victims of

---

[17] Aristotle *Rhetoric* 1415a10–11. At 1414b21–26, Aristotle compares the virtuoso flourishes in the typical flute-prelude to the epideictic orator's opening ad libitum. For "dithyrambic" extravagance in oratory, cf. Plato *Phaedrus* 238d; Dionysius *Lysias* 3 citing Timaeus on Gorgias.

[18] For Funeral oratory as epideictic, cf. Aristotle *Rhetoric* 1415b30–32. The Periclean Funeral Oration as epideictic, Wohl 2002:38–39.

[19] See Alexiou 1974:14–23 for *polis* regulation of funerals. Alexiou remarks that "these exaggerated displays . . . must have excited a state of frenzy." Funeral regulations could have been instituted to restrict vendetta killings in response to mourners' calls to avenge murder victims.

[20] The carnivalesque banquet as a celebration of "life, death, struggle, triumph, and regeneration" (Bakhtin 1984b:282) resonates with Pericles' praise of the richness of Athenian life, a richness vouchsafed by the heroism of the fallen, in the Funeral Oration.

[21] Frangeskou 1999:328 points out the stylistic features (repeated ô, balanced phrases, assonance, exaggeration, etc.) in key passages of Lysias' *Funeral Oration* aimed at inducing something resembling the ecstasy that affects Socrates in the *Menexenus* (235a–c). Cf. the preserved specimen of Gorgianic funeral oratory, fr. 5 D-K.

a crushing defeat (Chaeronea, 338 BCE), that speech contains sentiments whose extravagance prompts the speaker to beg the pardon of his audience:

> And may no ill will attend my speech. For it seems to me that if someone were to say that the valor of these men was the soul of Greece, he would only be speaking the truth. For as soon as these men breathed their last, then was the pride of Greece laid low. Perhaps I will seem to speak extravagantly (*huperbolên ... legein*), but it must be said all the same. Just as, should someone rob the world of its light, all remaining existence would become for us a grievous burden, so the loss of these men has brought low the onetime ambition of the Greeks and wrapped it in gloom.

Demosthenes 60.23–24

Doubtless our speaker apologizes for the bleak import of his words. But those sentiments would not have packed the punch they do without the extravagant comparison framing them.

If the speaker just quoted risks "speaking extravagantly," he is in good company. In another funeral oration and in a not dissimilar vein, Hyperides likens Athens, judge of humanity and defender of Greece, to the sun that regulates and nourishes the world (oration 4 cols. 2–3). By his own account, Hyperides will not hesitate (*ouk oknêsô*) to venture the comparison, an admission designed in this case not to apologize for, but to highlight, the audacity of the rhetoric. Indeed, Pericles himself, renowned in antiquity for bold comparisons, outdid himself in one funeral oration that likened the loss of Athens' young men to the loss of springtime from the year.[22] Philip Stadter points out the sophistic basis of the logic in this last comparison,[23] and it could well be in the area of just that kind of exhibitionism that ceremonial epideictic and sophistic *epideixis* ("demonstration") overlap.[24] Still, at least one epideictic genre strongly suggests the aptness of Aristotle's comparing epideictic with dithyramb. For funeral oration targets not so much the rational faculties of its audience as their passions and emotions. Indeed, Socrates in the *Menexenus*

---

[22] Aristotle *Rhetoric* 1365a31–33, 1411a2–4; cf. Plutarch *Pericles* 8.9 = Stesimbrotus *FGrH* 107 F 9 (war dead like divine immortals); see Stadter 1989:110.

[23] Stadter 1989:110.

[24] Cf. Cleon's "spectators of words and listeners to deeds" (Thucydides 3.38.4) and "spectators of sophists rather than deliberators of policy" (3.38.7). To that kind of listening corresponds the *epideixis* of bribed speakers, 3.42.3 (Diodotus mocking Cleon's line of attack).

claims that funeral oratory produces in him a kind of patriotic rapture (*Menexenus* 235a–c), what Loraux calls "the spell of an ideality."[25]

But the magic of Pericles' Funeral Oration by no means restricts itself to abstract idealities. Material Athens, a land of plenty and a city distinctive for its appreciation of recreation and festivity, also figures.[26] So, too, does a tendency to aristocratize the Athenian Everyman, to instill in him a sense of himself as the *crème de la crème*, even in the face of obvious wealth- and social disparity.[27] As we shall, paradox spikes the heady cocktail that is this speech.

Erôs and Revalorization

Erôs-vocabulary in ancient Greek is connotationally complex. It denotes desires whose satisfaction will bring pleasure to the desirer. Yet key aspects of *erôs* — the experience of being in its grip, the things it leads one to do — arouse anxiety, even dread, in our sources. To paraphrase Sophocles, *erôs* drives men mad, makes criminals of the just, and ruins them (*Antigone* 787–793). In Hyperides, a speaker observes that *erôs* in concert with feminine wiles upsets a man's natural equilibrium (*phusis*) and so brings about his undoing (Hyperides 3 col. 1, sect. 2; cf. Demosthenes 40.27). Hence in the courts erotic passion adduced as an excuse or explanation, like drunkenness or ignorance, for bad or unseemly behavior.[28]

Do the orators ever place an overtly *positive* construction on sexual passion? One example comes from a court speech, Aeschines' *Against Timarchus*, in the course of which the orator launches into an extended, and for judicial oratory, unparalleled, eulogy of pederasty, an older man's attraction to, and pursuit of, adolescent males (136–159). Why that eulogy? Aeschines, whose case against Timarchus hinges largely on matters of sexual misconduct, expects that an opponent will enter a counterplea defending, even praising, the sexual liaisons formed by the defendant, and will try to defame Aeschines, the prosecutor, as a sexual predator (132–135). But the fact that Aeschines disparages as encomium his opponent's anticipated praise of Timarchus

---

[25] See Loraux 1986:263–338.

[26] Thucydides 2.38, 2.40.1. Here my emphasis will differ from McGlew 2002:32–34. McGlew describes Pericles' privileging of duty over pleasure as a "Spartan-like project" (41). I would agree that Pericles undertakes to please a variety of constituencies, even "conservatives," but he also engages in explicitly counter-Spartan eulogy of Athens' charms.

[27] Wohl 2002:36–37, 49–51; cf. Kallet 2003:131–137; McGlew 2002:30–42.

[28] Demosthenes 21.38; 54.14, 20; Lysias 3.4; Anaximenes *Rhetorica ad Alexandrum* 7.14; Simonides 541 *PMG*.

(*enkômiasetai*, 133) provides us with a way of thinking about the exceptional nature, and encomiastic character, of Aeschines' own tribute to *erôs*.[29]

Indeed, praise of *erôs* seems to show a special affinity for speeches and related prose of an epideictic cast. Thus Gorgias in the *Funeral Oration* praises the honored dead for, among other things, "legitimate lust" (*nomimôn erôtôn*). In the *Helen*, a speech mixing praise with apologetic with theoretical speculation, the same writer cites *epithumiai erôtos*, the "longings for sex" felt by Helen's admirers, as incitement to distinction in a variety of worthy pursuits (fr. 11.4 D-K). And well the orator should if he is to achieve his stated aim of rehabilitating Helen's reputation. Yet in so doing, he stands established tradition on its head, tradition that denounced Helen as a "Hell . . . to ships, Hell to men, Hell to cities."[30]

So, too, Isocrates in his own *Helen* challenges commonplace notions, this time, through deliberate echoes of both Thucydides and Euripides:

> And not just Greeks and barbarians, but gods, too, were smitten by lust (*erôs enepesen*) for the hardships of that expedition, a lust so great that the gods did nothing to stop their own sons from taking part in the contest for Troy. On the contrary, Zeus, though he had been forewarned of Sarpedon's fate, and Eos of her son Memnon's, and Poseidon of Cycnus', and Thetis of Achilles' — all of them urged their sons on and sent them off *en masse*, deeming it a finer thing (*kallion*) for them to die fighting for the daughter of Zeus than to live without having risked danger for her sake. . . . And indeed, they reached the right decision (*eulogôs . . . egnôsan*). So, too, have I the right to describe the woman in such extravagant terms (*têlikautais huperbolais*).

> Isocrates 10.52–54

Like Thucydides and Euripides, Isocrates characterizes an adventurous, ambitious spirit as *erôs*, one that befell (*enepesen*) a whole group of individuals. But Thucydides and Euripides present that *erôs* as deeply problematic — Euripides, as a *deinos erôs*, a "fierce" or "frightening lust."[31]

---

[29] Among the epideictic features of Aeschines 1.136–159: citation of mythological and historical *exempla* (Achilles and Patroclus, Harmodius and Aristogeiton), the alleged inadequacy of praise rhetoric (*tois enkômiois*) to the task at hand. Cf. the similarly epideictic detour in Lycurgus 46–51, a mini-funeral oration.

[30] Aeschylus *Agamemnon* 689–690, trans. Smyth; Homer *Iliad* 6.344; Euripides *Orestes* 741, 743; *Electra* 213–214.

[31] Euripides *Iphigeneia at Aulis* 808–809; Thucydides 6.24.3. Euripides borrows *deinos erôs* from Aeschylus *Eumenides* 865, where a "fierce lust for renown" threatens *stasis* if given free reign at home. In Euripides, it suggests the stasiastic restlessness of idle Greeks.

Isocrates sees it, or at least, "spins" it, differently. For Isocrates, the *erôs* prompting the whole Trojan War needs to be understood as ambition of heroic proportions, an *erôs* ennobled by the gods' "rational decision" (*eulogôs ... egnôsan*) to risk the lives of their children, the half-gods who would fight before the walls of Troy. And their decision serves to rationalize the orator's own decision to praise Helen's beauty, and the *erôs* aroused by it, as "extravagantly" as he does (54–55).

We find a repeat performance in the same writer's *Antidosis*, where *erôs* likewise figures into Isocrates' self-referential rhetoric. Thus the orator, warning his audience that he will speak "counter intuitively" (*paradoxa*, 272), begs them not to dismiss him outright for "madness" in challenging cherished beliefs (273). Having thus prepared us, he proceeds to use the language of censure to commend the ambition to become a skilled orator, and to explain the advantages eloquence confers:

> I feel ... that people would become better and worthier if in the matter of speaking well they were to adopt an ambitious frame of mind (*philotimôs diatitheien*), and lust (*erastheien*) for the ability to persuade their listeners, and furthermore, lust to gain the advantage (*tês pleonexias epithumêsaien*), though not in the way that the foolish think of it (*mê tês hupo tôn anoêtôn nomizomenês*), but in the truest sense of the term.
>
> Isocrates 15.275

"To gain the advantage" translates *pleonexia*, a word whose negative connotations Isocrates both flags and derides as "the way that the foolish think of it." How *do* the "foolish" think of it? As the unprincipled pursuit of personal gain, in a word, "greed," or so Isocrates implies (276). But that is just how *pleonexia* was commonly understood.[32] We are, then, dealing with an explicitly counterintuitive construction of *pleonexia*, one as positive as "vulgar" notions of it are negative. So, too, the notion of a "lust" or *erôs* for the power to persuade (*tou peithein dunasthai ... erastheien*) will have carried with it a certain shock value. Evoking popular mistrust of the technologies of persuasion,[33] it challenges common notions.

---

[32] See Balot 2001.

[33] Regulations, ideologies stipulating proposals only for the good of the city; risks of public rhetoric; conflict of interests, corruption: Monoson 2000:59–60; Christ 1992; Ober 1989:170–174; Harvey 1985; chapter three below.

What have we learned? We have learned that the more showy and risky sort of rhetoric associated with epideictic could seek out and exploit a fraught sort of *erôs*, that the construction the "show" orator places on such *erôs* breaks with received notions, as in the case of Isocrates. Yet Isocrates finds in revalorization a powerful social dynamic. Through revalorization, he invites us to join his privileged speech-community, a community within which *erôs* counts as rational (cf. 10.54), and *pleonexia* as virtuous — counterintuitive to the many, but perfectly logical to the few. Still, revalorization like that is, in Isocrates' words, "hyperbolic": it shoots beyond some acceptable boundary. How is that a good thing? Vološinov, we recall, describes the "ideological sign" (i.e. the utterance) as Janus-faced, that is, as looking backwards and forwards as it crosses thresholds separating speech-communities and value systems.[34] What Isocrates does, then, is to invite us to cross that threshold, to join him in the pursuit of *philosophia*, his word for the higher rhetoric. In so doing, our outlook will be reframed, and concepts like *pleonexia*, re-evaluated.[35] But let us never forget the "transgressive" character of what we do. We need that to set us apart.

Returning, then, to the Periclean Funeral Oration, I suggest that Pericles employs a similar strategy of implanting in citizens a city-love fueled by ideologically dissonant values, a city-love where value-reversal at one level of analysis translates as value-affirmation at another. And he does so within a strategy of re-fashioning civic conflict into *concordia discors*, a harmony oblivious to the very real divisions inside itself.

Pericles' Problem

When in 431 BCE war between Athens and the Peloponnesians broke out, the strategy devised by Pericles was to defend only the city, not the surrounding countryside. Hiding behind the city's virtually impregnable defenses, and exploiting their control of the sea, Athenians would not be risking a pitched battle on home turf against superior forces. The catch was, of course, that rural Athenians would have to evacuate their lands, which they were understandably loath to do.[36] But when the expected invasion force came, its commander, the Spartan king Archidamus, adopted a clever plan. By occupying the outlying town of Acharnae and ravaging its territory, he hoped to estrange the

---

[34] See p. 8n31 above.
[35] Reframing: Neuman and Tabak 2003; Billig 1996:253–286.
[36] See Rusten 1989:116–117, 120–121.

Acharnians from other Athenians, that is, to induce *stasis*, division among the citizenry (2.20.4).

It soon became evident that his plan might succeed:

> They [the Athenians] found themselves divided and seriously at odds with one another. Some urged an attack outside the walls, certain others resisted such a course. Soothsayers began to recite all sorts of oracles, which people interpreted as the inclination took them. As for the Acharnians (who deemed themselves no inconsiderable part of the Athenian body politic), since it was their land that was being ravaged, they pressed the hardest for a sortie. Thus in every way the *polis* had been thrown into an uproar.
>
> Thucydides 2.21.3

It could not have been easy for Pericles to rally the support he needed. Pericles himself, in the speech Thucydides assigns him near the end of book one of the *History*, remarks that "farmers are the sort of people who will more readily expose their bodies than their possessions to the hazards of war" (1.141.5). The context of that generalization concerns Peloponnesians,[37] but Pericles generalizes; he could just as easily have been referring to the middling farmers of Attica, citizen-soldiers frustrated at not being allowed to defend their farms.[38] Those farmers probably would not have been alone in their disaffection. Important, too, would have been the landed gentry, who, as cavalry, carried the burden of protecting the city, but on top of that assumed burdens of a financial character.[39] By contrast, the *thêtes*, the landless poor, would have had less to complain about.[40] Yet Pericles, in his attempts to conciliate the others, could not risk alienating *thêtes* viewed by one writer as the mainstay of Athens' maritime empire and radical democracy (Pseudo-Xenophon).

We see, then, that any speech to rally support would have needed to address not one but three constituencies: the largely rural hoplite class, the landed gentry, and the landless poor. How to address those diverse and, to

---

[37] Crane 1992 on that mentality; cf. Hanson 1995:331 (agrarian hoplites willing to die "for a few acres on their own border"), 338–343.

[38] Sicking 1995. Subsistence farmers were at the time the majority: Crane 1992:252.

[39] Spence 1990 for the stiff resistance offered by the *hippeis* to the invading Peloponnesians.

[40] Kallet 1998 for the ideological connection between poorer Athenians and the empire; Jordan 1975 for the makeup of the trireme crews.

a certain degree, conflicting interests? And how to guarantee that the *dêmos*, the voting public meeting as a body, would not rashly elect to abandon Pericles' plan?

Pericles' Solution

One expedient at Pericles' disposal was to avoid having the matter of his war policy come up for debate. To quote Sicking, "When the fury and irritation in the city had reached its peak, he had refused to summon an assembly for fear that such an assembly would, swayed by anger, take the wrong decisions."[41] Another would have been to use the public funeral, held every winter for the city's war-dead, as a bully pulpit from which to pitch his case — not, as in an assembly speech, to propose and defend policies, certainly not as warm-up for an up-or-down vote (no such vote would have been taken), but to rally support and to remind Athenians what they were fighting for.

Curiously, Pericles' speech, amid all its rallying and reminding, goes in for quite a bit of intricate finessing. Thus Ober remarks on the "deeply complex and often seemingly deliberately ambiguous" nature of passages devoted to praise of the city and its institutions.[42] Indeed, he points out how, in Pericles' description of Athenian democracy (2.37.1), evasions and nuance can leave readers of the *History* wondering how well balanced the system really was — whether the speech as we have it might not serve to comment on class conflict threatening to develop into out-and-out *stasis*.[43] James McGlew, addressing the orator's circumspection on the subject of civic freedom, argues that "Pericles is careful to restrict the idea of freedom and free behavior . . . to public activity," a reflection of the war-footing the city was on at the time.[44] Victoria Wohl, also on the subject of freedom, notes how Pericles equivocates with the term *eleutheros*, "free." Political freedom all citizens possessed; *economic* freedom was less evenly distributed, though Pericles does not let that fact "dim the aristocratic brilliance of the demos as a whole."[45]

---

[41] Sicking 1995, 412 and n35, commenting on Thucydides 2.22.1. Hamel 1998:8–12 suggests that the moratorium on *ekklêsiai* during the first invasion of Attica should be viewed not as active interdiction but as weathering the storm.

[42] Ober 1998:84.

[43] Ober 1998:86–87.

[44] Quote, McGlew 2002:33; see 25–42.

[45] Wohl 2002:37.

What the aforementioned readings share is a focus on what nowadays would be called "spin": in Ober's reading, the historian's spin on the "fragility" of Athenian "greatness"; in McGlew's and Wohl's, the dramatized speaker's effort to spin the city's image in rhetorically expedient ways. Building on all three views, I suggest that spin here addresses the rhetorical challenges mentioned earlier. That is, its evasions and equivocations offer listeners, especially propertied interests and the politically disaffected, a chance to hear in Pericles' rhetoric a message to their liking. Thus we can understand that rhetoric as give-and-take within a social context, as a performance shaped by the speaker's grasp of the addressivity of his audience, the ideological stance conditioning how different sorts of listeners will have listened to him speak.[46]

We need, in other words, to understand these speech-acts as interactive, as *dialogical*. Bakhtin, commenting on externally directed action as, virtually by definition, *inter*action between actor and environment, will be our guide:

> . . . what I grasp is not the object as an externally complete image,
> but rather my tactile experience corresponding to the object,
> and my muscular feeling of the object's resistance, its heaviness,
> compactness, and so forth.[47]

Action responds. Its directedness shapes itself to the world experienced within the perception-horizon of the acting subject — it is, in its way, dialogical. If speech is a form of action, then any given set of speech-acts, even a rhetorical monologue like Pericles', will likewise shape itself to the contours of the world — the audience — it confronts.[48]

And so it does in Pericles' praise of Athenian democracy, where the speaker's substitution of *oikein* ("to administer") for *kratein* ("to rule," "to exercise power") glosses over what the Theban Herald in Euripides' *Suppliants* finds so galling about democracy (411), a feature underscored by the word itself: sovereign power (*kratos/kratein*) vested in the *dêmos*.[49] Yet the democracy in "democracy" is further mitigated by the orator's discussion of office-holding, specifically, its egalitarian character at Athens:

---

[46] Addressivity: p. 85 below.

[47] Bakhtin 1990:43.

[48] For the applicability of this principle to rhetoric, Billig 1996:224–227, 264–265.

[49] Under democratic ideology, the *kratos/kratein* of the *dêmos* represented legitimate sovereignty: Ober 1994:108. For the Herald, it is mob rule.

On the one hand (*men*), in name (*onoma*) our constitution is called "democracy" because of majoritarian administration (*es pleionas oikein*) in preference to that oriented to the few. On the other hand (*de*), all have equal recourse to the laws for settling private disputes. Yet a man here receives preferment on the basis of merit, as each stands in the public eye. For us, it is excellence (*aretê*) mostly (*to pleon*), not portion (*meros*), that qualifies one for service to his city (*es ta koina*).

Thucydides 2.37.1

For readers of Thucydides' *History*, those words will resonate with the historian's characterization of Periclean democracy as "democracy in name (*logôi*), though in fact (*ergôi*) rule (*arkhê*) exercised by the first man" (2.65.9), a words-versus-deeds antithesis privileging deeds as the more reliable criterion.[50] So, too, in the Periclean Funeral Oration, we have in Pericles' definition of democracy a words-versus-deeds antithesis, only here, the "reality" proves subtly meritocratic. By the 430s, all nine major archonships at Athens were filled by lottery from a pool more or less coextensive with the body politic; virtually anyone might serve. Though archons so selected will have played a largely ceremonial role in many respects, the egalitarian character of their selection was, nevertheless, regarded as a defining feature of democracy at Athens.[51] But that is not what the orator highlights. Rather, he alludes to the fact that unpaid officials chosen by ballot, the generals especially, actually ran things — a fact earning grudging admiration for Athenian democracy from an otherwise antidemocratic text dating from the late 400s.[52] It is, then, striking that Pericles similarly contrasts the name "democracy" with the all important fact that, "for the most part," not just anyone (as might be inferred from the name given to Athens' constitution) but persons judged qualified were chosen "for public service."[53]

Which brings us to ambiguity stemming from *meros*, which I translate as "one's portion." Does it, in other words, refer to election by lottery, a feature that, along with pay for, and general access to, office, set Athenian

---

[50] For which, Parry 1981:15.

[51] *Thêtes* (the lowest economic class) may have had access to all paid archonships by the late fifth century; see generally Ober 1989:79–80.

[52] Pseudo-Xenophon 1.3. The generals and their role: Hamel 1998. The generally elite character of the leadership class: Ober 1989.

[53] Cf. Adam Parry's paraphrase, 1981:162: "Our state is called a democracy . . . , but its reality is a political equality where rank is based on merit."

democracy apart? Or does it refer to the principle of rotation, what Aristotle calls "being ruled and ruling in turn" (*en merei, Politics* 1317a41–1317b3)? Or might it conceivably offer a subtle nod in the direction of a (by then, mostly obsolete) wealth-qualification?[54] I would suggest that it allows the listener to hear in it what he or she will.

Thus Pericles, in his praise of the Athenian constitution, does not simply buoy up the self-image of the *dêmos*; he negotiates the misgivings of democracy's critics, as, notably, in the following, perhaps the single most famous sentence in the entire *History*:

> We indulge our love for things of beauty without great expense, and our love for wisdom without softness.

> Thucydides 2.40.1

Rusten, pointing out that the artistic and architectural amenities of Athens could not have come cheap, prefers to take *philokaloumen* as "we seek what is *noble*" as opposed to expensive.[55] Yet given the city's financial reserves, amenities like the temples on the Acropolis arguably would have represented no crushing burden.[56] In any case, we can think of the phrase as directed to aristocratic critics of the city's democratic building program, as an attempt to convey to those critics the sense that city does not allow its aesthetic or intellectual pursuits to bankrupt either the city's coffers or the manhood of its citizens.[57]

More generally, we can think of Pericles' praise of Athens as an almost collaborative effort. Writes Aristotle, "It is necessary in each and every situation to speak of everything that one's audience honors as reality, whether that be among Scythians, Spartans, or philosophers" (*Rhetoric* 1367b9–11). Addressing that need, Pericles offers listeners the leeway to hear him praise that version of Athens that each severally prizes, or at least feels most comfortable with. In the process, listeners do not listen passively. Rather, they consummate the rhetoric; they participate in fashioning whichever vision each feels prompted to imprint

---

[54] "By lot" or "by turns": LSJ s.v. μέρος II.2; Rusten 1989:145–146; Gomme et al. 1970–1981:vol. 2 p. 8; Flashar 1969:18. Wealth or social qualification: Sicking 1995:414 and n42; Harris 1992:164.

[55] 1989:153; Rusten 1985:18.

[56] For a summary of Athens finances, Kallet 2003:127.

[57] The building program as democratically marked: Kallet 2003:128–131. Oligarchic-aristocratic response: Plutarch *Pericles* 12.1–2; Kallet 2003:131–136 (on this passage); Stadter 1989:130–187; Andrewes 1978; Wade-Gery 1958. Aristocratic appeasement in the Periclean Funeral Oration: McGlew 2002:39 citing Roberts 1994:43.

on it. But Pericles does not simply pitch his message to appeal to all and sundry. He must also foster in listeners the sense that "my" Athens, the city "my kind" identifies with, is the same Athens that we *all* identify with. This he does through insistent use of the first-person plural: *we* indulge our love for things of beauty, *our* city is the education of Greece, and so on.

Words Fail

But the careful negotiation of diverse interests is only part of the plan. Another part is the negation of rhetoric itself. Thus Pericles leads off by deprecating the hazards he faces: of saying the wrong thing, of not being believed, of saying too much or too little, of arousing ill-will (2.35). Later, we hear about how he will not bore his audience with the usual history lecture (2.36.4), how the city's power speaks louder than words (2.41.2), how no poet need eulogize the city (2.41.4), how consolation is difficult to offer (2.44.2), how Pericles has spoken only as well as he could (2.46.1).

Ober understands all this self-deprecation as an internal gloss, the historian's commentary on the unreliability of rhetoric in comparison to deeds and facts, to scientific historiography.[58] But in the Periclean Funeral Oration, the speaker's diffidence is itself thoroughly rhetorical. On one level, it seeks to diffuse envy. It functions, therefore, as *captatio benevolentiae*, self-presentation designed to win a favorable hearing from listeners — standard procedure for praise poetry as for oratory of all sorts.[59] But it also represents a strategy to control the reception of Pericles' speech. If *no one's* words, not even the speaker's, not even the words of a poet like Homer (2.41.4), are adequate to the task at hand, then whose words are left to carry any weight at all? In default of the ideal orator, we must live with the orator we have.

This self-referential, anti-rhetorical rhetoric comes to a head when Pericles, having just discoursed eloquently on the heroes' choice to die (2.42.4), ceases to assert and begins to exhort. In the process, he deprecates *logos* (rational calculation, argument) as insufficient to convince "you," the living, to live up to the example set by the dead. "No, you must actually gaze daily upon the city's power and become lovers of it" (2.43.1). But where can this *epitaphios logos*, this "speech at the graveside" go if speech will no longer suffice? I suggest that in the Periclean Funeral Oration, *erôs* takes *logos* to a whole new level.

---

[58] Ober 1998:84–86; also Wohl 2002:38–39.
[59] Pindar *Pythian* 1.81–84; Aeschines 1.140 (in an epideictic vein); Rusten 1989:138–139.

Erotic Ambiguity

"Don't just calculate the benefits. . . . No, you must actually gaze daily upon the city's power and become lovers of it." Urging listeners to move beyond reason, *logos*, Pericles exhorts them to let passion, *erôs*, guide their judgment.[60] But what is it that listeners are supposed to feel so passionate about? Is this "it" (*autês*) to which Pericles refers the city or its power? Both candidates, city (*polis*) and power (*dunamis*), fit the syntax. Both have figured prominently in the run-up to this point; neither word order nor proximity tells decisively in favor of either. Hornblower remarks that "if the Athenians were being urged to become lovers of the *power* of Athens that would be an even more striking and aggressive idea" — more striking, that is, than if the city itself were the true love-object.[61] For power-lust was, we have seen, the mark of a tyrant. And tyrants were, so it was believed, democracy's nemesis.

It is hard to conceive of a democrat like Pericles trying to instill in listeners an *erôs* as subversive as that. McGlew, for whom this is, first and foremost, city-love, nonetheless detects here a hint of power-lust, an evocation of the tyrant as model for an empowered and privileged citizenry. Still, tyrannical implications are, for McGlew, balanced by the would-be citizen-tyrant's submission to a city that acknowledges his sacrifice and reciprocates.[62] Sara Monoson also elaborates a reciprocal model for the image. Taking "city" (*polis*) as love-object,[63] she suggests that citizens, like pederastic lovers, are encouraged to engage in reciprocal demonstrations of affection (*philia*) with their beloved.[64] There remain, however, difficulties. Whatever the antecedent to feminine *autês*, that, if personified, should, strictly speaking, be understood as female. Thus the protocols of the higher courtship, male-to-male (i.e. pederasty), will not exhaust this metaphor's resonances. But no resonance, however disquieting, should be rejected simply because disquieting. Indeed, dissonance between this image's multiple entailments may be just the point.

---

[60] Cf. Forde 1989:31: *philopoli* ("love of city") of the ordinary kind here needs the added boost of erotic *peithô*. For the *logos-pathos* antithesis in Thucydides, Immerwahr 1973:19.

[61] Hornblower 1991–:vol. 1 p. 311. Cf. Hussey 1985:125 ("something is rotten here"); Immerwahr 1973 (pathological surrender to the forces of unreason).

[62] McGlew 2002:41–42. Kallet 2003:131–137 argues that the Periclean Funeral Oration contests the notion of a tyrant *dêmos*.

[63] Monoson 2000:73: "Citizens become lovers of a specific object, the city of Athens, after having perceived that it possesses an exceptionally alluring quality, power."

[64] Stressing benevolent reciprocity, she notes the danger that such a relationship could deteriorate into exploitation: Monoson 2000:64–87.

Let us begin with city-love, *polis* as the object of *erôs*. As an *erastês* of his city, the citizen-soldier can be expected to manifest a passionately felt affection or *philia* for his *erômenê* or "beloved." Monoson's schema of a respectable, even ennobling, exchange of goods will at this point come into play. Under that schema, war becomes a means for citizens to "contribute to the common enterprise in the most glorious fashion imaginable" (2.43.1.), and with a just return to be expected. What sort of return? The glory that attends death in battle.

That "contribution" — in Greek, *eranos* — becomes the locus of citizen-city reciprocity.[65] *Eranos*, a word cognate ultimately with *erôs*, means no one thing, but seems in all its meanings to stress a division of shares.[66] In classical Attic, it regularly referred to a joint loan or investment.[67] Wohl suggests a further resonance, that of a wedding feast binding citizens and city, living and dead, in a beautiful union.[68] *Erôs* leading to *eranos* will, then, have manifested what I call "communal *erôs*," not a selfless, but a deeply self-*interested* desire for close-knit civic bonds, desire that finds validation and fulfillment in collective empowerment.

Still, "No one is so foolish as to feel *erôs* for death" (Sophocles *Antigone* 220). The city-loving soldier may not seek self-annihilation for its own sake, but how else can he consummate his love if not by dying? But who wants to die? That would be madness, the madness of *erôs*.[69] How, then, to overcome the citizen-soldier's hesitation in the heat of battle? In part, by fixing the inner gaze of listeners on the image-ideal offered by the fallen. Mirroring their fantasies of self-fulfillment, that image kindles longing to merge with it, to live and die as did the honored dead.[70] Still, however magnetic that image, "the hardships of campaign and the grisly reality of battle could overwhelm individual and group and lead to conspicuous lapses in valor."[71] How, then, does Pericles' rhetoric negotiate dissonance between, on the one hand, the instinct to self-preservation, on the other, the ideal of self-sacrifice?

To answer that question, we need to explore external factors complementing the internal dynamic described by Wohl — how, in other words,

---

[65] Monoson 2000:84.

[66] Weiss 1998:46.

[67] *Eranos* as charitable contribution, club dues, for-profit investment: Rusten 1989:169. *Eranos* as civic entitlement ("dues" paid to the city): Aristophanes *Lysistrata* 648–651; Hornblower 1991–:311–312 on the parallel with Thucydides 2.43.1.

[68] Wohl 2002:57.

[69] Pathological death-wish as *erôs*: p. 10n9 above.

[70] Wohl 2002:58–59.

[71] Quoting Christ 2006:90; see generally 88–142.

the image-ideal supplied by the fallen exerts a kind of peer pressure. For it kindles desire to join an elite company of warriors for whom the folly of self-immolation makes an exhilarating sort of sense. How does folly make sense? Through the reframing of paradox, and in a way already seen in Isocrates. Here, as there, genre counts — genre not as a literary construct, but Bakhtin's notion of speech genre, how a particular way of speaking or writing can seem to fit certain occasions, settings, or discourse-communities, but not others.[72] Just so here, the ambiance not of an assembly meeting but of the public funeral will prevail. Pericles, in urging listeners to become lovers, asks them to go beyond the calculation (*logos*) of advantage (*ôphelia*, 2.43.1). In effect, he asks them to transcend assembly-style deliberation, the weighing of alternatives with a view to their "expediency or harm" (Aristotle *Rhetoric* 1358b21–22 on political oratory). But will reason cease to play a role? Surely not. Pericles' listeners must still think: about the city's greatness; about the deeds of past benefactors, whose good judgment (*gignôskontes ta deonta*) offers listeners a shining example; about prosperity as contingent on freedom, and freedom as contingent on courage (2.43.1, 4).

But this higher *logos*, the *logos* of *erôs*, also demands that listeners transcend the logic of day-to-day. *Erôs*, we recall, is highly problematic, the epitome of irrationality. And so it remains here — by conventional standards. But those standards "we" as lovers (*erastai*) have left behind. Thus Pericles, by introducing *erôs* into the city's discourse, induces a kind of *stasis*. He transforms the *dêmos*; he lifts it up and out from its deliberative function and brings it into contact with another speech-community, the honored dead, whose implicitly *erôs*-driven logic of self-sacrifice will make eminent good sense to city-lovers among the living. Let me emphasize the social dynamic at work, how Pericles' rhetoric subtly pressures listeners to heed but one rationale, one *logos*: that of those other lovers, for whom death in battle represented no "mishap" but a golden opportunity.

So much, then, for the resonances of *erastas autês* as evocation of a unifying *polis*-love, a centripetal discourse of social coercion.[73] What about *dunamis*-love? If, as I suggest, we need as well to recognize that resonance, what will it have entailed? Thucydides himself provides the kind of parallel that can help. In Thucydides' narrative of the Sicilian debate, the historian, diagnosing the mood of Athenians galvanized by the prospect of conquest,

---

[72] Bakhtin, 1986:60–102.
[73] Cf. appeals to honor/shame, Thucydides 2.43.4–6.

states that "an *erôs* to sail fell upon all alike." So saying, he then dissects that *erôs* to show how different groups responded differently: the old were reassured by the scale of the mission; the young, expecting to come through safe and sound, were excited by longing for the exotic; the rank-and-file, eager for the short-term windfall the invasion seemed to offer, thought they could look forward to long-term pay stemming from an expansion of the city's power (6.24.3). My point: that in and of itself, a plea to feel *dunamis-erôs* must reach listeners at an individual, self-interested, even materialistic level.

Scholars who worry about that resonance have reason to. *Dunamis*-lust (*dunameôs epithumêsai*), specifically, desire for mastery of the sea, seduced the Spartans to their regret, according to Isocrates. For it destroyed their land-based hegemony (5.60) and corrupted them the way prostitutes ruin their lovers (8.103). Nor should we forget how Thucydides' "*erôs* to sail" offers an object-lesson in reckless deliberation (6.13.1, 6.24.3). But that same *erôs* also offers an object lesson in motivation: how calculation alone will not suffice to free us from our fears and inhibitions; how *erôs* does not really fall on all alike, but affects each of us differently and at an individual level. That side to *erôs*, the self-assertive side, thus provides the "hook" for Pericles' rhetoric. Through it, the speaker seizes hold of his listeners' imaginations and offers each of them a sense of tangible rewards: the city's power and the attendant perks. Admittedly, that will not sit well with Pericles' efforts to maneuver Athenians away from a selfish, risk-benefit calculus.[74] But the city's attractions here do not operate on a purely abstract or spiritual plane. Considering that it will take an eyeful of the city's *dunamis* to spark a citizen's *erôs*, we must keep in mind that Pericles refers to the concrete and very visible manifestations of the city's power and prosperity.[75] I am referring, of course, to the public-works program from which the *dêmos* derived pay, prestige, and aesthetic pleasure, a program prompting Pericles' critics to compare Athens to a dolled-up woman.[76]

Dunamis becomes, then, the beauty that draws the lover's eye, the goods lovers seek to possess and enjoy. As for connections between this more narrowly selfish *erôs* and the *erôs* of self-sacrifice, one last parallel will help. In Xenophon's *Anabasis*, we read how a certain Episthenes, panicked lest a Thracian ruler execute a handsome boy, extended his neck and offered to die in the boy's place. "'Strike,' he said, 'if the boy so bids and will feel grateful

---

[74] Among the fallen, poor and rich alike ignored material considerations, Thucydides 2.42.4. See McGlew 2002:32–34.

[75] *To eudaimon*, Thucydides 2.43.4. Monuments as tokens of *dunamis*: Ober 1998:84–85.

[76] Plutarch *Pericles* 12.2.

for it.' " When the boy begged that the two of them be spared, Episthenes, putting his arm around him, challenged, apparently in jest, the Thracian to fight for the lad (*Anabasis* 7.4.7–11). Though Episthenes in Xenophon's narrative offers his life for the boy's, that gesture is still deeply self-interested. He is, so we are told, a *paiderastês*, a lover of boys, and it is his *tropos*, his "inclination," that explains his behavior. *Erôs*-driven, this *tropos* is to be understood as less than fully rational, yet militarily valuable: Episthenes once assembled a crack regiment based on physical beauty alone. Yet even if Episthenes were to have been killed, in his fantasy, he still would have got what he wanted: the boy's thanks, which in pederastic terms translate as sexual gratification.[77] Just so, the citizen-warrior, in his fantasy of reciprocity, will receive the "tangible" rewards of heroism: a noble burial, an orator's praises, the gratitude of all. And it is this gratitude that the city-lover desires more than anything else, the bliss of knowing that, by having saved the city, he holds it in his debt forever.[78]

Erotic passion as the higher reason, self-sacrifice as self-gratification — Thucydides neglects to tell us what effect this *logos* of *erôs* produced in mourners. Nor does he reflect on its implications for the future course of the war — not explicitly, at least. But he might less obviously. Thus for some readers, the plague narration, following, as it does, directly on the heels of Pericles' speech, casts a shadow over the idealism that seems radiate from the orator's every word.[79] On the other hand, speech and plague occurred in just that order and within a matter of months; perhaps there is no more to it than that. But whatever the significance of that juxtaposition, Thucydides provides us with a kind of "control group" when, in the course of narrating the Sicilian Debate, he revisits the *logos* of *erôs* in the context of assembly speeches whose dissonant resonances arrest the mind the same way that the conflicting, disorienting stimuli of *erôs* overwhelm both mind and body. Did, then, our funeral orator set his city on a dangerous path by infusing *erôs* into the city's discourse? Whether he did or not, Thucydides paints the portrait of a statesman uniquely equipped to steer the *dêmos* through stormy moodswings and passionate longings, an example his successors would have done well to follow had they but the will to try and the know-how to pull it off.

---

[77] For the passage, Dover 1989:51.

[78] Cf. McGlew 1993:188: "*Erastês* — the word Thucydides' Pericles uses for lover — hints at a relationship that is not only intimate but active and passionate. The *erastês* is devoted to his beloved, but is also possessive, domineering, and prone to jealousy. He cares for his lover and is personally interested in her welfare, but he demands exclusive attention."

[79] Cornford's highly influential 1907 reading.

3

HE LOVES YOU, HE LOVES YOU NOT
DEMOPHILIC COURTSHIP IN ARISTOPHANES' *KNIGHTS*

I N THE *ACHARNIANS* OF 425 BCE, Aristophanes promises to "shred" the leather
merchant Cleon, a political bigwig and a thorn in the playwright's side.[1]
Delivering on that promise the very next year in *Knights*, Aristophanes
portrays Cleon as a repulsively obsequious, yet violently quarrelsome house-
slave named Paphlagon. But to exact full poetic justice, the playwright
evidently felt he needed to create a character in whom this stage-Cleon would
more than meet his match. Hence the Sausage-Seller, a disreputable street
vendor vying with Paphlagon to win the affections of the significantly named
Demos ("The-People, " from *dêmos* "citizenry"), an elderly householder and
Paphlagon's master. Indeed, the pair profess love — *sexual* love — for their
incongruously superannuated love-object, but why? What could they, or, for
that matter, the playwright, hope to gain from staging a thinly veiled political
rivalry as a tawdry love triangle?

Whatever it is, students of the play would do well to pay heed. For sexual
imagery runs through the goings-on like an *idée fixe*, at times sounding the
dominant note, at times playing counterpoint to other themes.[2] Yet this
imagery has, at least until recently, mostly gone unnoticed.[3] When scholars
comment, they tend to focus on one or another of two "logics." Thus Dover,
pointing out how each of Demos' two "lovers" stands to benefit from coming

---

[1] Aristophanes *Acharnians* 299–302. Aristophanes' troubles with Cleon and related matters: Olson
2002:xxix–xxxi, xlvi–xlvii, l–li; Atkinson 1992; Sommerstein 1986.

[2] See Landfester 1967:55 on "die Darstellung des Politischen im Erotischen für die weitere
Handlung als konstitutiv"; cf. Hubbard 1991:67–68.

[3] But see Ludwig 2002 (consult index); Wohl 2002:73–123; Henderson 1991:66–70. Landfester
1967:50–60, 73, 100–101 provides detailed analysis; his focus on passivity looks forward to
Dover 1989 and Foucault 1990. Neither Rosen (1988:59–82) nor McGlew (2002:86–111) addresses
the politician-as-lover conceit. For recent work on political themes in the play: McGlew
2002:86–111; Hesk 2000:255–258, 289–291; Riu 1999:143–154; Yunis 1996:50–58.

across as the more generous, and therefore more deserving, "suitor," alludes to some of the more elevated components — the ameliorating reciprocities — of classical Athenian pederasty.[4] That, however, cannot be divorced from another, equally important "logic." Thus Henderson connects *erôs* imagery to Paphlagon as "violator of the people";[5] I would further assert that *dêmos*-"buggery," which is quite as organic to the *erastês* (male lover) conceit as any positive connotation, needs to be understood within a larger system of reversals and incongruous revalorizations. Curious, and too little studied, is the fact that Paphlagon and the Sausage-Seller pursue their quarry by means of *kolakeia*, obsequious cajolery at odds with the dominance usually associated with being an *erastês*. More curious still is it that Demos, elsewhere a gullible victim, in the lyric interlude at lines 1111–1150 rationalizes his passively mercenary stance vis-à-vis his lovers.

I shall, then, be taking a closer look at still unresolved problems relating to the politician-as-lover conceit in Aristophanes' *Knights*. In so doing, I part company with those who start from the assumption that the image mimics the purportedly "demerastic" (*dêmos*-besotted) rhetoric of a Cleon. I, too, see oratorical practice as the starting point. But the image itself I read as comically absurdist reification inspired by the "demophilia topos," a well-attested blame motif attacking court and assembly speakers for attempting to seduce the *dêmos* with specious claims of affection. By sexualizing the topos, Aristophanes discovers within the dysfunctional give-and-take of "demophilic" politics a whole tangle of contradictory reciprocities, symmetries, and asymmetries — strategies, in other words, whereby power is got through surrender, and dominance through subservience. Overlooked in all this has been the role of Demos, who, in the crux passage mentioned earlier (1111–1150), admits to feigning ignorance and passivity so as to screen his own aggressively exploitative stance toward would-be "buggerers." Strife and conflict therefore underlie the amicable veneer. Comically dressed-up as pederastic *kolakeia*, this dystopian vision of political friendship presents Athenian democracy as fraught with category slippage and revalorizations symptomatic of *stasis*.

---

[4] Dover 1972:91: ". . . for lovers try to outbid one another in generosity to the person whom they love." Cf. Sommerstein 1981:181; Connor 1971:96–98 and sources cited p. 97n14.

[5] Henderson 1991:69; cf. Monoson 2000:86–87. Brock 1986 and Landfester 1967 connect Demos-*erômenos*' passivity to the "Souveränitätsproblem." Wohl 2002:73–123 reads *Knights* as reversing a constructive leadership-erotics suggested by Cleon's Mytilenian speech, Thucydides 3.37–40.

Demerastic Rhetoric?

To make sense of sexual imagery in *Knights*, we should first turn to the play's finale, where the Sausage-Seller, setting aside all pretense that Demos is anything but the sovereign *dêmos* of Athens, or that the courtship of Demos was anything but a political contest, demonstrates the sort of assembly rhetoric that previously so enthralled his new master:

Sausage-Seller:

First of all, whenever an assembly speaker would say, "O Demos, I am your lover (*erastês*), and I love (*philô*) you and care for (*kêdomai*) you, and no one else counsels you the way I do" — whenever they'd start their speeches like that, it would set you flapping your wings and tossing your horns.

Aristophanes *Knights* 1340–1344

It would seem that Demos had, prior to his transformation, been an easy mark for the highly emotional, even erotic, brand of audience-bonding favored by the city's politicians. Or so claims the Sausage-Seller as he pointedly shifts our attention from the dramatic illusion to the "realities" of public oratory — realities supposedly illustrated by verbatim quotation of a few, choice phrases.

But how close to reality are we? Certain scholars, pointing out similarities between the love language famously scripted by Thucydides in the Periclean Funeral Oration ("You must daily gaze upon the city's power and become lovers [*erastai*] of it," 2.43.1) and the erotically inflected love declarations in our play (732–737, cf. 1341), detect in the latter a snapshot of late fifth-century practice — "flowers culled from the oratory of Cleon," as some have put it.[6] There is, however, reason for doubt. In the surviving corpus of Attic oratory and related evidence (speeches in Thucydides, Plato's *Apology*, sophistic exercises), we find no instance of, nor reference to, speakers wooing audiences with professions of *erôs*. In fact, we find but a single, rather unusual instance (Plato *Apology* 29d, though cf. Thucydides 2.60.5) of an emotional effusion at all

---

[6] Connor 1971:97, quoting Rogers 1910:188; see also Ludwig 2002:145 (cf. 151); Monoson 2000:66; Crane 1998:318–319; Dover 1972:91; Gomme et al. 1970–1981:vol. 2 pp. 135–137; Burckhardt 1924:40; Neil 1901:175. Wohl 2002:92–93 suggests that *erôs*-rhetoric could have figured in the historical Cleon's attempt to bind "demos to demagogue in a relation of mutual desire without mutual degradation."

like what the Sausage-Seller reports — that is, one where a speaker professes a heartfelt attachment or partiality (*philia, kêdos*) to his audience ("you"), or to the collectivity (*polis, dêmos*) to which that audience belongs.[7] That should arouse our curiosity, given the frequency with which speakers attribute such love talk to *others*. Why, then, all those claims that "so-and-so says he loves you" if matching instances of same fail to materialize in the evidence?

The Demophilia Topos

We can begin to answer that question by looking more closely at how speakers both did and did not conduct their audience-bonding — I shall use the technical term *captatio benevolentiae*.[8] Thus we note that democratic sympathies, patriotism, a favorable disposition toward "you," the audience — none of that in and of itself would have been taken amiss.[9] On the contrary, audiences seem to have demanded of speakers just those sorts of assurances, whence the practice of, for instance, listing one's own or one's forebears' civic-minded accomplishments,[10] or representing one's friendships and hatreds as identical to those of one's listeners (Demosthenes 18.280–281; cf. Aristophanes *Acharnians* 509–512; Aristotle *Rhetoric* 1381a7–19), or, with varying degrees of obliquity, implicating oneself in patriotic sentiments of various sorts.[11] None of that is, however, quite as blunt or direct as what the Sausage-Seller quotes. To be sure, speakers show little reluctance to profess civic goodwill (*eunoia*),[12] though we shall see how *eunoia* could be viewed differently from *philia* (affection, love, friendship) in terms of emotional intensity. Lysias, Aristides tells us, "professed himself to be a friend (*philon*) in common of the *polis*" (Aristides 3.607 Behr = Lysias fr. 109b Albini), though

---

[7] For the affective register of *philia*, below; for *kêdesthai*, Landfester 1967:101; Neil 1901:175.

[8] "Currying of favor," phrase first used Boethius *In topica Ciceronis* 1042d, 1043a Migne, but cf. Cicero *Officia* 2.48. Standard term of rhetoric since Alberic of Monte Cassino (eleventh century ce): Murphy 2001:205–206.

[9] See Ober 1989:336; Connor 1971:99–108; Landfester 1967:53–55; Burckhardt 1924:40–46.

[10] Antiphon 6.45; Andocides 1.141–143; Lysias 25.12; Demosthenes 18 passim; see Ober 1989:226–247, cf. 266–270.

[11] Isocrates 8.39 ("such is my task, just as it is of every other man who cares about his country [*tôn allôn tôn kêdomenôn tês poleôs*]"); 20.1 (*eleutherias makhometha kai tês dêmokratias epithumoumen*, "we fight for freedom and desire democracy"); Demosthenes 23.190; Dinarchus 1.92 ("if we care for our homeland"); Aeschines 2.152; Lycurgus 3.

[12] Andocides 2.25; Aeschines 1.159; 2.118, 181; Demosthenes 18.1, 8, 286. Similar are first-person affirmations of civic *prothumia*, "zeal" or "commitment": Lysias 12.99; 20.19, 33, 35; Demosthenes 18.286.

just what Aristides quotes, and how accurately, remains a puzzle. Pericles, in the last of the speeches assigned to him by Thucydides, affirms himself to be *philopolis*, "partial/devoted to the city" — in other words, a patriot (2.60.5). But in tandem with his patriotism Pericles notes his incorruptibility, seemingly as if to thwart suspicions the first claim might tend to raise (see further below). Nor do we find a fully applicable parallel in the Periclean Funeral Oration (Thucydides 2.43.1), where Pericles affirms no city-*erôs* of his own, but urges it on others. As for the warm expression of *philia* in Plato's *Apology*,

> If then you would, as I said, acquit me on these conditions [viz., that I give up philosophizing], I should answer you, "Men of Athens, I do indeed love you dearly (*egô humas, ô andres Athênaioi, aspazomai men kai philô*), but I shall obey the god rather than you."

Plato's Apology 29d

that does not so much express democratic sympathies as it does a rather elaborate, and somewhat ironic, "No thank you."[13] As for speakers declaring *erôs* for audience, *dêmos*, or the like ("I am your lover [*erastês*]," "I desire/lust for [*erô*] you"), that does not happen in our sources — except, of course, in Aristophanes' *Knights*.[14]

What, then, to make of some twenty-odd instances of speakers warning audiences not to trust an *opponent's* love-talk — instances like the following:

> Why in the world is it, men of Athens, that you, whose interests are on the lips of all, are generally no better off now than before, while these men whose every word hangs on your welfare, never their own — why is it that they have gone from poor to rich? *Because, men of Athens, though they say they love you, it is not you they love, but themselves.* (*hoti phasin men, ô andres Athênaioi, philein humas, philousi d' oukh humas all' hautous*)

Demosthenes Exordia 53.3 (my emphasis)[15]

Similar is Isocrates' warning to an imagined assembly audience "not to pay heed . . . to those who claim to love the *dêmos*, yet bring it to utter ruin" (*tois*

---

[13] Cf. the use of *philein* with requests (LSJ s.v. I.7.), demurral (Plato *Phaedrus* 228d–e).

[14] Demades fr. 78 de Falco, in which the speaker claims to be a cowardly *erastês* of peace, is spurious.

[15] Authenticity: Yunis 1996:287–289 with references. Selfishness theme, cf. Aristotle *Nichomachean Ethics* 1168b15–25; Lysias 20.17.

47

philein men ton dêmon phaskousin, 8.121), or another speaker's to ignore "those whose words speak of love for you" (*tous men phaskontas toutous tôi logôi philein humas*) but whose deeds, we gather, speak otherwise.[16] We are, then, dealing with a variation on the familiar words-versus-deeds antithesis, with the emphasis placed, as usual, on deeds as the more truthful signifier.[17]

But it would seem we are also dealing with a red herring of sorts if, as we saw earlier, matching instances of speakers actually saying such things in so many words fail to materialize in the expected contexts. I would therefore posit an element of exaggeration, even distortion, for what I shall call the "demophilia topos" ("So-and-so claims to love you/the *dêmos*/the *polis*, but in fact does not").[18] True, it prefers indirect over direct, verbatim quotation. But we should not for that reason regard it as mere shorthand for an adversary's audience-bonding. It is, rather, a rhetorical move, a way to impute certain sentiments, even language, to targeted speakers.[19] Thus when a plaintiff in the corpus informs the jury that the defendant "will be telling you he loves you (*phêsei humas philein*) second only to his relatives" (Demosthenes 58.30; cf. 28–29), the intimacies implied by *philia* are key to the sarcasm of the speaker's quip.

But why the apparent reluctance to profess in one's own behalf the sort of *polis*-oriented *philia* readily attributed to others (e.g. Isocrates 16.28)? Dionysius, commenting on Pericles' avowal of *polis*-love in Thucydides' *History* ("I am *philopolis*," 2.60.5), faults it as vulgar, inappropriate, and squandered, inasmuch as singing one's own praises tends to provoke annoyance and resentment, not sympathy, especially before a political or courtroom audience (Dionysius of Halicarnassus *Thucydides* 45). Plutarch, though he also recognizes the risks inherent in self-praise, nevertheless cannot criticize Pericles' gambit: the statesman had no choice (Pericles in Thucydides 2.60–64 is under attack), nor does he lie (*Moralia* 540c–d). So, too, Demosthenes, needing to defend honors he has received, mentions the disadvantage self-commendation places one in (Demosthenes 18.3–4). In another speech, Demosthenes clearly

---

[16] Isocrates 8.127; 12.141; Demosthenes 3.24; 22.66 (*kêdemôn*, "one who is solicitous for your welfare," sarcastic); 26.23; 58.30; Aeschines 2.8; Dinarchus 1.100; 3.22; Plato *Apology* 24b.

[17] See Parry 1981:15.

[18] Cf. *Knights* 870, 946 ("you have enraged me with your claims that you love [*philein*] me [sc. the *dêmos*]").

[19] Direct quotation only by the Sausage-Seller (Aristophanes *Knights* 1340–1344). Cf., however, direct quotation of an allegedly impassioned (*aei boai*, "always shouts") and bogus *eunoia* claim at Demosthenes 25.64; for derogatory *boai*, Bers 1997:187 and n110. See Bers 1997:134 on emotive indirect discourse; 115–128 on direct quotation in Aristophanes; 224 on direct versus indirect quotation.

relishes the opportunity to rake Charidemus (mercenary commander and honorary citizen) over the coals for a letter combining, so we are told, fulsome self-praise (23.160–161) with a bogus profession of "love for you."[20]

Use of *dêmotikos*, "true-blue democrat," *Volksfreund* (Wankel), offers further clues.[21] Commendable though it was to be *dêmotikos*, bluntly first-person affirmations of the type "I am *dêmotikos*" are difficult to confirm.[22] Still, the charge that "so-and-so falsely claims to be *dêmotikos*" appears to have been commonplace, as when Aeschines alleges some such claim to be Demosthenes' mantra.[23] Later in the same speech, Aeschines disparagingly observes that "goodwill (*eunoia*) and the name 'the people's friend' (*to tês dêmokratias onoma*) are common property, yet those whose conduct least fits the description are usually the first to seek refuge there" (3.248). Whatever its accuracy, this last observation suggests that listeners could at least be induced to regard self-commendation in a demophilic vein as *ipso facto* suspect.

Noteworthy is the psychagogic power speakers sometimes ascribe to patriotic posturing. Thus Aeschines alerts listeners to the danger of being deceived by the pleasant sound (*euphêmian*) of Demosthenes' claim to being *dêmotikos* (3.168). In a similar vein, the speaker in *Against Aristocrates* warns his audience not to let Charidemus' fraudulent friendship "cloud" their wits (Demosthenes 23.184). Relevant to these psychological considerations is the matter of wording, the "spin" affective vocabulary could place on allegations of patriotic posturing.[24] What sort of spin? For that, we can turn to Aristotle. Contrasting *eunoia* (goodwill) with *philia* (affection, love, friendship), the former, he tells us, while it appears to be an element of the latter, differs in possessing neither "tension" (*diatasis*) nor "desire" (*orexis*), these last being concomitants of *philêsis*,

---

[20] *Philos einai phêsi phenakizôn humas*, "in saying he loves you he pulls the wool over your eyes," Demosthenes 23.184; cf. 23.174, 193.

[21] Thucydides 6.28.2 (Alcibiades' allegedly "undemocratic lawlessness") suggests *dêmotikos* as a potent slogan already in 415. See Wankel 1976:vol. 1 p. 138.

[22] Hoping to be recalled from exile, Andocides (2.26) assures listeners he likely, and sensibly, will be *dêmotikos*. Cf. the obliquity of Isocrates 18.62 ("you should regard as *dêmotikoi* not those who . . . but who" etc.). Note non-problematic third-person assertion ("So-and-so is/was *dêmotikos*"): Lysias 20.22; Isocrates 16.36; Demosthenes 24.134; Aeschines 1.173; 3.194.

[23] Aeschines 3.168: *nai, alla dêmotikos estin* etc. ("yes, but let's not forget he's 'the people's friend'" etc.); cf. 176, 248; Lysias 28.12; 30.9, 15; Isocrates 18.48; Dinarchus 1.9, 44, 78–79; *dêmizontôn* (those who "people-ize") in Aristophanes *Wasps* 699.

[24] "Spin" in Attic oratory, Hesk 2000:202–207, 213. Cf. in the "Hermagoreans" and Seneca the Elder the related idea of *khrôma* or *color*, the "color" or "complexion" one gave to a court case: Fairweather 1981:32–33, 166–178.

"loving."[25] A client of Lysias' appears to capitalize on just such a contrast when, having already commended victims of the Thirty for their *dêmos*-oriented *eunoia* (13.1; cf. 13, 93–94), he raises the rhetorical temperature by characterizing the relationship between the martyrs of democracy and "you" as *philia* involving the same obligations as those incumbent on "friends and intimates" (*philous kai epitêdeious*, 92; cf. 94, 96–97).

So, too, will speakers have capitalized on the voltage associated with *philia* — its "tension" and "desire" — when attacking others for demophilic posturing. That could have suggested a certain lack of decorum, an unseemly willingness to indulge in over-emotional speech, on the part of alleged demophiles.[26] But we should remember that the problem was not *dêmos*- or *polis*-oriented *philia* itself (ordinarily highly commendable), but the notion that a speaker would go before an audience and declare, "I love you" (*philô humas*) or the equivalent. Such a sentence conveys information (the fact that I love you), but it also performs in the Austinian sense: it enacts an emotional bond, namely, *philia*, between speaker ("I") and addressee ("you") — so especially in the case of the Greek verb *philein* ("to love"), whose semantic field extends to the performance of *philia* through kissing.[27] Thus when I say, "I love you," I may be lying, *but something still happens.*[28]

Of course, the demophilia topos performs this verbal kiss only at a mimetic remove; through it, a speaker avers that someone else, not himself, declares audience-love. Does that indirectness rob this speech-act of its performative power? Without rehearsing the whole debate over the representation of performative speech,[29] we need to keep in mind the social-performative component intrinsic not only to the reported speech-act itself *but to the very act of reporting another's speech.* For such an act

> takes into account a third person — the person to whom the reported utterances are being transmitted. This provision for a third

---

[25] Aristotle *Nichomachean Ethics* 1166b30–34; see Konstan 1997:74.

[26] Cf. Bers 1997:147–148; Bers 1994b on care taken by courtroom speakers to project an appropriate social personality. See also Roisman 2005; Worman 2002.

[27] Speech-acts (Austin's "performatives") include sentences like, "I bet you X dollars" and the response, "You're on!" — sentences that do not so much describe as enact a fact (a bet, a marriage, etc.). See Ober 1998:36–38; Ober 1994; Petrey 1990:5–7; Austin 1975:13–14.

[28] See Neuman 2004:63.

[29] Its power to perform if abstracted from its proper setting, as in the case of speech-acts quoted, narrated, fictionalized: Petrey 1990; Derrida 1982:307–330; Austin 1975.

person is especially important in that it strengthens the impact of organized social forces in speech reception.[30]

The reporting of speech, insofar as it invites others to join in scrutinizing someone else's words, is social and ideological all at once: social in terms of the sharing involved, ideological in terms of values put into play. It is, in short, its own speech-act. Where reported speech directly concerns addressee, affect will likely play a part. And that is how our topos must have worked. Implicating listeners as victims of demophilic posturing, the topos will have targeted their sensibilities at the level of what Aristotle calls *thumos*, the soul's "spirited" dimension and seat of *philia*. Concomitant impressions of *philia* betrayed will then have stirred the *thumos* to anger.[31] Particularly galling would have been the gullibility this topos at times imputes to listeners. So, for instance, in Demosthenes' *Third Olynthiac*, the current generation, doting as it does on the ingratiating love-talk of corrupt politicians, fails to measure up to the *dêmos* of yesteryear[32] — precisely the Sausage-Seller's point, as it is also the playwright's in much of the comic business soon to be examined.

Friends, Lovers

The play opens with two house slaves complaining of a third, Paphlagon, a newcomer who will stop at nothing to make himself the favorite of Demos, the master of all three. To rid themselves of the Paphlagon-nuisance, the first two slaves enlist the aid of a nearly perfect rogue, the Sausage-Seller, in hopes that he, by dint of utter shamelessness (that is, by fighting fire with fire), will replace the upstart as manager of Demos' household.

A contest pitting Paphlagon against the Sausage-Seller is ushered in with love declarations that place a decidedly pederastic complexion on what follows:[33]

---

[30] Vološinov 1986:117.

[31] *Philia* and *thumos*: Aristotle *Politics* 1327b40–1328a3; Ludwig 2002:194–195 and n98.

[32] The speakers of yesteryear "did not habitually gratify or love (*ouk ekharizonth'... oud' ephiloun*) your forebears the way those we've got now do you": Demosthenes 3.24; cf. 3, 13, 21–22, 25–26, 30–31.

[33] Cf. Landfester 1967:51–52 on the programmatic force of these lines; 50–60, 73, 100–101 for erotic evocations generally in *Knights*. Andrew Lear has sent me the intriguing suggestion, more plausible, I think, than others, that Aristophanes here parodies not a Cleon professing *dêmos-erôs*, but one accusing others of doing so.

Demos:

Why Paphlagon, who's been wronging you?

Paphlagon:

Him! Him and his boys have been beating me up, all because of you.

Demos:

But why?

Paphlagon:

Because I love you, Demos. Because I'm the one who's hot for you. (*hotiê philô s', ô Dêm', erastês t' eimi sos.*)

Demos:

Okay, so who are *you*?

Sausage-Seller:

I'm this guy's rival (*anterastês*). I've pined forever for you, wanted to treat you nice (*erôn palai sou boulomenos te s' eu poiein*) — I and a lot of us respectable types (*kaloi te k'agathoi*) have. But we can't. *He* won't let us.

Aristophanes Knights 730–736

By identifying himself, however incongruously, with the *kaloi k'agathoi* ("respectable types"; contrast 185–186) wishing to benefit Demos ("treat you nice," *s' eu poiein*), the Sausage-Seller hints at shame-honor protocols again evoked when Paphlagon, some ten lines later, urges Demos to choose his favorite within the formal setting of an *ekklêsia*, a meeting of the *dêmos* sitting as a political body:

So hurry up, Demos! Call an assembly, so you can decide between us who's more caring and give him your love.

Aristophanes Knights 746–748

In relation to the *erôs* declarations uttered just lines earlier, "love" (*hina touton philêis*, "so you can give him your love") in requital for "kindness" (*hopoteros . . . eunousteros*, "which one of us is kinder") can be understood as the reward a successful suitor can expect from a compliant beloved; our sources show it could stand for sexual gratification.[34] Yet the venue — a political

---

[34] Dover 1989:49–54.

assembly — for the upcoming contest leaves no doubt as to the dual character (political-pederastic) of the anticipated courtship.

But why choose a "more caring" suitor in the first place, and "more caring" as opposed to what? It was, we have seen, benevolence (*eunoia*) and good services (*eu poiein*) that legitimized the persuasive efforts of politicians. Much the same can be said for lovers, who were expected to prove their worth through the guidance and mentoring they offered their respective beloveds. Take that away, and the reciprocities of pederasty amounted to prostitution.[35]

In Aristophanes' *Knights*, it is Demos' honorable standing that is on the line, and the enticements offered by each of his lovers that are on trial. Whoever puts on the more compelling display of *eunoia* will win a crown from Demos; that recalls the practice of awarding crowns to politicians and others for civic or *polis*-directed goodwill.[36] But the sparring of our two candidates also foregrounds what Demos can expect from an *erastês* whose *peithô* falls short in the *eunoia* department. Thus Paphlagon advises Demos not to heed the Sausage-Seller's oracles lest they turn him into a "worn hide" (*molgos*, 962–963), meaning, arguably, a male willing to submit to sexual penetration.[37] The Sausage-Seller counters that listening to Paphlagon's oracles could spell circumcision for Demos (963–964),[38] a barbaric indignity for any Greek man.[39] Elsewhere in the play, Paphlagon boasts that he can make a fool of Demos *ad libitum* (713), and that his skills include the ability "to make the *dêmos* expand and contract on cue" (719–720). Quips the Sausage-Seller, "Even my ass-hole knows that trick" (721), as if to imply that Paphlagon's vaunted skill at *dêmos*-manipulation will habituate Demos to a degrading docility analogous to the Sausage-Seller's own sexual passivity.[40]

All of this connects with the demophilia topos in fairly obvious ways. "Spinning" civic *eunoia* as a more intimate, and in context more disquieting,

---

[35] Cf. Pausanias in Plato *Symposium* 184b, 184e–185a; Demosthenes 61.5 (*erôs* without shame); Aeschines 1.137. See Dover 1989:49–54 for the redeeming power of *philia* in pederasty, 202–203 for the educative role played (ideally) by the *erastês*. Aristophanes *Wealth* 153–159, though cynically treating honorable pederasty as dressed-up *porneia*, acknowledges a notional distinction between the two. See further Konstan 1993:8; Foucault 1990:204–214; Dover 1989:145–147.

[36] Cf. e.g. Isocrates 18.61; Demosthenes 18. For evocations of honorary crowning in *Knights*, Yunis 1996:54. For honorary decrees (including those involving crowns), Hedrick 1999:410; Veligianni-Terzi 1997; Henry 1983.

[37] I find Henderson 1991:68–69, 212 and the parallels adduced there persuasive. Henderson 1998:347 translates "a mere balloon"; Sommerstein 1981:195 understands as "flayed alive."

[38] So Henderson 1998:347; Sommerstein 1981:195.

[39] See Henderson 1998:78–79n30 on *Acharnians* 155–163; Dover 1989:129–130; cf. Herodotus 2.37.2.

[40] Landfester 1967:11, 59 notes thematic resonances (viz., the "Souveränitätsproblem") of *erômenos*-Demos' passivity; Henderson 1991:66–70 discusses details of active-passive role-playing in the courtship.

philia, the topos exaggerates the emotional side to a speaker's audience-bonding. Spinning demophilia as *erôs*, the playwright renders the Demos-bonding of Paphlagon and the Sausage-Seller more disquieting still. Yet this politics-pederasty equation, when looked at closely, reveals cracks in its ideological underpinning. Democracy presupposes a sovereign *dêmos*, and one therefore dominant over individual citizens, including the leadership elite. Pederasty assigns to the *erastês* seniority in a relationship assigning to his junior a subordinate role should the relationship take a sexual turn.[41] Thus in our play, politics-as-pederasty, insofar as it *subordinates* Demos, which is to say the sovereign *dêmos*, to his lover-politicians, necessarily subverts at least as much as it ratifies democratic values.

Flatterers

But it also matters *how* Demos' lovers go about wooing their beloved. We get a foretaste of that strategy when, early on in the play, Slave 1 complains of the kind of antics resorted to by Demos' new slave, antics foreshadowing the direction the courtship will take when it later begins in earnest:

> Slave 1:
>
> Well, this Paphlagon tanner-fellow, once he'd sized up the old man, fell at our master's feet and began to wheedle (*êikall'*) and cajole (*ethôpeu'*) and flatter (*ekolakeu'*) and gull (*exêpata*) him with scraps of leather. And he'd say things like, "Demos, let's keep your jury service to one trial, then a bath. Then, a little something to eat, devour, munch. Don't forget your jury pay! Would you like me to serve you dinner?" Paphlagon's next move is to filch whatever one of us is cooking, and present it, complements of himself, to the master.

> Aristophanes *Knights* 46–54

No single term quite does justice to the constellation of behaviors that the speaker attributes to Paphlagon. Our sources do, though, suggest that just such groveling, gratifying, and gulling converge in the figure of the *kolax*, or "flatterer," whose *kolakeia* ("flattery") would seem to supply the model for persuasive strategies to which one or another flattery label is affixed at various

---

[41] On pederastic asymmetry and its problematics, I mostly side with Foucault 1990:215–225; Halperin 1990:88–112; Dover 1989:103–109. For useful critiques of an unnuanced approach, Davidson 1997; Thornton 1997; Cohen 1991.

points in Aristophanes' play.[42] So, for instance, when the Sausage-Seller offers Demos a pillow to cushion the latter's heroic derrière ("No rump that saw action at Salamis should have to feel sore," 784–785), Paphlagon cannot help but marvel at Demos' vulnerability to trifling "cajoleries."[43] *"That's* what I call a truly noble demonstration of democratic devotion!" gushes a grateful Demos (*alêthôs gennaion kai philodêmon*, 787), as if to make sure no one misses the political subtext to *kolakeia* in the play, or the connection with yet another blame motif prominent in the orators:

> It is, in fact, through political speeches of an excessively gratifying sort that they put you in a frame of mind to give yourself airs at assembly meetings, and to feel flattered (*kolakeuesthai*) hearing all that pleasing talk (*panta pros hêdonên akouontas*).

> Demosthenes 8.34

To the extent that Paphlagon and the Sausage-Seller flatter and cajole within a political framework, they evoke what Demosthenes labels "sweet-talking the people" (*pros kharin dêmêgorein*, 3.3), and, in the passage just quoted, outright *kolakeia*.[44] This image of the politician-as-*kolax* presents, we note, much the same jaundiced view of an opponent's *captatio benevolentiae* as we get in the demophilia topos, though with added emphasis on the *dêmos* and its vulnerabilities.[45]

One cannot easily miss the political resonances of *kolakeia* in *Knights.* What, if anything, does it mean that Demos' lovers are also his *kolakeuontes*, his "flatterers"? Paphlagon, so he tells us, can humiliate the *dêmos* at will, knows the kind of crumbs it likes to feed on, and, to top it all off, can make

---

[42] *Kolakeia* generally: Ribbeck 1883. Surveys of *kolakeia* (*thôpeia*, etc.) evocations in *Knights:* Tylawsky 2002:19–27 (Cleon in *Knights* and *Wasps*); Brock 1986:18–21; Dover 1972:91–92; Landfester 1967:57–59. Landfester notes, though he does not fully explore, the connection to pederastic courtship.

[43] *Thôpeumatia*, a flattery term: Aristophanes *Knights* 789; cf. 216 ("tasty-tidbit sweet-talking"), 776 (*kharioimên*, "gratify"), 890 (*thôpeiais*, "cajoleries"), 1031 (*sainôn*, "wagging the tail," "fawning"), 1116 (*thôpeuomenos*, "flattered"). For the offer of a cushion as *kolakeia*, cf. Theophrastus *Characters* 2.11; Aeschines 3.76–77. For fussy attention to grey hairs et sim., cf. Aristophanes *Knights* 908 with Aristophanes fr. 689 *PCG*; Theophrastus *Characters* 2.3.

[44] Cf. Euripides *Hecuba* 257; *Suppliants* 412–416; fr. 1029 Nauck (*thôpeias okhlou*, "flattery directed at the mob"); Aristophanes *Acharnians* 370–374, 633–658; Thucydides 3.42.6, 7.8.2; Isocrates 15.133; Demosthenes 3.24; 4.51; *Exordia* 28.1; Aeschines 3.127, 226, 234; Aristotle *Politics* 1292a4–38; Plutarch *Pericles* 11.4. See Konstan 1997:102–103 with notes.

[45] The flattery and demophilia *topoi* merge in Isocrates 8.121; Demosthenes 3.24–26; cf. Demosthenes 23.179 (*kolakeuôn kai phenakizôn humas*, "flattering and cheating you") in connection with the false-*philia* theme.

it "expand and contract on cue" (713–720). Turning to Euripides' *Suppliants*, a play also dated to the 420s, we note how the Theban Herald implies Athens to be a place where politicians, in quest of personal gain, lead by "puffing up" (*ekkhaunôn*) the citizens with speeches (412–413), and by providing them with momentary gratification (*to d' autikh' hêdus kai didous pollê kharin*, 414), which is to say, through means recognizable as *kolakeia*.[46] Comparing that to *Knights*, we see how Paphlagon's Demos-manipulation exploits puffery and deflation — that is, flattery and censure — along with outright gratification. Remembering the Sausage-Seller's caustic rejoinder to Paphlagon's boast ("Even my ass-hole knows that trick," 721), it becomes evident that both here and elsewhere in the play, as indeed elsewhere in Aristophanes' *oeuvre*, "flattery" (*kolakeuein*, *thôpeuein*, etc.) can serve as the medium for a covertly aggressive form of seduction hazardous to a beloved's autonomy and honorable standing.[47]

Hence a contradiction. Flatterers (*kolakes*, *thôpes*, etc.) were as a class debased figures.[48] The relationship of flatterer to victim of flattery was, not unlike that of pederastic lover to his beloved, a relationship of unequals, though with status values reversed. That is, the flatterer, the *active* participant in the arrangement, was viewed as inferior to the passive recipient, the target of flattery.[49] That contrasts with pederasty, where, as we have seen, the sexually *inactive erômenos* was conventionally understood as subordinate to the active *erastês*. The lover-as-flatterer thus presents us with the paradox of a senior partner subordinating himself to his junior.

That paradox, insofar as it highlights a kind of *jouissance* in the abjectivity *erôs* reduced one to, could be said to encapsulate what it meant to be in love. By which I mean that it encapsulates not the sheer joy of *erôs*, but all the ambivalence the lover's plight could evoke.[50] For clarity on how that relates to our play, it will help to look more closely at flattery, Paphlagon's and the Sausage-Seller's preferred mode of courtship, as a strategy itself fraught with problematic ambiguity. On the one hand, flattery (*kolakeia*, *thôpeia*) empowered one to coax compliance out of one's betters, as when a girl in Menander successfully

---

[46] Cf. Plutarch *Alcibiades* 6.4 (puffery and deflation). See Yunis 1996:45 ("This passage contains many of the standard charges against the demagogue" etc.).

[47] Cf. Aristophanes *Acharnians* 634–638 (flattered Athenians sit up on the "tips of their little behinds"); see Olson 2002:117; Hubbard 1991:51.

[48] Ranked with *thêtes* and slaves: Aristotle *Nichomachean Ethics* 1125a1–2; cf. *Rhetoric* 1383b32–35.

[49] Under the mature democracy, treating fellow citizens deferentially could be viewed as *douleia* or *kolakeia* out of step with democracy: Konstan 1996a:10–11.

[50] This is the Lacanian view of jouissance, for which Homer 2005:88–91.

"flatters" gods whose aid she seeks (*kolakeuous'... pepeiken, Dyscolus* 36–39). But the empowering modalities of *kolakeia* also point to problem areas. Thus we encounter *kolakes* who con their way into inheritances.[51] In Antisthenes, both *kolakes* and *hetairai* prey on victims whose deficiencies in good sense they seek to exploit (fr. 132 *SSR*; cf. Eupolis fr. 172.7–8 *PCG*). In Antiphon Sophist, a very similar deficiency induces the victims of flattery to eschew even the companionship of friends:

> Many, though they possess friends (*philous*), fail to acknowledge the fact; rather, they consort with fortune-hunting toadies (*thôpas ploutou*) and opportunistic flatterers (*tukhês kolakas*).

> Antiphon Sophist fr. 65 D-K

Whether or not these last *kolakeuomenoi* suffer from a true cognitive failure or have simply shut their eyes to their friends, the passage just quoted illustrates a dichotomy that will prove thematically important in *Knights*: the contrast between the genuine *philos* and the *kolax*-poseur, a rather slippery sort of contrast since, by playing the *philos*, the *kolax* blurs the difference between himself and his opposite number.[52] Ordinarily, the *philia* aped by the *kolax* will have been of a deferential, inferior sort (cf. Aristotle *Nichomachean Ethics* 1159a14–15). Yet Paphlagon incongruously boasts that Demos will find "no better friend than me" (860–861) — incongruously because this slave and flatterer *par excellence* uses language (*philon beltion'*, 'better friend') evoking the familiarity, mutuality, and parity usually associated with the kind of friendship meant when nowadays we say, "You and I are good friends."[53] Should Paphlagon get caught playing false with this "friend" of his, he doubtless will come across as having violated the golden rule of Greek popular morality: help friends, harm enemies. Or so one assumes ancient audiences would have responded.[54]

We have seen that Demos' lovers, through their antics and attack rhetoric, bring to light the play between *philia* and its quasi-opposite, *kolakeia*. But

---

[51] *Tais kolakeiais... psukhagôgoumenoi*, "inveigling their victims with flattery," Demosthenes 44.63; cf. 45.63–65; Isaeus 8.37; Plato *Laws* 923b

[52] For friends-versus-flatterers, cf. Euripides fr. 362.18–20 Nauck; Aristotle *Rhetoric* 1371a23–24; Xenophon *Memorabilia* 2.9.8.

[53] Konstan 1997:52–92; Konstan 1996b. *Philos* in *Knights* 861 = noun "friend"; note that Aristophanes has *philon beltion* ("a better friend"), not *philteron* ("more dear"). Cf. the "good friend" (*philos agathos*) in Plato *Lysis* 211e; Xenophon *Memorabilia* 1.6.13, 2.4–6.

[54] Archilochus 23.14–15; Solon 13.5 West; Sappho fr. 5.6–7; Xenophon *Memorabilia* 2.6.35; Plato *Republic* 332a–b; Blundell 1989:180–184; Dover 1974:180–184.

erôs, too, reveals within itself a similarly ambiguous play of opposites. When felt by male subjects, *erôs* often comes across as desire not just to enjoy but to possess and dominate.[55] Yet *erôs* masters those in its grip: as Socrates explains, the supposed freedom of tyrants is actually a form of slavery, for the tyrant is himself tyrannized by *erôs* (Plato *Republic* 572e–573b). But lovers beware: to kiss a pretty face is to let oneself be instantly enslaved.[56]

Inextricably linked in *Knights*, pederasty and *kolakeia* are not often part-nered elsewhere. Yet partnered they are, and often enough for us to detect a pattern. In Plato's *Phaedrus*, Socrates at one point claims that male lovers, like flatterers and prostitutes, offer their beloveds harmful, albeit pleasurable, companionship (240a–b). Socrates does not, of course, really believe what he is saying, but that does not mean that others would have found such a senti-ment wholly implausible. Clearchus of Soloi defines the lover (*erastês*) as a "flatterer" (*kolax*) seeking the "affection" (*philia*) of one possessing beauty or youth (fr. 21 Wehrli = Ath. 255b). In Plato's *Symposium*, the behavior of lovers can smack of slavish flattery (183a–b, cf. 184c). If Pausanias, Plato's speaker, empathizes with these lover-flatterers, Plutarch in his *Life of Alcibiades* seems not to when he disparages the mass of Alcibiades' lovers (not Socrates) as mere flatterers whom the youth despised. Yet in so characterizing them, the biographer has in mind no aberrant or anomalous *erôs*, but the instabilities and contradictions that *erôs* for an Alcibiades could evoke.[57] Hence the *kolax-erastês* both is and is not a contradiction. By playing the *kolax*, he seems to overturn pederastic hierarchies. Yet what else but *erôs* drives him to play that role?

And that just about sums up Paphlagon, who, as Demos' slave, lover, and *kolax*, flouts status disparities fundamental not just to pederasty, but to the very structure of Athenian society.[58] Add to that hinted aspersions against his sexual conduct,[59] and this allegorized leader of the democracy begins to

---

[55] Dominance and the male sexual role, Cohen 1991:186–187; Dover 1989:103–109. Power-lust, tyranny-lust: Archilochus 19.3 West; Herodotus 1.96.2, 3.53.4, 5.32; Isocrates 8.65, 113; McGlew 1993:183–212; Rothwell 1990:37 and nn67–68.

[56] Xenophon *Memorabilia* 1.3.11; cf. *Symposium* 4.14, 26; *Cyropaedia* 5.1.12; Plato *Symposium* 183a; *Phaedrus* 252a; Aeschines 1.42 (enslavement to lusts); see Foucault 1990:78–82.

[57] Plutarch *Alcibiades* 4.1, 6.1, for which Wohl 2002:124–170.

[58] Athenian law forbade slaves to "love" (*eran*) free boys or to "follow after them," a role Aeschines understands as reserved for free males (1.139). See also Wohl 2002:226 on Plutarch *Solon* 1.6.

[59] Cf. Aristophanes *Knights* 75–79 (elaborate punning on sexual passivity and political corrup-tion), 377–381 (anus-scrutiny turned against Paphlagon), 765 (Paphlagon is "noblest" after Lysicles and two prostitutes); *Acharnians* 664 (Cleon as coward and bugger). See Wohl 2002:90.

mirror the very "buggers" (*kinoumenous*) whom he, as the people's "watchdog," hounds out of political life.[60] Many (not all) of the same attributes also appear in the Sausage-Seller. However benign his ultimate aims (he will emerge as Demos' savior), the idea that he, a sexually compromised street vender,[61] would pursue pederastic politics with a view to becoming a "real man, a major player" (*anêr megistos*) riding roughshod over Athens and much else (157–178, 356–358), brings him uncomfortably close to his rival. Indeed, it presents us with a grotesquely exaggerated version of the demophile's reckless egocentricity. To gain power over Demos, *both* lovers paradoxically stoop to *thôpeumata*, the tricks of the flatterer, thereby calling their love into question. Yet in so doing, they both seem unaware of the even more paradoxical assist provided by the object of their attentions.

Stasis

If nothing else, Aristophanes' play leaves a vivid impression of Demos' weakness for the enticements offered by Paphlagon and (for the purpose of ousting Paphlagon) by the Sausage-Seller as well. Thus we hear of a Demos who can be won over by the mere gift of a cushion (784–788), a "slack-jawed" Demos abjectly dependent on jury pay (*kekhênêi*, 804; cf. *têi kekhênaiôn polei*, Athens as "city of slack-jaws": 1263), a naïve Demos, for whom the Sausage-Seller's exposé of past idiocies is pure revelation (1337–1355) — a Demos, in short, defenseless against lies and trickery of all sorts.

What, then, to make of the following, in which an oddly savvy Demos admits a kind of complicity in the questionable practices of his lovers?

Chorus:

O Demos, you possess a fair empire, for everyone fears you like a big-shot tyrant. But you're easy to trick, and you love flattery and being duped, always gazing in a slack-jawed stupor at whoever is giving a speech. And that brain you've got there, it's just not there!

---

[60] Aristophanes *Knights* 876–880, 1017–1024. Ex-prostitutes were forbidden to address the assembly or play other public roles: Halperin 1990:88–104; Winkler 1990:54–64; Dover 1989: 19–39, 102–104.

[61] Sausage-Seller as sexually compromised: Aristophanes *Knights* 417–426 (hiding stolen meat between one's buttocks implies sexual passivity, which in turn implies a future in politics), 721, 1242. Note how the Sausage-Seller's political disqualifications (above note) become ironic qualifications. See further Wohl 2002:81–86; Henderson 1991:66–70.

Demos:

But it's you with no wits under those fair locks of yours if you think I'm witless. No, I *allow* myself to be gulled; I *like* bawling for my daily chow. I *want* to maintain a thievish political leader. So I raise him up, and when he's had his fill, I strike him down.

Aristophanes *Knights* 1111–1130

At a point just before the final, decisive contest, with Demos' lovers momentarily offstage, the Chorus notes the baffling juxtaposition of Demos' king-like qualities with his idiotic vulnerability to flattering speeches. Demos takes issue with very little of it, countering only that his imbecility is merely a pose, one that he assumes willingly. So long as a given leader responds satisfactorily to his infantile cries (*brullôn*) for handouts, he will fatten the politician as if for the sacrifice (1127–1140) — that is, allow him to steal (1127, 1149) from state coffers until the inevitable corruption trial (1150). Thus Demos tolerates bad behavior from his leaders in a way that, for its cynically self-interested willingness to accommodate, at least up to a point, those who care little for his well-being, exhibits patterns of prostitution. I repeat, up to a point: Demos surely stops short of that boundless forbearance one poet attributes to the "bugger" (*kinaidou*) and the "whore" (*pornês*), kindred souls (*isos ... ho nous*) willing to do anything for cash (Archilochus 328 West, spurious). Still, Demos gives them a run for their money. Ever ready to gratify the thievish lusts of his flatterer-lovers so long as *he* stands to benefit, Demos has long since, and with eyes wide open, embraced a *modus operandi* that he has more than once been warned against, and in suggestively sexual terms.[62] But, as Landfester points out, Demos shows complicity in behaviors — theft of public funds, deception of the *dêmos* — treated under Athenian law as offenses of the highest order.[63] Thus citizen Demos pursues self-interest at the expense of Demos-the *dêmos* personified. Whatever his gains, they inevitably translate as loss.

At this point we begin to notice a strange symmetry of deception, manipulation, and exploitation between Demos and his lovers, a travesty of reciprocities whereby leaders and led in the democratic polity "struck and

---

[62] Cf. Aristophanes *Knights* 719–721, 962–963. Citizen-male prostitution as self-compromise: Aeschines 1.22, 29, 54–55; Scholtz 1996. Greedy, predatory *hetairai/pornai*: Archilochus 302 West (spurious?); Aristophanes *Assemblywomen* 1161–1162; Hyperides 5.1–3 Jensen; Isocrates 8.103; Plato *Phaedrus* 240b; Anaxilas fr. 22 *PCG*; Konstan 1993:6–12.

[63] Landfester 1967:72–73.

maintained a viable social contract in part through the discursive operations of public oratory."[64] But one term of that contract was non-negotiable. Under a system where, as David Konstan puts it, "the sovereign δῆμος was the unique entity toward which a citizen was expected . . . to show deference,"[65] even the elite had to submit to what Josiah Ober calls the "ideological hegemony of the masses."[66] Granted, Paphlagon and the Sausage-Seller fall over each other being submissive. But their flattering attentions (even the Sausage-Seller's) are easily read as subversion and subjugation, even a kind of buggery, and thus deviate from the protocols governing the system within which they operate.[67] Telling is the implied perversion of democratic checks and balances. Filtered through a sexual lens, the non-negotiable sovereignty of the *dêmos* becomes a male citizen's sexual autonomy set in phallic counterpoise to threats like those posed by would-be tyrants and oligarchs.[68] Yet when leaders from outside the ranks of the *kaloi k'agathoi* want to have a go at Demos, he seems willing to negotiate in ways that efface distinctions between those threats and the resistance he offers.

For perspective, we can turn to the "Old Oligarch," who likewise has the Athenian *dêmos* showing shrewdness, if not exactly wisdom, in its preference for "bad" men as leaders useful to its interests.[69] Though Pseudo-Xenophon's speaker mostly detests democracy, he grudgingly admires how well it meets its objectives, namely, unambiguous empowerment for the poorer, "worse," element (the *dêmos*), whom the system sets free to rule (1.8). He even allows that the *dêmos* exercises foresight at least insofar as it elects its generals and other unsalaried officials not from its own ranks, but from the "elite" (the *dunatôtatoi*, 1.3). By contrast, Demos in *Knights* "plays" the system in ways strikingly ambiguous by any standard. Nor would the "Old Oligarch" award high marks for elevating characters like Paphlagon-Cleon (i.e. *worse* than Demos) to the generalship.

But more than that, the whole tenor of the play's satire cuts to the material heart of the late fifth-century democracy. Jury pay, the spreading round

---

[64] Ober 1996:91 describing Ober 1989; see also Ober 1994.

[65] Konstan 1996a:11.

[66] Ober 1989:332.

[67] Henderson 1991:68 suggests that a sexually passive Sausage-Seller is "at one with the people," whereas Paphlagon-Cleon is the aggressor-buggerer. But both suitors resort to nearly identical, highly questionable tactics.

[68] The "phallic" democracy at Athens: Halperin 1990:88–112. Cf. *dêmos* as *turannos-erastês*: McGlew 1993:183–212.

[69] Pseudo-Xenophon 1.1. The pamphlet's connection to political currents: Rosenbloom 2004a:87–90; Brock 1986:25–26; Forrest 1975.

of imperial profits — rewards, in other words, deriving from policy aimed at benefiting the masses — these are, according to the "Old Oligarch," spoils to all appearances rightfully (*dikaioi*) accruing to the rank-and-file citizenry, the mainstay of Athens' imperial might (1.2). In a not dissimilar vein, Pericles expatiates on the many blessings Athens offers its citizen-fighters, blessings rendering the city a fit object of citizen *erôs* (Thucydides 2.38–41), a place, the orator means, far superior to enemy states like Sparta.[70] In *Knights*, however, such advantages tend to come across either as handouts used by the leadership elite to scam a gullible Demos, or else as handouts actively sought after by a corrupt Demos cynically scamming those who would scam him.[71]

Perhaps not surprisingly, the disclosures of lines 1111–1150 have proved singularly challenging to commentators, who often treat them as an antidote to criticism of Demos as foolish elsewhere in the play — an antidote that would seem not to sit very well with the miracle cure — the rejuvenation and re-education of decrepit, dim-witted Demos — still to come.[72] While I would not deny certain inconsistencies in plot and characterization,[73] I would argue that inconsistency here enriches the texture of comic reversal. For it demands we rethink the entire scheme of sexual-political debauchery, a scheme that, in light of these disclosures, suggests nothing so much as a kind of covertly waged internecine war, in a word, *stasis*.

Stasis, civic discord, was, of course, the great nightmare of ancient Greek politics. Yet stasis, unlike, say, the plague of 430–426, could furnish raw material for comedy.[74] And so it does in *Knights*, where the playwright satirizes

---

[70] The utopian thrust of the Periclean Funeral Oration, and funeral oratory generally: Loraux 1986.

[71] E.g. jury pay (recently raised by Cleon): Aristophanes *Knights* 51, 255. Various items: 1019, 1078–1079, 1090–1091, 1100–1106, 1125–1126, 1163–1220, 1350–1354 (back-reference to pay).

[72] Yunis 1996:57–58. Landfester 1967:72–73 argues that a Demos boasting complicity in serious political offenses parades his immorality without diminishing his foolishness, Reinders 2001:192 that the passage attacks the *dêmos* "ruthlessly" even as it seeks to inoculate itself against formal charges of slandering the *dêmos*. Brock 1986 takes the claims at face value as an intermediate ending helping Demos save face. According to Rosen, a Demos alert to his leaders' misdeeds draws audience attention to "the way the demos ought to behave" (1988:79–80). According to Hesk 2000:289–291, the interlude foregrounds the ambiguities inherent in *dêmos*-power and in rhetoric and counter-rhetoric. McGlew 2002:101–104, noting the disjuncture between the wily Demos of the interlude and the "confused and regretful" Demos of the finale, observes that the interlude looks ahead to vengeance against Paphlagon.

[73] E.g. the Sausage-Seller as both vulgar demagogue and *kalos k'agathos* hero. See especially Brock 1986 for the play's ambiguities, to which Brock applies the solution of a double plot movement.

[74] Cratinus satirizes Pericles as a Zeus-like tyrant, son of Stasis and Time. This "Zeus" takes Aspasia, daughter of "Rear-Entry" (*Katapugosunê*), as his "Hera" (frr. 258–259 *PCG*). Cf. e.g. Aristophanes *Thesmophoriazusae* 788 (women chafe at being blamed for *stasis*, discord et sim.); *Wasps* 488–499, subversion-tyranny paranoia, for which MacDowell 1971:180; *Wealth* 944–950.

Cleon's demagoguery as disturbance (*tarakhê, polupragmosunê*) in conflict with the quietism (*hêsukhia, apragmosunê*) embodied by the aristocratic Knights and, finally, Demos.[75] But *stasis* in real life involved more than conflicts of interest or ideas; it involved conflict *between persons*. And so we should not gloss over the lyric interlude, revealing, as it does, mutuality of deception and aggression, leaders versus led. To some that will seem a rather eccentric sort of *stasis*, at least insofar as it drives a wedge between the demagogues and their constituents, the *dêmos*. But that is how it often is in Old Comedy.[76] Nor are we dealing with any literally factionalized *polis*. Rather, we are dealing with a comic trope treating the whole give and take of democracy as conflictive and dysfunctional to the core.

We can better appreciate how that works by noting category-slippage symptomatic of *stasis* in other sources. Thus the poet of the *Iliad* connects a collapse of legal restraints and social and familial mores to *erôs* for internecine war.[77] Developing that idea further, Theognis rails against the vulgar herd (*kakoi*) gaining the upper hand over their betters (*agathoi*), and doling out justice (*dikas*) in favor of the unjust (*adikoisi*) for the sake of private gain and personal power. Hence *stasis*, murder, and despotism (39–52 West). Notes Veda Cobb-Stevens,[78] that litany of reversed expectations in Theognis looks forward to similar reversals in Thucydides' famous description of the mindset and discourse typifying *stasis* at Corcyra and elsewhere:

> Speakers, too, altered as they saw fit the value associations words ordinarily brought to bear upon things (*tên eiôthuian axiôsin tôn onomatôn es ta erga*). Thus reckless audacity was deemed the courage of a loyal adherent, and cautious hesitation, specious cowardice. Good sense became a screen for spinelessness, and the effort to see all sides to an issue, sheer laziness. To strike out rashly was to act like a man; to plan from a secure footing, a fine-sounding excuse for desertion.
>
> Thucydides 3.82.4

---

[75] Edmunds 1987; cf. Rosenbloom 2004a; Rosenbloom 2004b.

[76] Cf. Rosenbloom 2004a:88 on "comedy, which plots to sever the bond between *ponêroi* and demos and to restore the ancestral/moral order of *chrêstoi* to hegemony."

[77] "Without clan, law, or hearth is he who loves dire war among his own people," *Iliad* 9.63–64. Cf. reversal and disintegration in Hesiod *Works and Days* 182–201, for which West 1978:199 adduces Near Eastern and other parallels.

[78] Cobb-Stevens 1985:165–166 et passim; see also Konstan 1997:49–50; Edmunds 1987:35–37. For the pathology of *stasis* and similar matters, Price 2001; Kalimtzis 2000; Gehrke 1985:245–254.

And so on. Like many a Thucydidean sentence, the one at the start of the passage just quoted lends itself to no easy translation. Particularly difficult is the noun *axiôsis*, often taken to refer in context to verbal denotations altered to serve factional interests (e.g. LSJ s.v ἀξίωσις IV.). Reading on, though, we note the degree to which linguistic instability resides in the affective *impact* of words,[79] and in the attitude shifts reflected by altered labels for things ("You call it 'good sense'? *We* call it 'spinelessness'!").[80] Judging from the historian's examples, this "rhetoric of *stasis*," as it has been called,[81] opportunistically revalorized actions and attitudes by painting factional or personal interest in the colors of received ideals.[82] But it also served to reconfigure identity. By talking a talk that broke with the usual value associations, speakers effectively severed prior ties and ratified new ones (cf. 3.82.6). Revalorization functioned, then, not just semantically; it functioned socially and symbolically.

By now, it should be apparent that the rhetoric of *stasis*, Thucydides' topic in the passage quoted above, was largely a matter of *spin*. And spin, I would suggest, aptly describes what Demos and the Chorus are up to when Demos justifies, and the Chorus applauds, the *modus operandi* of the former. For Demos shows little shame when he strikes the pose of a passively mercenary *erômenos* (1162–1163), indiscriminate in his choice of lovers (738–740), and a sucker for flattery and deceit (1115–1120, cf. 1340–1355). This pose the Knights praise as *puknotês*, a pun on Demos' rootedness in democratic tradition.[83] Yet the noun denotes the cunning with which Demos outwits, exploits, and ultimately destroys leaders. Buttressed by cunning such as that, Demos' sovereignty, though the very yardstick of political and juridical legitimacy at Athens, recalls what Thucydides, still on the topic of *stasis*, deplores as "intelligence recognized as superior because it prevailed through treachery" (3.82.7) — a striking contrast with simplicity (*to euêthes*), the better part of

---

[79] I mostly agree with Price 2001:41–42 on the meaning of *axiôsis* in this passage, though its use here is less unparalleled than Price suggests. *Axiôsis* mostly has to do with "worthiness," "merits," and the like (see LSJ s.v.); at Thucydides 2.88.2, it means "conviction" or "belief" relative to the merits of a course of action — so, too, more or less, in Thucydides 3.82.4.

[80] Dionysius glosses thus: "changing the usual words for things to be called by, they [those embroiled in *stasis*] saw value in calling them differently" (*Thucydides* 29.4). I.e. things were renamed as factional or personal interests dictated.

[81] Kalimtzis 2000:11.

[82] Cf. Price 2001:39–67, 81–189 on "transvaluation"; Neuman and Tabak 2003:260 on "positive reformulation"; Billig 1996:170–185.

[83] The Pnyx (stem *Pukn*-) being the hill where the Athenian assembly — the *dêmos* — met. Cf. *Dêmos Puknitês*, 42.

nobility according to Thucydides (3.83.1).[84] As for the aristocratic Knights, siding with Demos, they commend a course of action contradicting not just democratic values, but those, too, of oligarchy, the constitution with which the wealthy were liable to be associated. For a Demos cleverly and aggressively arranging matters to keep himself on top, albeit through a show of submissiveness, replicates vulgar Paphlagon's style of *polupragmosunê*, the impertinent political meddling detested by *kaloi k'agathoi*, "well-bred gentlemen," like the Knights.[85]

So, too, the play's representations of demagoguery, from both a political and a pederastic viewpoint, involve no small element of revalorization. Thus policy favoring the *dêmos* — for instance, the *per diem* raise from two to three obols awarded jurors (doubtless encouraging a broader spectrum of Athenians to serve) — becomes vulgar *kolakeia*. Conversely, an exemplar of vulgarity like the Sausage-Seller is hailed the city's destined savior (147–149), and vaunts himself a *kalos k'agathos* lover of Demos (733–735). Indeed, a whole range of ideologically crucial polarities — free versus slave, dominant versus submissive, *philia* versus *kolakeia*, *kalon* (honorable) versus *aiskhron* (disgraceful) — becomes blurred as a consequence of the passive-aggressive contacts transacted within this *ménage à trois*.

But I would further suggest that in *Knights*, the whole image of politics as *erôs* connotes disruptions of a stasiastic cast. To begin with, the association of *erôs* with *stasis*, or with *stasis*-like disruption, was a commonplace. Homer, we have seen, speaks of *erôs* for internecine strife (*Iliad* 9.63–64). In Sophocles' *Antigone*, the Chorus reflects on the universal reach of Eros, the god who maddens the wits of mortals and immortals alike, drives the just to injustice, and has "stirred up this strife of kindred men," which is to say, set father against son.[86] Echoing Sophocles, but evoking more explicitly political associations, Aristophon describes Eros as having been "justly" and "reasonably voted out" of the company of the gods for "stirring them up" and "fomenting *stasis*" whenever among them. Stripped of his wings, Eros has been exiled to the human realm (fr. 11 *PCG*).

How, then, within that realm might politically inflected *erôs* prove "stasiastic"? In Aristophanes' *Frogs*, "*epithumia* (desire) for personal gain," in

---

[84] Following Hornblower vol. 1 p. 486 ad loc. on *metekhei*.

[85] Though nowhere referred to as *kaloi k'agathoi*, the Knights in *Knights* are styled *andres agathoi*, "noble men," at 225. In context, that conveys much the same information. *Kaloi te k'agathoi* will join forces with the Knights (227), not, apparently, as a class wholly distinct from them, but similar in sensibilities and aims. Labels for the 420s upper crust: Rosenbloom 2004a:88n125.

[86] Sophocles *Antigone* 781–794; cf. fr. 684 Radt; Theophrastus fr. 107 Wimmer.

a word, greed, can impel one to foment "hateful *stasis*" and behave disagreeably toward fellow citizens (359–360). In Thucydides, a pleonectic (*pleonexia*, "greed") component to *erôs* proper emerges from the Mytilenian debate, specifically, from Diodotus speech. There greed (*pleonexian*) based on wealth (*exousia*), arrogance (*hubrei*), and pride (*phonêmati*) numbers among the "incurable" (*anêkestou*) passions that, overmastering human beings, cause them to throw discretion to the wind — a pattern with close affinities to the process, discussed in the very next sentence, whereby *elpis* and *erôs*, hope and lust, drive people to seek out fortune's riches at any cost.[87]

Foucault can help clarify the relationship between *stasis* and the pleonectic dynamic within *erôs*. Though focusing not on politics *per se*, but applying a political metaphor to the ethics of pleasure, Foucault argues that classical Greek thought viewed sexual lust as a need similar in many respects to other physical appetites (hunger, thirst), though different from them in the degree to which the pleasurable satisfaction of the need creates a desire for more. This inability to achieve satiety can lead to "rebellion and riotessness . . . the 'stasiastic' potential of the sexual appetite," and with that, ill health.[88] Foucault uses the adjective "stasiastic" in a non-political, metaphorical, sense. But we can just as well apply his schema to politics, where *erôs*, the untrammeled, essentially pleonectic desires of citizens and leaders, cause the city to spiral into *stasis*, the political malaise *par excellence*. Thus Thucydides locates the causes of *stasis* in greed (*pleonexia*), ambition, and competitiveness guided by the desire for pleasure (3.82.8) — a recognizably erotic mix of motivations, and powerful enough to dissolve civic *philia*, the glue holding the city together and guarding it against *stasis*.[89]

"Though they say they love you, it is not you they love, but themselves" (Demosthenes *Exordia* 53.3). In Aristophanes' play, *erôs* — not feigned *erôs* for a decrepit old man, but real, pleonectic *erôs* for power and wealth — are what drive Paphlagon and even the Sausage-Seller to court Demos in ways blurring the distinction between *philia* and its evil twin, *kolakeia*. But Paphlagon and others like him need to watch out, too. For Demos-*erômenos* revalorizes passive gullibility as a cunning guise to thwart

---

[87] Thucydides 3.45.4–5; cf. e.g. Solon 4 West; Euripides *Suppliants* 238–239. See Balot 2001:38–39, 79–98, 156–159, 194.

[88] Foucault 1990:49–50.

[89] Cf. Aeschylus' "spirit of common love" as antidote to *stasis* in *Eumenides* 984–985; Aristotle *Politics* 1262b7–9, 1295b23–24; Demosthenes 18.246 (*rhêtôr*'s duty to promote civic *homonoia* and *philia*). See further Kalimtzis 2000; Konstan 1997:69–70; Hutter 1978. For this passage and the themes of *stasis*, *pleonexia*, etc., Balot 2001:137–141; Price 2001:6–67.

attacks on his supremacy, a screen behind which to hide his own ambitious lusts. This tango of desire, deception, and manipulation may have Demos and his lovers moving in sync, but its undertone of aggression sounds a dissonant note. A democracy in name, the reality on stage suggests nothing so much as a stealthily run rat race.

Conclusions

To sum-up, just as the demophilia topos sought to destabilize an opponent's patriotic self-representations, so Aristophanes' image of the *erastês tou dêmou*, the "people's lover," discovers and amplifies within demophilia an erotic dynamic, "the 'stasiastic' potential of the sexual appetite." Put differently, this vision of political *erôs*, despite obvious affinities with Pericles' famous directive that Athenians "daily gaze upon the city's power and become lovers (*erastai*) of it" (Thucydides 2.43.1), exposes paradox and contradiction at which the Periclean conceit can only hint. However much Pericles' metaphor seeks to exploit connotationally divergent resonances (a lover's generosity toward his beloved, a lover's self-centered pursuit of a love-object), the work it performs needs to be understood in relation to the challenge faced by the orator, namely, to unite Athenians, and to inspire them to give up their lives for their beloved city. By contrast, erotic metaphor in *Knights* creates, rather than responds to, an atmosphere of uncertainty and crisis. For when the city's leaders fix their gaze on the sovereign *dêmos* and become lovers of *it*, they become as much potential buggerers as benefactors. Troubling is Demos' role. However proactive in his efforts to police corruption, he plays the system by feigning ignorance and vulnerability, while his self-centeredness combined with his dual character — citizen Demos, the *dêmos* personified — underscores the fragility of ties binding individual to group.

That leaves us with a striking redefinition of "normal" and "deviant" democracy. The norm, reinstated for the play's finale (1316–1408), presents us with a transformed Demos, boiled down, rejuvenated, and beautified through the Sausage-Seller's magic. Decked out in all the finery befitting the "monarch of Greece and of this land" (1330), Demos has returned to a nearly mythic past, when the citizenry, like the aristocrats they supposedly were, still wore golden cicadas in their hair.[90] Deviant is the here-and-now of jury pay, *misthos*

---

[90] Cf. Aristophanes *Knights* 1331 with Thucydides 1.6.3. Other tokens of archaic luxury in Aristophanes *Knights*: purple robe (967); "frog-green" cloak (formerly Paphlagon's, 1406). See Sommerstein 1981:195, 220.

(wages) for the poor, and all the rest — the *erga* of the radical democracy, here reduced to *logos*, tricks by which demerastic leaders court a willing *dêmos*. Thus Aristophanes targets not just Paphlagon-Cleon, but the whole rhetorical basis of Athenian democracy, a system under which demagogues plead devotion to a public complicit in the their leaders' efforts to manipulate them. Yet Aristophanes does not simply administer an antidote to demophilic rhetoric. Attacking the substance — the *erga* — conveyed by advice cloaked in all that seductive *logos*, the playwright envisions a regime under which the operations of the radical democracy will be circumscribed, and its belligerent imperialism curtailed (cf. 1300–1315).

As for the Sausage-Seller, he has repeatedly distinguished himself in the role of plain-speaking demophilia-debunker (cf. 1340–1344 with e.g. 792–796), forcing his rival again and again to up the demophilic ante. Demos has, in fact, long since acknowledged the Sausage-Seller as true-blue Demos-lover (786–787), and addresses his benefactor now as "dearest of men" (1335) — no hypocrite, but the real McCoy. But rather than accept the compliment graciously, the Sausage-Seller, if anything, goes the demophile one better: "You mean me? My dear fellow, you've no idea what you were like before, or what you did. Else you'd think me a god!" (1336–1338) — a comic bit of self-aggrandizement, but ironic as lead-in to the Sausage-Seller's lecture on demophilic speechifying.[91] Yet the Sausage-Seller's miracles amount to little more than a beauty treatment, and have already been adumbrated for what they really are: *kolakeia*.[92] There are, however, more surprises in store. As we have seen, the Sausage-Seller, unlike the orators, adds an erotic layer to his version of the demophilia topos ("Whenever an assembly speaker would say, 'O Demos, I am your *erastês*, . . .' " 1340–1344). But further on into his lecture, the Sausage-Seller spins the topos in a most unusual direction. In the orators, the topos alarms listeners with the thought of their being taken in by someone's insincere love talk, or else chides them for having done so. It shames them, in other words, into thinking for themselves. By contrast, the Sausage-Seller absolves Demos from all blame: too senile to resist his leaders' blandishments, Demos failed to notice the subtly phallic threat those blandishments posed (cf. 1356–1357).

---

[91] Anticipated by "epiphanies" (Aristophanes *Knights* 149, 458, 836) and by the Sausage-Seller's "providential" arrival (147); see Landfester 1967:36–37, 92–94, though I regard "apotheosis" here not as resolving earlier paradox (so Landfester), but as equivocal and ironic.

[92] Rejuvenating grey-hair plucking: Aristophanes *Knights* 908. Cf. p. 53n43 above.

But feebleminded Demos boiled down appears no better off intellectually than before. Whatever the merits of his new policies, impulsive decision-making has replaced deliberation and reflection. Indeed, Demos will banish the young from the agora, the school for aspiring orators, and will make politicians give up legislating for hunting (1357–1383). Thus *logos*, elsewhere praised as the essence of Athenian democracy,[93] will have no place at all under the new order. This Athens of the ancestors has, with good reason, been likened both to oligarchy and to Eastern despotism as the Greeks imagined it.[94] In the end, though, the play's vision of the "noble simplicity" has elided the *polis* altogether. Indeed, it returns Demos — or *seems* to return Demos — to a bygone Golden Age, where human beings (Demos), perpetually young (cf. Hesiod *Works and Days* 113–115) and untroubled by politics (*Knights* 1373–1383), enjoy good things without toil (a magic makeover, catamite "chairs," peace-treaty concubines; cf. Hesiod *Works and Days* 116–118) through the good offices of the gods (the Sausage-Seller), with whom the mortal race, restored to pristine innocence, may again consort.[95] This arresting vision of bygone Athens could well have aroused powerful yearnings in a war-weary audience, but its *peithô* deviously taps into an atavistic urge for infancy.

Though one might wonder how well so unflattering a treatment of the democratic *status quo* would have played to the Athenian *dêmos*, it could not have played *too* badly. *Knights* did, after all, win, nor should we second-guess the public's tolerance for being satirized, especially amid the carnivalesque revelry of the Dionysian festival. But what about the apparent inconsistency in Aristophanes' characterization of Demos, whose brief moment of candor (lyric dialogue 1111–1150; see above) jars with his transformation from superannuated naïf to the rejuvenated and supposedly reformed Demos of the finale? On the one hand, we can take that transformation at face value, and assume that cunning, crafty Demos has ceased to figure within the dramatic reality. Alternatively, we can assume that Demos continues to "play the babe" to the very end, thus making a mockery of the Sausage-Seller's exertions in

---

[93] Thucydides 2.40.2–3; Lysias 2.19; Isocrates 4.47-49; Demosthenes 19.184 (Athens' "government in words"); Roisman 2005:139.

[94] Oligarchy: Ludwig 2002:61–62. "Costume monarchy" with overtones of eastern despotism-tyranny: Wohl 2002:110–114.

[95] Cf. Hesiod fr. 1.6–7 Merkelbach-West; *Theogony* 535–536 with West's note. The schema in *Knights* reprises elements of Cratinus' *Ploutoi* (frr. 171–179 *PCG*), which seems to have decried a present made corrupt by a recently deposed tyrant Zeus (read Pericles), and to have sought to revive an idealized, aristocratic Golden Age. See *PCG ad locc.*; Ameling 1981:400–402; Schwartze 1971:43–54.

his behalf. Neither alternative completely satisfies. Yet a comic dénouement featuring an ironically *equivocal* return to the "noble simplicity" would hardly be at odds with the bizarre twists taken by flattery politics in the play. Demos remains a creature of his appetites (1384–1392), and let us not forget how important those appetites have been in luring him to his senses. Whether a reformed Demos has finally shed his much vaunted cunning, or whether cunning Demos, in taking up with a new favorite, simply begins the cycle anew — none of that is clear. Nor can we know for sure how things will turn out for this new favorite once the honeymoon is over.

4

FORGIVE AND FORGET
CONCORDIA DISCORS IN ARISTOPHANES'
ASSEMBLYWOMEN AND *LYSISTRATA*

I N Aristophanes' *Assemblywomen*, salvation — *sôtêria* — for Athens and its citizens dominates the agenda, not just of the political meeting whence the play's title, but of the play as a whole.[1] To an Athenian audience, that will have suggested a city in crisis,[2] but what kind of crisis? We hear of a *dêmos* coddled by demagogues, of the city's straitened finances, of a widening gulf between rich and poor, of Athenian selfishness generally.[3] But how does that, business as usual, some might call it, make for a crisis on the order of, say, the ravages of war, the precariousness of peace, the misrule of a grotesquely corrupt and corrupting leader, the plight of a poorly led city facing immanent defeat and possible destruction — the sort of crisis, in other words, the poet's earlier plays would have led us to associate with measures as drastic as those enacted here?[4] For what could have been more drastic than for the city's men first to surrender power to women, then to acquiesce to a generalized sharing of property, spouses, children, everything?[5]

---

[1] *Sôtêria* 'safety, deliverance from danger' on the agenda: Aristophanes *Assemblywomen* 396–397; cf. 202, 209, 233–234, 401–402, 412, 414. Oaths sworn by Zeus *sôtêr*, "Zeus the Savior": 79, 761, 1045, 1103.

[2] Emergency meetings with *sôtêria* at stake: Aeschines 2.72; Demosthenes 18.248; 19.123; Aristotle *Constitution of the Athenians* 29.2; Sommerstein 1998:176; Hansen 1987:28–30; Rhodes 1985:233–235.

[3] Demagogues and the *dêmos*' preference for them: Aristophanes *Assemblywomen* 176–182. Selfishness, cynicism, greed, inconstancy, (reckless) innovation, poverty, insensitivity to same, class tensions: passim. General corruption: Saïd 1996:284–286.

[4] Chronic-endemic character of troubles in *Assemblywomen*: Foxhall 2002; Henderson 2002:415; Reinders 2001:1249. Sense of crisis in Aristophanes' *Knights*: Anderson 1995:10–13. In *Frogs*: 687–688, 736–737, 1418–1423, 1435–1436, 1446–1450.

[5] Women's rule in *Assemblywomen* as reversal: Sommerstein 1998:8 citing Aristotle *Politics* 1259b1–3, 1260a8–13.

This curiously overdetermined yet underwhelming crisis we can connect with an interpretive "enigma" the play has long posed: the question of what it is all about.[6] One recurrent observation, that material issues — "Demon Poverty" and wealth-disparity — are central to the play's theme, receives ample justification within the text itself.[7] Yet the crux of the matter lies not with poverty *per se* but with its discontents. According to Isocrates, privation leads to a breakdown of inter-personal ties, indeed, to violent conflict: war or civil strife (4.174). Thus in a play produced in or about the year 391 BCE,[8] when Athens was still recovering from military defeat, loss of empire, and its own, rather traumatic encounter with civil strife, there can be no clean break between themes of socio-economic health and those of political health. And in that period, questions of political health lead almost inevitably back to civil strife and its avoidance.

So my question is whether issues of civic concord and discord do not figure in the crisis at hand, and if so, how.[9] My starting point for this investigation will be textual clues suggesting as much. Reading those clues against the cluelessness enacted onstage, I suggest resonances with the widely praised, yet problematic, amnesty ratified in association with the restoration of democracy in 403 BCE.[10] Civic harmony predicated on collective forgetting thus provides Aristophanes with a theme. For he "hears" in this harmony an ideologically charged point of contention between, on the one hand, a discourse of democratic consensus as antidote to civic unrest, on the other hand, a discourse of civic-phallic autonomy as bulwark against antidemocratic *hubris*.

To see how that works, it will help to consider *Assemblywomen* in relation to the playwright's earlier drama of women taking charge: the *Lysistrata* of 412 BCE. Bringing to bear Bakhtinian ideas on the sociality of language, I shall explore how Praxagora in the later play harmonizes the city's discourses, and in so doing, realizes Lysistrata's dream of a close-knit civic order. Yet Praxagora, in order to form a more perfect union, must resist resistance and

---

[6] Since at least 1836, the year of Zastra's dissertation. For the interpretive "enigma" (Sommerstein's term): Reinders 2001:243–251; Ober 1998:150; Sommerstein 1998:18; Sommerstein 1984:314–316; Hess 1963:i–xiii.

[7] Socio-economic themes in *Assemblywomen*: Sommerstein 1998:18–22; Saïd 1996:299–301; Taaffe 1993:103, 130–131; David 1984; Sommerstein 1984 (whence the phrase "Demon Poverty"); Foley 1982:14; Ussher 1973:xxix–xx. "Relative unity and moderate (if not universal) economic recovery" in the post-403 period: Rothwell 1990:2; cf. Reinders 2001:247–251; Funke 1980.

[8] Date: McGlew 2002:191; Sommerstein 1998:1–8.

[9] Cf. Ober 1998:133: "They (Athenian women) seek a new ground for Athenian *homonoia* in a radical homogenization of material and familial benefits."

[10] For which, Ober 2002; Quillin 2002; Tieman 2002; Wolpert 2002a; Wolpert 2002b.

dissent with dissent. Hence *concordia discors* in *Assemblywomen*, whose crisis turns out to be nothing less than a clash of values: same-thinking, the city's saving grace, versus the different-thinking implied by free speech, a value long central to the democratic franchise, yet sidelined under the new regime.

Stasis as Subtext?

To get at the root of the dilemma in *Assemblywomen*, we need to look not just to the text itself but beyond it for concerns in the air in the later 390s, the period of the play's first production. Still recovering from catastrophic defeat at Spartan hands a decade earlier, Athens was coping as well with the aftermath of a brief but violent episode of oligarchy following that defeat (404). Not to be overlooked, then, are ways in which *Assemblywomen*'s action and dialogue suggest connections with issues of civic strife (*stasis*) and civic concord (*homonoia*), which contemporary sources often juxtapose with what is, clearly, *Assemblywomen*'s dominant preoccupation: *sôtêria*.[11]

But can *stasis* provide material suitable for comedy? Alan Sommerstein writes that, like the plague of 430 (never mentioned in comedy), the *stasis* of 404/3 would have triggered memories too painful for an early fourth-century audience to tolerate.[12] Still, we should not underestimate comedy's capacity to treat difficult topics, including the nightmare of *stasis*, a theme central to Aristophanes' *Knights* of 424.[13] In *Assemblywomen*, *stasis* plays just beneath the surface of Praxagora's two assembly speeches: her rehearsal speech, performed on stage (171–240), and the actual speech, reported indirectly (427–453). Both speeches impute to men, and deny in women, qualities resonant with the dysfunctional state and civic discord. Thus women, as conservative as men are restlessly innovative, do not divulge state secrets, cheat, engage in judicial blackmail (sycophancy), or dissolve democracy, the clear implication being that men do. By contrast, women do — and, therefore, men do not — behave cooperatively and trustingly with one another, behavior reflecting the kind of *philia* that holds the city together and *stasis* at bay.[14]

Does that, though, allude to the revolutions of 411 or 404? Themes of constitutional subversion, and fear thereof, surface with some frequency

---

[11] *Sôtêria, homonoia*, amnesty: Andocides 1.73, 76, 81, 106–9, 140; Lysias 18.18–19; 25.23, 27. *Sôtêria*, civic affection (*philia*), *homonoia* versus hatred, *stasis*, disagreement (*dikhonoia*): Plato *First Alcibiades* 126a–c.

[12] Sommerstein 1998:154.

[13] See "*Stasis*," chapter 3 above.

[14] Aristophanes *Assemblywomen* 214–228, 435–453; cf. the Chorus, 300–310.

in Aristophanes, for instance, in *Wasps*, which satirizes the habit of finding a subversive under every rock (345, 417, 463–507, 953). Sources from the period before 411, when addressing such matters, very often speak of "conspiracy" or the attempt to establish tyranny; after 411 and 403, when democracy really *was* dissolved, charges of oligarchy (i.e. of favoring one) or of aiming to dissolve the democracy (*ton dêmon/tên dêmokratian kataluein, katalusis tou dêmou*) come to the fore.[15] In surviving comedy, this last charge, that of dissolving democracy, crops up twice: once in each of Aristophanes' surviving post-403 plays (*Assemblywomen* 452–453; *Wealth* 948–949). So the discourse would seem to have changed — oligarchy now, not tyranny, as scare-image — in response to recent events. But does *Assemblywomen* evoke a real-life dissolution from a decade before? We need to consider what an early fourth-century audience would have pictured while listening to Chremes' *reportage*: an assembly speaker (Praxagora in disguise) no longer addressing an irrational fear (contrast *Wasps*), but insinuating that the *dêmos* does something that it in fact did, and twice, the last time barely a decade or so ago — an action whose memory would haunt the *dêmos* for years to come, namely, to vote itself out of existence.[16] And so, when this comedy plays women (cooperative, trusting, sharing, *non*-contentious, *non*-litigious) off against democracy-dissolvers like the city's men, that likely would have touched a nerve, and would have resonated with a topic much in the air at the time: *homonoia* (concord) as an essential ingredient to civic well-being — as essential as *stasis*, its opposite, was felt to be detrimental.[17]

Yet Praxagora's picture of women's political quietism raises questions.[18] Hitherto, women may not have had either the opportunity or the inclination to intrigue against the political status quo, but what are they doing now if not just that? No surprise, then, that Praxagora's scheme carries its own, stasiastic resonances. To begin with, she refers to herself and her co-conspirators as *hetairai*, "companions" or "comrades" (feminine gender):

> Sun's just about up, meeting's about to begin. Time they snagged our
> tails (*hedras*) — I mean, time us professional girls (*hetairas*) — uh, time

---

[15] Sartori 1999:148–149; MacDowell 1971:180.

[16] In 411 and 404, the *dêmos* was forced into complicity with processes leading to its dissolution: Wolpert 2002b:16–20, 35–36, 41–42; Price 2001:304–312. Cf. Aristophanes *Wealth* 947–950 (democracy-dissolution assumed to require legislative approval); Xenophon *Hellenica* 2.3.45 (*dêmos* persuaded to dissolve democracy to appease Sparta); Aeschines 3.234 (*dêmos* "flattered" into complicity).

[17] Andocides 1.140; Lysias 18.17–18; 25; Isocrates 4.174; 18.44; Xenophon *Memorabilia* 4.4.16, 4.6.14; Archytas fr. 3 D-K; Aristotle *Nicomachean Ethics* 1155a24–26; Ephorus 70 F 148.7, 149.6–7 *FGrH*; Loraux 2002:109, 256–257, 262; Ludwig 2002:19, 193–194, 342–343; Ober 1989:295–299; Funke 1980. Cf. Loraux 2002:116–119 on *harmonia*.

[18] Cf. Sommerstein 1998:180.

our "professed sisterhood" (*hetairas*) snagged some seats (*hedras*) and
secretly settled into place, if you get my drift. And you would if you
remembered Phyromachus' slip-up.

Aristophanes *Assemblywomen* 20–23

The reference to Phyromachus' famous slip-up, evidently, *heteras* "others,"
mispronounced as *hetairas* "prostitutes," flags what precedes as an elaborate
pun on the noun *hetaira* (a) in the neutral sense of "companion," (b) in the
sexual-professional sense of "call girl" (cf. *thêkas*, "seats" or "derrieres": LSJ
s.v. ἕδρα III.), and (c) in the political-social sense of members of a *hetaireia* or
sunômosia, a "club" leaning toward, or committed to, anti-democratic politics.[19]
Whatever else, Praxagora playfully stumbles over resonances suggesting
comparison between this revolution in the works and earlier conspiracies.

As to the *tolmêma*, the bold, even reckless deed these women feel driven
to dare, Praxagora makes no bones: they shall seize control of the city, albeit to
do the city good (105–109; cf. 287–288). At least part of the problem the women
want remedied has to do with assembly pay introduced and then raised by
Agyrrhius. So divisive has the measure been that the man who gets his pay
"praises" Agyrrhius "to the skies," while the man who gets none condemns
payees to death; having thus cheapened the exercise of one's civic right, these
policies and their author provide the stated motivation for the women's coup.[20]

Are we, then, dealing with yet another demagogue play, *Knights* reworked for
the 390s? Critics rightly caution against reading *Assemblywomen* as little more than
that. But William Hess has a point, even if he overstates it.[21] *Ponêros* ("bad," 185),
effeminate (102–103), demagogic, and stasiastic, Agyrrhius re-embodies qualities that, to an earlier generation of conservatives, defined the likes of Cleon and
Hyperbolus.[22] Thus when the Chorus of Women, waxing nostalgic for a bygone age,
deplores the mercenary civics of the here-and-now, it all begins to sound familiar:

---

[19] *Hetaira* here as feminine of *hetairos*, "club-member," "conspirator." In Aristophanes *Assemblywomen*
110, the women form a *xunousia*, an organized association. Revolutionary *sunousiai* in Lysias 8:
Todd 2000:88. *Hetairoi, hetaireiai* (political clubs or "action committees"), *sunômosia* ("conspiracy"),
oligarchy: Thucydides 8.54.4, 65.2, 81.2, 92.4; Lysias 12.43; Aristotle *Constitution of the Athenians*
34.3; McGlew 2002:112–138; Hall 1993:269–270. The pun in *Assemblywomen*: Sommerstein
1998:139–140; Ussher 1973:75–76.

[20] Aristophanes *Assemblywomen* 184–188; Hess 1963:17–18, 87. Ecclesiastic pay: Sommerstein
1998:154, 167 with references. Unpaid were non-attendees and late arrivals (beyond the six-
thousand quorum).

[21] Hess 1963 takes *Assemblywomen* as a post-imperial *Knights*, and Agyrrhius as its Cleon, but see
Rothwell 1990:5–7; Ussher 1973:101.

[22] Agyrrhius' career: Sommerstein 1998:147–148; Hess 1963:18–29. Pay for political-judicial
service ran counter to oligarchy: Ostwald 2000:27. On *ponêroi*, Rosenbloom 2004a.

But that was *not* the case when noble Myronides held sway. No one got paid to govern then. No, you'd come with your own bag-lunch: something to drink, some bread, two onions, three olives. But see how today's lot lines up for its three obols just for doing a turn in office. Like a pack of ditch-diggers! (*pêlophorountes*, 'clay-haulers')

Aristophanes *Assemblywomen* 304a–310c

Contrasting the vulgar crassness of today's democracy with the aristocratically inflected Athens of yesteryear ("noble Myronides," active 470s–450s), these women hearken back to similar nostalgia in *Knights*, and to late fifth-century Athens' preoccupation with what it called the "ancestral constitution" (*patrioi nomoi, patrios politeia*), the restoration of which provided a rallying cry for oligarchic "reformers" in 411 and 404.[23]

So we have reason to be confused. Speaking the language of democratic reform and moderation, the women institute one *key* reform, equal redistribution of property, that carries with it more than just a whiff of democratic extremism. As David Braund has shown, speakers in the courts could invoke material egalitarianism — the belief that luxury should be shared, not hoarded — as an ideological value, if not a constitutional imperative, under Athenian democracy.[24] Of course, the democracy never actually went so far as to impose the kind of equalization envisioned by Praxagora, whereas the oligarchs of 404, driven by both greed and need, *did* pursue confiscation, and with gusto (see further below). Still, in Euripides' *Suppliants*, the Herald, a recognizably oligarchic reactionary (even if he is, for the purposes of the play, a monarchist), seems to take it for granted that confiscation and democratic *hubris* go hand in hand.[25] That association, we should note, will carry over into fourth-century sources.[26]

---

[23] Xenophon *Hellenica* 2.3.2; Aristotle *Constitution of the Athenians* 29.3, 34.3, 35.2; Wolpert 2002b:35–42; Ostwald 1986:337–411. Myronides as exemplar of manliness and ferocity in battle: Aristophanes *Lysistrata* 801–803; commands held by him, Sommerstein 1998:167.

[24] Braund 1994.

[25] Have-nots motivated by envy and deceived by democratic leaders (*prostatai*) to apply the "savage lash" to haves: Euripides *Suppliants* 240–243. *Hubris*-resonances in the preceding: Michelini 1994:224–225; Fisher 1992:418–424.

[26] Redistribution (*anadasmos tês gês*) and cancellation of debts (*apokopê khreôn*) in connection with democratic coups and the like: Plato *Republic* 565e–566b; Aristotle *Politics* 1305a2–7; *Constitution of the Athenians* 40.3 (Athens the exception); Isocrates 12.259 (*stasis*, redistribution unknown in Sparta); Gehrke 1985:323 and n76 with passages cited there. Saïd 1996:303 notes in *Assemblywomen* resonance with the system of requiring the rich to fund public projects. Wealth-inequality as itself a cause of *stasis*: Isocrates 4.174; Archytas fr. 3 D-K.

Praxagora's program of confiscation and communalization will, then, have resonated with ideas of what radical democracy could be all about; it certainly takes Evaeon's "extremely democratic idea" — free coats and lodging for everybody (408–426) — to the next level. Still, aspects of Praxagora's program also run in a *counter*-democratic direction. Decreeing an end to lawsuits (655–671), and re-commissioning courtrooms and porticoes as public banqueting halls, and the assembly-speaker's platform as a wine-bar and recital stage (675–680), Praxagora effectively dissolves the principal organs of democracy: the people's assembly and courts (cf. Aristotle *Constitution of the Athenians* 9.1 on courts). Adjusting for comic exaggeration, we hear in this echoes of the Oligarchy of the Thirty.[27]

Which is not to reduce Praxagorean gynaecocracy (women's rule) to oligarchy plain and simple. Praxagora does not speak in terms of limiting the franchise to an elite whom she terms the "best" (*khrêstoi, aristoi*, etc.), as the "Old Oligarch" might have done. Nor do her policies target the lower orders; on the contrary, she sets out to insure that a wealth-elite will never again take shape. Yet she also applies certain Spartan touches to her overall design. In so doing, she reminds us a little of Critias, notorious oligarch and admirer of all things Spartan (Critias fr. 6, 32–37 D-K; Xenophon *Hellenica* 2.3.34). Athenians will, then, dine together at public banqueting halls dubbed *sussitia,* "common messes," as at Sparta, where a military ethos will prevail (676–692, 714–717, 834–852), arguably in imitation of Spartan practice. Athenians, like their Spartiate counterparts, will have unfree laborers do all the farming (651–652), and will share possessions and spouses in ways that could have echoed popular views of Spartan customs (590–710). As for gynaecocracy itself, valuing, as it does, the political wisdom of women, it too could have savored more than a little of Laconism.[28]

The aforementioned resonances seem, however, to go right over the heads of most of *Assemblywomen's* male characters. So, for instance, Praxagora's Neighbor, completely sold on communalism's perks, pronounces communalized sex "a downright democratic idea" (*kai dêmôtikê g' hê gnômê,* 631), yet no one notices *un*democratic policies like court- and assembly-closings.[29] Still,

---

[27] Krentz 1982:62–68 with sources cited. Restriction of the franchise and oligarchy: Ostwald 2000:27–28.

[28] Pomeroy 2002:75–82, 92–93; Dettenhofer 1999:102–103. Spartan resonances generally: Sommerstein 1998:16; Rothwell 1990:10. Marriage arrangements at Sparta: Pomeroy 2002:37–45 and see index s.v. "marriage." Praxagorean spouse sharing does not replicate Spartan customs exactly.

[29] I cannot fully agree with Ober 1998:149 that this line is "funny, but not crazy in an Athenian context." If, as is likely, the Neighbor (not Praxagora) speaks (Sommerstein 1998:194), it is at least deeply ironic that the speaker will have had to pay for wealth-equalization with virtual disfranchisement.

material egalitarianism on this scale, surely the answer to destitute Evaeon's dreams, carries with it, as we have seen, undeniably democratic associations.

And yet it also represents a break with values enshrined in oaths rich with meaning under the restored democracy. Thus whenever a new "archon eponymous," the chief official at Athens, entered office, he would, so we are told, proclaim his intention to respect private property (*hosa tis eikhen*) for the duration of his term (Aristotle *Constitution of the Athenians* 5.2). So, too, would jurors swear, among other things, not to cancel debts, redistribute property, or dissolve democracy ("Heliastic oath": Demosthenes 24.149–151). Why such oaths? Whatever their origin or original intent, under the post-403 democracy, they arguably would have been viewed as countermeasures to the kind of brutality and greed unleashed by democracy's demise in 404 BCE.[30] Hence contradiction underlying Praxagora's program. On the one hand, it aims at a democratically inflected equalization to foster civic concord. Yet it breaks with ideologies associating democratic stability with respect for the individual citizen's person and effects.

To this last topic we shall presently return. But what about communalism as stasiastic on top of everything else? We gather from Aristotle that have-nots do not always take to the idea that their peers politically may have more than they materially, and that *stasis* may seem a way to remedy the situation. Note that Aristotle is, in a sense, speaking of a factionalized state of mind: warring cognitions to be harmonized through revolutionary wealth-redistribution.[31] Just so a factionalized state of mind propels the action in *Assemblywomen*. Only there, Praxagora's revolution, though likewise intended to resolve dissonant cognitions produced by wealth-disparity in the face of political equality, triggers other dissonance, other *stasis*, as it enacts a wealth-equalization at once oligarchic and democratic, stabilizing and disruptive.

Of course, Praxagora intends just the *opposite* of *stasis*. As antidote to the selfish, divisive energies men display in the public sphere, she promotes traditionalism, cooperation, and sharing, values practiced by women in the home,[32] and values eminently adaptable to eliminating social discontent, as Isocrates shows:

---

[30] Lysias 12.36, 83, 95–98; 13.43–48; 18.17; Xenophon *Hellenica* 2.3.21, 38–42, 2.4.1; Aristotle *Constitution of the Athenians* 35.4; Diodorus 14.5.5–7; Wolpert 2002b:15–24; Gehrke 1985:210–214, 325.

[31] Aristotle *Politics* 1302a24–26 ("Those who seek equality take part in faction (*stasiazousin*) if they think that they have less, yet feel themselves on a par with those whose with more"); see Kalimtzis 2000:112–115.

[32] Foley 1981a:1–6, 16–21; cf. Rothwell 1990:20–21.

... and when we have freed ourselves of material privation, which dissolves comradeship and drives kin to become enemies and incites all humanity to war and *stasis*, then there will be no avoiding concord among us (*ouk estin hopôs oukh homonoêsomen*) or genuine good will.

Isocrates 4.174

Isocrates is not, of course, in the passage just quoted addressing gynaecocracy. Still, his comments on the benefits of eliminating want will clarify for us the unstated goal of Praxagora's revolution: concord and the avoidance of *stasis*.

But the point here is not whether Praxagora does or does not set out to fight *stasis*, nor whether *stasis* as means to an end is a compromise Praxagora is willing to make. It is, rather, that Aristophanes has dramatized a kind of cognitive dissonance illuminated by Michael Billig in his study of the often discrepant strands of thought shaping human consciousness. Billig calls these the "contrary topics of common sense," by which he means the almost instinctively felt pros and cons with which people often react to perfectly commonplace situations or notions — how, for instance, one and the same discourse community can subscribe to "truths" as incompatible as "the best things in life are free" and "you get what you pay for."[33] Of course that "how" will vary, instance to instance. But it typically involves social factors, the need to fit one's own representations into the ebb and flow of the ambient discourse. Hence in our play discrepant evaluations of gynaecocratic communalism, a system variously radical and moderate, disruptive and stabilizing, depending on speaker, audience, situation, and so on.

We can, if we like, think of that as a kind of discursive *stasis*, spin, in other words, as an ideological investment automatically generating its own counterspin, its own counterdiscourse — so especially in the dissonant valuations Praxagora herself brings to the idea she has birthed. Thus in the speech she tries out on her friends, we hear much to recommend women's rule, but we also hear of women's bibulousness, lasciviousness, and infidelity (224–228), credentials seemingly at odds with the case Praxagora wants to make.[34] Reprising the misogynistic humor of Aristophanes' *Lysistrata* and *Thesmophoriazusae*, these vices seem to have been slipped in as a sop to men expecting that kind of joke from our play. But they also highlight ambivalence

---

[33] Billig 1996:232–238.
[34] For these dissonant resonances of gynaecocracy: Rosellini 1979.

in the enunciation and reception of gynaecocracy, a system capitalizing on women as steady anchors of the home, yet worrying because of its reliance on women and power wielded by them. So, for instance, Chremes reports to a sympathetic Blepyrus the grumbling of Attic farmers when the latter first hear about Praxagora's proposal (432–433; cf. 471–472), while Blepyrus himself worries lest politically empowered women impose excessive sexual demands on men (465–475). How, then, will Praxagora sell the city — the *whole* city, not just the women — on her idea? As we shall see, what matters are the cognitive filters through which men are made to take it all in.

Forgive and Forget

Still recovering from catastrophic defeat at Spartan hands a decade earlier, Athens in the late 390s was coping as well with the aftermath of a brief but violent episode of oligarchy following that defeat.[35] One coping mechanism, the Amnesty of 403, stipulated that all Athenians wishing to join the reconstituted democracy had to swear an oath whose central term was *mê mnêsikakein*, "not to remember wrong." This verb, *mnêsikakein*, holds close affinities to the violence of factionalized politics (LSJ s.v. I.). Thus to forego *mnêsikakein* is to forego reprisal. Yet one hesitates to treat *mnêsikakein* simply as revenge. Within the context of reconciliation, the negation of *mnêsikakein* means not just the avoidance of violence, but the hope of freeing the mind of poisonous thoughts (*ou mnêsikakêsô*, 'I shall be mindful of no evil').[36]

That hope — that need — did not suddenly come about with the restoration of democracy in 403. Phrynichus, one of the city's more important playwrights, in 493 produced a play, the *Capture of Miletus*, for which he was fined one thousand drachmas. Why that fine? Phrynichus had, so we are told, "reminded his audience of misfortune that hit home (*anamnêsanta oikêia kaka*)"; the play itself no one thenceforth was allowed to produce ever again. In Herodotus' telling, it was collective memory embodied in the *theêtron*, the massed assemblage of spectators, that needed to be shielded from destructive grief.[37] For Plutarch, that measure carries political resonance. Along with the

---

[35] Upwards of 1,500 Athenians, perhaps as much as five percent of the citizenry, killed, not to mention non-citizens: Wolpert 2002b:22nn67–68; Krentz 1982:79.

[36] Andocides 1.90; Xenophon *Hellenica* 2.4.43; Aristotle *Constitution of the Athenians* 39.6; Dionysius *Lysias* 32; Loraux 2002:246–248; Ober 2002; Quillin 2002; Tieman 2002; Wolpert 2002a; Wolpert 2002b; Dorjahn 1946:1–6. Members of the regime's inner circle were additionally required to submit to an audit.

[37] Herodotus 6.21.2, for which, Loraux 2002:146–154, 181, 295n58, 311n51.

403 Amnesty and other measures, it shows Athenian statecraft: the city taking steps to inoculate the collective consciousness against inauspicious news or memories.[38]

It is significant that salutary forgetting could resonate within Athenian myth and cult. According to Plutarch, Athenians maintained an altar to Lethe, "Goddess Oblivion," in the Erechtheum, the temple shared by Athena and Poseidon, onetime rivals for lordship over the city. Now Athenians, as is well known, cherished the memory of the contest that gave them the horse and the olive. Why, then, the altar? It was because of Lethe's role in keeping the peace in the aftermath of a contest so divisive even in its remembrance that Athenians subtracted its date from their calendar. Likewise should we consign to *amnêstia*, "non-remembrance," the anniversary of any quarrel with family or friends. Or so advises Plutarch (*Moralia* 489b), who also draws attention to the parallel with the 403 Amnesty.[39] So remember Oblivion, remember to forget. Else suffer the consequences.

But what kind of forgetting is that? If, as George Lakoff points out, "negating a frame activates the frame," then focused forgetting necessarily entails a paradoxical kind of remembering: "If you tell someone not to think of an elephant, he'll think of an elephant."[40] Still, in the tense atmosphere of the post-403 period, that "elephant," citizens' complicity in violence against citizens, needed desperately to be ignored. One approach, fear as *aide-mémoire*, earns praise from a source recounting how the Athenian Council executed a democrat who "had begun to remember past wrongs," which is to say, was bent on revenge. The upshot: no one ever again "held a grudge," no one forgot to forget.[41] But whatever that measure's actual effect, it is certainly striking that so pacific an act of forgetting as the Amnesty, closely tied as it was to concord (*homonoia*) and the avoidance of renewed *stasis*, could be viewed as buttressed by that ultimate focuser of thoughts: the threat of death.

Even so, it was hard to forget, as narratives of ongoing recrimination and reprisal attest,[42] not to mention court cases where the issue at hand provided a thin veil for political revenge.[43] How, then, did this altogether equivocal

---

[38] Plutarch *Moralia* 814b–c, for which Loraux 2002:148, 300n11.
[39] Plutarch *Moralia* 741a–b; Loraux 2002:43–44, 171–190. The historicity of the subtraction remains vexed.
[40] Lakoff 2006.
[41] Aristotle *Constitution of the Athenians* 40.2; Wolpert 2002a:115–116.
[42] Xenophon *Hellenica* 3.1.4; Nepos *Thrasybulus* 3.3; Krentz 1982:114–122.
[43] Assorted speeches of Lysias and early Isocrates; Andocides 2; Quillin 2002:72–73; Wolpert 2002a; Wolpert 2002b:48–71; Krentz 1982:114–117. Stone 1988 and Dover 1975 suggest political motivation for Socrates' impiety trial.

forgetting, one effectively breached in the very observance, come to win the admiration it did?[44] To Andrew Wolpert, Athenians gathered around it as a kind of social construct upon which to rebuild a shared identity:

> ... since so many were either complicit in the atrocities of the Thirty or failed to rally behind the democratic exiles, it was actually easier for the Athenians to imagine the *dêmos* to have been united in its opposition to the Thirty than for them to acknowledge their own failings or to recognize the divisions that still existed in the community after the reconciliation, divisions that threatened the stability of the restored democracy.[45]

Further insights come from discourse analysis. According to John Shotter and Michael Billig, memory and remembering — how the past is constructed — can be understood in social-discursive terms. When we remember, we adopt a stance not just to the past itself, but to what it symbolizes for us and others. Memory thus represents a field within which we demarcate our ideological investments and social alignments.[46] That will, naturally, involve rejection as well as identification, social blindness as well as shared cognizance. And so it did in 403 BCE, when, if one wanted to take advantage of the chance to rejoin the Athenian *dêmos*, one had to jump through one very important hoop: to swear to ignore whole areas of active memory. That gained one entry into a community of individuals like-minded on at least one crucial point: that "we," committed democrats (for such we are in swearing not to remember), refuse to acknowledge divisive thoughts within our midst.

But could the city think as one *and still think*? So *Assemblywomen* seems to ask. To be sure, the play nowhere refers explicitly to the *stasis* of 404, to the Amnesty of 403,[47] or to residual tension in the post-403 period. Yet it need not have. Remedying civic restiveness with distractive pleasures, and pulling the plug on dissent by "re-purposing" venues for same, Aristophanes' play engages themes of salutary forgetting when it stages a revolution designed to erase all reminders of division within the city. Yet divisions persist — why? To understand why, it will help to consider an *action directe* staged by women in *Assemblywomen*'s similarly themed forerunner: the *Lysistrata* of 411.

---

[44] Andocides 1.140; Lysias 2.64; Xenophon *Hellenica* 2.5.43; Aristotle *Constitution of the Athenians* 40.2; Wolpert 2002b:48, 159n2.

[45] Wolpert 2002a:111.

[46] Shotter and Billig 1998:17–18.

[47] Though cf. Aristophanes *Wealth* 1146, an explicit reference to the Amnesty of 403.

Peithô on Trial: *Lysistrata*

Still reeling from the Sicilian disaster of 413, and harried year-round by enemy encampments within Attica, Athenian husbands in 411 BCE watched as their wives — or rather, male actors *portraying* their wives — joined forces with their enemies' "wives" to end the decades-long war with Sparta.[48] Under the direction of Lysistrata, the heroine of Aristophanes' like-named comedy, these women vow to withhold sex from their husbands until the latter cease fighting. In addition, Lysistrata dispatches a contingent of Athenian women to occupy the Acropolis, where the city's financial reserves are kept. Starved for sex and cash, the men of Athens at last agree to lay down arms, as do their sex-starved foes.[49]

That fairly well sums up what has made *Lysistrata* famous as a "peace play," but it tells only part of the story. Another part has to do with gendered politics and dialogics: how male and female transact power and influence within the city and within the city's constituent households. Gender politics in the play are, of course, nothing new to critics. Thus M. Shaw some time ago discovered within *Lysistrata* a more or less Hegelian dialectic — a clash, that is, of values, female-domestic versus male-public, triggered when a "female intruder" ventures outside the house and into the life of the *polis*.[50] To Shaw's rather starkly drawn opposition Helene Foley applies a corrective. In their bid to end the fighting, the women in *Lysistrata* have, to be sure, crossed a threshold. But in a larger sense, they affirm their rightful place in the public sphere: they restore the social order, thrown into disarray by men and their war, to the *status quo ante*.[51]

But what about those moments of destabilization and dramatic tension, transitional between a before-and-after normalcy? Let us start with spatial issues. Michèle Rosellini underscores the fact that, for a comedy, *Lysistrata*'s action exceptionally plays out in a public space, specifically, the Athenian Acropolis.[52] In seizing it, women have not simply cut off men's access to

---

[48] Metatheatrical resonances of female impersonation by male actors on the ancient Attic stage: Bassi 1998; Taaffe 1993.

[49] Presumably, husbands with sufficient means could have found extramarital outlets, though the play glosses over that. Still, for ordinary Athenians, conjugal sex probably represented, among other things, a genuine erotic outlet: Fowler 1996. Cf. the recent "crossed legs" strike staged by Colombian women fed up with gang violence: NPR *Morning Edition* 15 September 2006.

[50] Shaw 1975.

[51] Foley 1982:7. Women's roles outside the house (e.g. public cult), men's with respect to the house (e.g. maintaining material wellbeing): Cohen 1991:70–83, 150–154; Foley 1982:1–5.

[52] Rosellini 1979:13.

Athens' war chest. They have grounded their case, both argumentatively and topographically, upon this vitally important symbol of women's contribution to public cult. But they have as well seized the *rhetorical* high ground, a symbolically appropriate platform from which to make their case.[53]

But how to get men to listen? Partly through physical *peithô* ('persuasion') — seduction, intimidation, humiliation, even extortion in the form of a dual embargo, sexual and financial. But women also deploy verbal argument, both to justify this new role they have taken on (588–590, 638–657), and to propose a scheme to transform *polis* and empire into a broad-based coalition of shared goodwill (567–586). Not just peace, then, with Sparta, but an ambitious program for reform rides on women's success at getting their message across. To do that, women cannot simply use coercive means, their dual embargo. They must as well engage men in genuine dialogue. They must *communicate*.

This challenge, that of forging a discursive connection with men, goes to the very heart of what speech is all about. According to Vološinov, speech happens neither as pure expression of an individual soul, nor as something meaningful only because it obeys certain abstract rules. Rather, it happens as speech-acts transacted between persons. As such, it presumes and anticipates reception, evaluation, response. In its effort to forge what Vološinov calls an "ideological chain" between speakers, the speech-act is shaped by, and reshapes, not just lexicon and grammar, but also the common store of images, assumptions, and attitudes within which the discourse of the city happens.[54]

Speech represents, therefore, a fundamentally *social* phenomenon. But the sociality of speech will not be all of a piece and will depend in large measure on the central term in the transaction: evaluation. At its most basic, social evaluation of another's utterance operates according to a binary code: positive/negative, acceptance/rejection, Us/Other. If the effort to forge an "ideological chain" — to open a channel to one's discursive partner — meets with success, that in and of itself will betoken some level of social connection. But there's the rub: if speakers sense no common ground between them, if they feel alienated before even saying a word, then they have little chance of initiating any real dialogue.

What can interfere? Let me try a computer analogy. Computers seeking to connect over a network will typically engage in what is known as "hand-

---

[53] Cf. Rosellini 1979:12–15. This is, of course, a staging ground less politicized, or masculinized, than the Pnyx, the regular venue for assembly meetings.

[54] See "Dialogical Reading," chapter 1 above.

shake," through which they negotiate the communication protocol they will use for exchanging data. In human communication, that "handshake" can be analyzed into a pair of elements, the one termed "manifestation" by Deleuze, the other, "addressivity" by Vološinov and Holquist. Manifestation is the "I" in communication: it is my pushing myself and my message into your world. Deleuze illustrates by quoting Lewis Carrol's Alice: "if only you spoke when you were spoken to, and the other person always waited for *you* to begin, you see nobody would ever say anything . . ." — manifestation, in other words, as a necessary precondition for communication.[55] But there is another element to the bargain: addressivity. If your computer is not in the "ready" state, it will "hear" no incoming message. Nor will you if your posture as listener, your "addressivity," cannot be made to fit with my manifestation.[56] At its simplest, speaking is itself manifestation, and listening, addressivity: my speaking says to you "listen," and your listening says to me "speak." Operating outside of the purely semantic content of a message, those "metacommunicative messages" ("this is a joke," "this is between friends," "*this* is serious") frame content.[57] We can, then, view handshake as that shared sense (entirely subjective, validated only by the dynamics of communication itself) that a connection has been made — the sense, in other words, that we can *talk*. Anything amiss within the metadiscursive frame, even the merest impression of an improper fit, say, between speaker and message or message and addressee, can cause one or both of us to lose the signal.[58]

Returning to *Lysistrata*, movement toward dialogue is both initiated and hampered by the women's manifestation. Thus women in the play, to finesse a connection with their male interlocutors, "take on some male characteristics while outwardly emphasizing their inherent femininity."[59] Decked out in all their seductive finery, they try to lure men away from war[60] even as they "man" the ramparts and speak and fight like their opposite numbers (e.g. parallel disrobing, 614–690). Of course, women, through their "manning," speaking, and fighting, place themselves in a conflictive stance toward men.

---

[55] Deleuze 1990:17; also 13–18. Cf. Vološinov 1986:83–90 on "expression" and "orientation."

[56] Addressivity: Holquist 1990:27, 48; Vološinov 1986:85–87.

[57] Bateson's metacommunicative messages (gestural, facial, intonational, verbal): Neuman 2003:68; cf. Vološinov 1986:87, 103–104. "Content" and "meta-" are relative terms: content can frame; frame always involves some sort of content.

[58] Cf. Neuman et al. 2002:95–96, which see generally on the orator's need to enter into his audience's "collective self — their group membership or identity" (94).

[59] Taaffe 1993:59.

[60] For this tactic, especially Bassi 1998:107–108.

But in so doing, they also assimilate themselves to the opposite sex: they re-orient their dialogical outreach, their manifestation, to spaces where male-male dialogue, not just conflict, is transacted. Yet the sexual side to the women's *peithô* runs at cross purposes with their efforts to reach out. Dolling themselves up to intensify their husbands' lust, the women transform themselves into hyper-women, and their men into hyper-men, victims now of an exaggerated and painful Priapism. Eventually, men will have to give in. But until then, these transformations serve only to underscore and exacerbate discursive polarization.[61]

Exacerbating it further is male prejudice and intransigence. Thus the Commissioner (*Proboulos*), branding the women's *action directe* "sheer hubris,"[62] remains adamantly unreceptive. So, too, do the men of the Chorus in condemning the women's "unbridled vice" (*toiaut'... akolastasmata*, 398). Indeed, merely by speaking out, these women provoke male hostility, as calls for them to shut up attest (364, 590; cf. 515–516). Significantly, the Men's Chorus Leader compares the women to Amazons and Artemisia, who for him exemplify the female Other at its most bellicose and threatening.[63] Significantly, too, the Old Men of the Chorus describe the firepots they carry as Lemnian (*lêmnion to pur*, 299), ostensibly because their eyes are "bleary" (*lêmai*) from all the smoke. Yet their choice of adjective speaks of deeper worries: that women might be planning a coup like that staged by the husband-slaying Lemnian women of myth.[64] For they clearly fear coup d'état, an assault on democracy by would-be tyrants seeking to "ride saddle" against the city (Hippias = "Horseman"), that is, come out on top, sexually and politically.[65]

Which is to say, the men are panicked. But more than that, they can form no coherent idea of what their women are up to. Reacting to this ostensible coup as if to attempted castration at the hands of a murderous band of Lemnian Amazons commanded by a latter day Artemisia bent on reinstating a dynasty of Athenian tyrants,[66] the men respond not to *stasis* before their eyes

---

[61] A return to normal levels of gender-polarization accompanies the eventual resolution of tensions: Taaffe 1993:51–52.

[62] *Hubris ... pollê*, Aristophanes *Lysistrata* 658–659; cf. 400. See Fisher 1992:118 and n231.

[63] Aristophanes *Lysistrata* 671–679. Artemisia commanded pro-Persian forces at Salamis (480 BCE); the Amazons, barbarian warrior-women of myth, attacked Athens: Bremer 2000; Dorati 1998:46–48; Henderson 1987:160.

[64] Dorati 1999; Taaffe 1993:53; Henderson 1991:98; Henderson 1987:105; Martin 1987.

[65] Aristophanes *Lysistrata* 616–679. Cf. *PMG* frr. 893–896; see Henderson 2000:355n57; Loraux 1993:154–157.

[66] Castration: Henderson 1987:161. Women "dousing" men's sexual-military encroachments: Aristophanes *Lysistrata* 254–386; Dorati 1999:84; Henderson 1991:98.

but *stasis* in their heads. Admittedly, these paranoid responses of theirs are spread out over the course of several scenes (254–681). But in the compressed span of some ten lines (671–681), it comes at us thick and furious: women turning from infantry assaults (grabbing a "handhold," *labên*) to naval assaults to cavalry assaults; women trading an Artemisian persona for an Amazonian persona; women as literal warriors, as sexual "warriors."

To that jumble of misconceptions we can add those of the Commissioner. Blaming men for failing to police their wives' sexuality (403–420), he compares the present crisis to an assembly vote botched when an assembly speaker, effectively "channeling" his wife's frenzied cries to Adonis, carried his motion, the ill-omened Sicilian Expedition of 415–413 (387–398).[67] But that is, of course, nothing like the present situation. Women in *Lysistrata* do not dole out sexual favors; they withhold them. Nor do men "channel" women; women speak for themselves. None of which speaks well of the men's addressivity, their capacity to "get" the messages women are sending.

Still, at two points in the drama, Lysistrata is able to command the Commissioner's attention: first, as he unsympathetically listens to her complain about being silenced by her husband (503–531), then, as she offers a suggestion at once visionary and self-defeating. Thus Lysistrata, using imagery derived from the world of women's work, explains how men should "weave" together a single "garment" (*khlaina*) of shared goodwill (*koinên eunoian*) centered on the *dêmos*, but uniting various disparate "threads": metics, *xenoi*, all who are friendly to Athens and capable of benefiting it (565–586).

That plan, inspired and breathtaking though it is, manages only to alienate the Commissioner. Assimilating male statecraft to women's handicrafts, Lysistrata allows the Commissioner the leeway to read her plan as a feminization — men metaphorically carding, spinning, weaving — on a par with the legislative fiasco he decried some lines before.[68] So our Commissioner takes it quite amiss: "Terrible, terrible, how they batter and bobbin us!" For it speaks, so the Commissioner thinks, to women's insensitivity to the war-burden men have shouldered (587). But when Lysistrata counters by noting her and her associates' contribution of sons, the Commissioner will have none of it. "Silence!" he commands, "Don't go there — bad memories!" (*siga, mê mnêsikakêseis*, 587–590). Earlier, Lysistrata's counsel merely alienated the

---

[67] The Commissioner probably means that the women cast a funereal pall over the expedition with their lamentations; cf. Plutarch *Alcibiades* 18.2–3.

[68] Cf. barbaric gender reversal: Sophocles *Oedipus at Colonus* 337–343; Herodotus 2.35.2; Hippocrates *Airs Waters Places* 22; Dorati 1998:43–44; Cohen 1991:79–80.

Commissioner. Now, it hits home with truth too painful to bear: a war that has cost Athenians dearly in lives. In silencing Lysistrata, the Commissioner uses an expression, *mnêsikakein*, "to remember past wrongs," "to hold grudge," with, we have seen, affinities to the violence of factionalized politics. Memory and grief, powerful arguments against war, the Commissioner would suppress as stasiastic.[69] But so would he *any* effort by women to address policy recommendations to himself and his fellow men. Despite women's efforts to reach out, and a limited effort on the Commissioner's part to pay heed, no ideological chain is forged, nor any line of communication opened. There is, it would seem, nothing either side can say that will help.

Where discourse fails, other means must prevail. Thus the Commissioner, who says he would rather die than heed women, undergoes a literal dressing down, first as a woman, then as a corpse.[70] As for the Men's Choristers, they positively collapse before the tender cajoleries of their women (1014–1042). Though the Men's Chorus Leader cites Lysistrata's *iunx*, her sexy persuasiveness, in connection with the rhetorical versatility the moment demands, Lysistrata herself knows all too well that it will take the mute but irresistible nakedness of *Diallagê*, feminine "Reconciliation" in the flesh, to get the two sides talking to each other (1108–1188).

But conciliatory forgetting, too, has a role to play, specifically, during the concluding love-feast, a lavish affair celebrating peace between states and rapprochement between the sexes. Thus when a guest launches into a war song (the *Telamôn*) when he should have been singing a peace song (the *Kleitagora*), that ill-timed reminder *could* have ruined the mood, and possibly even rekindled hostilities. Fortunately, the other guests, pleasantly inebriated, overlook the gaffe and applaud anyway, thereby demonstrating the benefits of wine as catalyst of a kind of social forgetting (1225–1240). Even the list of invited gods suggests the need to suppress unpleasant memories. Invoking Memory and her Muse, the Spartan Herald summons a divine cohort to which his Athenian counterpart adds the names of those "to serve as witnesses, constant reminders of the magnanimous tranquility that divine Aphrodite has fashioned for us" (1260–1290, 1296–1321). Yet we hear nothing about Athena Polias, the city's spear-wielding, city-protecting patron, whose rocky crag, lately the scene of inter-gender strife, provides the setting for the present love-feast. Thus the local Athena, eclipsed for the moment by her Spartan

---

[69] "To allow Lys. to complete her statement ('never to see them again') would indeed have evoked spectator resentments and in addition would have been ill-omened": Henderson 1987:145.

[70] Aristophanes *Lysistrata* 530–538, 599–607; Dorati 1998:50–53; Taaffe 1993:64–66.

counterpart (1299, 1320/1), will play no overt role in deflecting collective memory away from the recent war to an earlier one, when Spartan-Athenian friendship led the Greeks to victory against a foreign foe (cf. 1247–1272).

To sum-up, we seem to have in *Lysistrata* an essay not on the power of *logos* but on its limits: its inability to span too broad or too deep an ideological divide unassisted. Thus when women reach out to their male compatriots, or male Athenians to their enemies (cf. 1228–1238), the sober give-and-take of *logos* will need the boost it gets from judiciously dispensed, and withheld, doses of women's soothing and sexy ministrations (*thôpeia*, *iunx*) combined with the tranquilizing effects of drink. Men do, to be sure, eventually find ideological common ground in memories of past cooperation, but not before Lysistrata puts non-verbal persuasion into play. Returning, then, to *Assemblywomen*, Praxagora, we shall see, adapts this recipe to a revolution far more ambitious than anything tried in *Lysistrata*. Can it be made to work? That will depend on whether a restive citizenry can be made to *think* it does.

Synoecism

In Aristophanes' *Lysistrata*, the title character's dual embargo works wonders, though we get no sense that Lysistrata herself succeeds in her larger aim: to talk Athenian men into "re-stitching" a broader coalition — we might call it an empire — coming apart at the seams. Praxagora perforce sets her sights more locally: there is no longer any empire to re-stitch. There are, though, citizens desperately needing to regain a sense of common purpose. In addressing that need, Praxagora also talks. But her plan to tear down divisions on both the concrete and symbolic plane speaks just as eloquently as any speech she could give:

> For I intend to transform the town (*astu*) into a single domicile (*mian oikêsin*) by demolishing (*surrêxas'*) everything into a single entity, so everyone can walk into everyone else's house.

Aristophanes Assemblywomen 673–675

By cutting passageways between houses to form one vast residence, Praxagora will extend the principle of commonality (*koinê diaita*, "shared life") to all corners of the city (the *astu*). Given the centrality of this totalizing transformation, not just of residential architecture, but of a citizenry united as one, we can think of her achievement in Greek terms as *sunoikein*, "synoecism." This term's elements (*sun-* "together," *oikos* "house") can refer to the banding together of husband and wife to form a household, or of population units (households, villages, etc.) to form a civic community, a *polis* (LSJ s.v. συνοικέω I. 1., 2., II.). Thus Praxagora, mastermind of a politically transformative *oikos*-amalgamation, emerges as a latter-day Theseus, mythical king and orchestrator of Athens' legendary synoecism. We are told that Theseus, in carrying out the original merger (*sunôikise*) of Attic populations, made astute use of persuasion (Plutarch *Theseus* 2.2, 24.1–25.1), whose part in the merger he commemorated with a temple to Aphrodite Pandemos partnered with Peitho, persuasion personified (Pausanias 1.22.3). Which is to say that he recognized the role of a quasi-erotic, integrative dynamic in forging this union of demes. Just so Praxagora, insofar as she spares no resource of persuasion to reinaugurate the Athenian state, embodies a feminine-gendered *peithô* prized as the antithesis of political chaos and violence.[71] Herself a cross between Theseus and Aphrodite, she has hit upon a plan to form that more perfect union Lysistrata could only dream of (Aristophanes *Lysistrata* 565–586): take over the state for real this time, and take responsibility out of the hands of men. In the earlier play, Lysistrata floated an optimistic view of the *polis* as an extension of the feminine-private sphere.[72] In *Assemblywomen*, that vision translates into action.

Comparison with Euripides' *Medea* and Sophocles' *Oedipus at Colonus* sheds further light. In both plays, an extra-urban stream, the "fair-flowing," ever-flowing Cephisus, fosters a pure, inviolate beauty friendly to Aphrodite — beauty in which Athens itself basks, whether explicitly (*Medea*) or by association (*Oedipus*). Part and parcel with that is the *sophia*, the genius for intellectual and artistic achievement, with which Aphrodite's Loves are partnered, and on which a divinely begotten race feeds in Euripides' play. But it is fundamentally *harmonia*, not simply "harmony," but a shared existence of material blessings and aesthetic attractions, that renders Athens a refuge attractive, yet inhospitable, to a child-murdering foreigner like the same play's title character (Euripides *Medea* 824–845; cf. Sophocles *Oedipus at Colonus* 668–719).

So, too, in *Assemblywomen*, a shared existence (*diaitan ... koinên pasin*, 673–674) of material blessings (cf. 1112–1133) will conduce to the goal of banishing politically divisive individualism and greed.[73] Synoecism becomes, then, the tangible corollary of *homonoia*, the ideal of civic unity underlying

---

[71] Praxagora's *peithô*: Rothwell 1990:26–43 et passim.

[72] Foley 1982:7; cf. Konstan 1995:51–54; Rothwell 1990:21; Vaio 1973:372.

[73] Cf. Möllendorff 1995:121–122: Praxagora will reorganize the *polis*, the male, external world (identified with the here-and-now) on the model of the *oikos*, the female, internal world (identified with the past).

gynaecocratic communalism. Sexed-up as it is in our play (613–634), *homonoia* recalls Max Weber's "communism of love," under which an individual's uniquely forceful charisma gathers around itself a community based on the sharing of goods.[74] At the same time, this totalizing communalization carries with it Pythagorean overtones. Prompted by the teaching of their master, who declared the things of friends to be in common, and friendship to be equality (*koina ta philôn einai kai philian isotêta*), Pythagoras' disciples deposited all their property in a common store (Timaeus *FGrH* 566 F 13b = Diogenes Laertius). Just so do Praxagora's policies seek to reinvent Athens as a city of love and equality based on sharing. We have, therefore, in this communism of love envisioned by Praxagora the Periclean ideal reawakened, though in the absence of an empire on which to focus acquisitive lusts. This is, then, communal *erôs* in a form even purer than we saw in the Periclean Funeral Oration. With women enfranchised, *erôs* focused inward (among other things, citizens and foreigners may no longer mingle sexually, 718–724), and spouses to be shared, this marriage of citizens exemplifies synoecism in every sense of the word.

And in so doing, it concretizes what could be called a "poetics" of same-thinking, one that Bakhtin would characterize as centripetal or "center-seeking" in its tendencies. Why a poetics, and why centripetal? Poetry for Bakhtin, lyric poetry especially, illustrates how certain types of discourse can privilege finality of expression achieved through close harmonization of word with thought and word with word; with that contrast the center-fleeing ("centrifugal") interplay of discourses Bakhtin celebrates in the polyphonic novel.[75] Where discourses follow that single, guiding vision, they risk forgetting their "own history of contradictory acts of verbal recognition," their grounding within historical currents and conflicting perspectives.[76] That scheme will help us understand Praxagora's revolution, how it erects through discursive and non-discursive means an idyllic utopia designed not so much to *deter* divisive cognitions as to *distract* from them. Praxagora's idyll, a poem of a city, promises a union more perfect than any known till now, one offering a restive and self-centered citizenry a chance to transform the *erôs* of greed, ambition, and *stasis* into an *erôs* for community and cooperation. But it must,

---

[74] Weber 1978:1119–1120.

[75] Bakhtin 1981:275–288.

[76] Morson and Emerson 1990:319–325; Bakhtin 1981, 278. This scheme undeniably reveals critical bias on Bakhtin's part and ignores a great deal of poetry. Buts its usefulness emerges if we understand "centrifugal" as referring to the ways that discourse engages other discourses, "centripetal" to the ways that it engages its own production. Both dynamics surely operate all the time.

as Praxagora well knows, suppress all *logos* with the power to divide. Free speech must henceforth yield to same-thinking, just as property rights must to sharing.

Which brings us back to all that Praxagora wants to knock down and clear away, literally and figuratively. Literally, of course, she proposes demolishing *oikos* demarcations, party walls separating house from house. What did the Greek house represent? If nothing else, something that enclosed space, specifically, for those who had business being inside, family and guests. But the house also excluded; it set off an outside where outsiders were, unless invited in, expected to stay.[77] And so it is for Praxagora's "townhouse." In contrast to the confederation envisioned by Lysistrata, a "weaving together" of citizens and others, this amalgamation of public and private will remake Athens into a dwelling (*oikêsis*) for Athenians and, it seems, no one else. Foreigners, both free and slave, who earlier had, often to their material gain, provided Athenian men with a sexual outlet, must henceforth cease and desist (718–724). Apart from that, Praxagora does not elaborate on a role for non-Athenians. Still, the Heraldress invites none but citizens to dine in state (834). Even Praxagora's Maidservant, though a slave, seems to have entered the rolls and thus to have a place reserved for her (1115). Praxagora's "townhouse" will, then, both exclude and include. No castle in the clouds as in *Birds*, it actualizes a utopian "there" within the here-and-now.[78]

To build it, though, Praxagora will "demolish completely" not just inter-house demarcations (party walls), but family and chattel demarcations as well. This word "demolish completely" (*surrêxas'*, 675; cf. LSJ s.v. συρρήγνυμι) vividly suggests the violence and finality with which Praxagora would carry out renovations seemingly intended to enact a kind of poetic justice. To demolish a man's house symbolized the destruction of his family and place in the community. It was, as the relevant sources suggest, a punishment reserved for those viewed as guilty of egregious offenses — murder, tyranny, treason for profit. Thus in tragedy, the destruction of a royal household often represents payback for a family history of crime that has brought pollution upon the entire land.[79] Of course, Praxagora will not carry out a demolition quite on that scale: she does not intend to raze all domestic space to the ground,

---

[77] See Cohen 1991:70–97 for the house as "a physical embodiment of claims of privacy associated with the family" (84).

[78] Cf. Reinders 2001:277–279; Zimmermann 1983:74–75.

[79] See Connor 1985. This punishment might be visited upon the powerful, as in the case of certain oligarchs of 411. Cf. the destruction of Socrates' "Thinkery" in Aristophanes' *Clouds*.

nor to expel Athenians from their homes. But she will erase all evidence of the *Ancien Régime*'s — of men's — individual domains.

And in so doing, it would seem that she does away with some of their manhood. Ubiquitous and eloquent symbol of the house as an expression of manhood was the herm. Planted just outside street doors, these stone posts with their erect *phalloi* (cf. e.g. Thucydides 6.27.1) sent an unmistakable message: "Molest this house and I molest you."[80] For to trespass upon an Athenian man's house amounted to a personal violation, what the Greeks termed *hubris*.[81] Prosecuted by *graphê*, that is, by public writ, an act of *hubris* could be interpreted as a menace to the *polis* as a whole, so important was it to protect the dignity of individual citizens.[82] Thus Thucydides, though he does not specifically label as *hubris* the mutilation of the herms in 415 (Plutarch and Demosthenes do), conveys the impression that, at the time, Athenians associated that desecration with behavior of a hubristic cast, acts like the explicitly hubristic profaning of the Mysteries.[83]

That association suggests as well a political side to the mutilation of the herms. Symbolizing the castration of citizen-male householders,[84] it also could have presaged, at least in retrospect, plots to dissolve democracy. Thus scholars argue that under democracy, "the herm [expressed] the notional equality of each household, represented in the person of its patriarch and signified by a simplified image of a man."[85] Remarks Halperin,

---

[80] Thucydides speaks of the abundance of herms as a local idiosyncrasy at Athens, where they could be found at the entrance to both private and sacred space (6.27.1). The archaeological evidence for their presence in public spaces is excellent, less than excellent for them in front of private doors. Aristophanes *Wealth* 1153 illustrates the latter; some of these could have been of perishable wood. Their presence at house doors likely will have been commonplace if not inevitable. William Furley notes that the phallic potency of herms functioned in a triple capacity: to keep intruders out, to protect those within, to protect the latter when venturing forth from within (Furley 1996:19–20). See further McGlew 2002:132–138; Wohl 2002:21–25 and index; Furley 1996:13–30; Fehling 1988.

[81] Cf. Lysias 3.7. Integrity of the house and personal honor: Cohen 1991:147. Fisher (1992:1) defines *hubris* as "the serious assault on the honour of another, which is likely to cause shame, and lead to anger and attempts at revenge."

[82] *Graphê hubreôs*: Isocrates 20.2; Demosthenes 21; Fisher 1992:36–85. In Isocrates 20.1 (402–400 BCE), political freedom and democracy are there to protect the citizen's physical body against assault, a crime the speaker associates with the outrages of the Thirty (4, 10–11).

[83] *Eph' hubrei*, Thucydides 6.28.1. For the mutilation as hubristic, Demosthenes 21.143–147; Plutarch *Alcibiades* 18.4; Fisher 1992:145.

[84] So Wohl 2002:20. Thucydides 6.27.1 refers to damage to the faces of herms. Whether or not vandals also damaged the *phalloi* (as *Lysistrata* 1093–1094 may imply) makes little difference: "either way, the citizen body is mutilated" (Wohl 2002:154n79). Cf. Wohl 23–24 on the civic-emasculatory dimension of the mutilation of 415 BCE.

[85] Halperin quoting Winkler from the latter's unpublished Martin Classical Lectures; see Halperin 1990:104–105 and 188n112.

> The erection of herms many be another symptom . . . of the growing sense of masculine self-assertion and the new pride in masculine egalitarianism that accompanied the consolidation of the democracy at Athens.[86]

Let me be clear: I am not claiming that Praxagora's *oikos* amalgamation corresponds exactly to penetration of the house by would-be burglars, adulterers, or rapists, the sort of intrusion herms seem to have been envisaged as preventing. But it matters that she would tear down demarcations symbolizing an Athenian citizen's autonomy and masculine integrity. Though meant in the service of a higher egalitarianism, these demolitions would tear down the *old* egalitarianism, the patriarchal democracy. And that is, of course, just what gynaecocratic communalism intends, namely, to "unman" Athenian government for its own good; to end, once and for all, the divisiveness of egocentric, pleonectic *erôs*; to unite Athenians in the spirit of *koinônia*, a broad-based sharing. Thus Praxagora faces the challenge not just of planning the city's salvation, but of selling her plan to a citizenry with much to gain from it, though at a price all may not be willing to pay.

Peithô on Trial: *Assemblywomen*

In preparing for the assembly meeting that will make or break this revolution, it helps that Praxagora, its leader, has had the benefit of a rhetorical education, which she has got by living next to the Pnyx (the hill where the assembly met) and listening in on the proceedings there (241–244). In that and other respects, she stands apart from her co-conspirators, who, though disguised as men (Athenian politics being a men-only affair), cannot easily get the hang of swearing by male gods or otherwise signaling their membership in the appropriate discourse community: that of citizen men.[87]

But the women's lack of education and experience is at least partly made up for by natural aptitude. Thus in a variation on a familiar conceit, women, like the feminized youths they resemble (youths "who've been banged the most"), as public speakers enjoy an edge by virtue of their sexual passivity.[88] Indeed,

---

[86] Halperin 1990:104. Cf. Wolpert 2002b:90 on a herm erected beside the Piraeus walls rebuilt in 395/4 (Philochorus *FGrH* 328 F 40). The proliferation of herms in the city (versus the countryside) seems to accompany the introduction of democracy; see Furley 1996:17–21 with references.

[87] Aristophanes *Assemblywomen* 88–165, 189–191, 285–299. Women (not Praxagora) as masters only of "gossip" (*lalein*): 119–120; Beta 1999:61.

[88] Aristophanes *Assemblywomen* 111–114; cf. 102–104, 427–432. For the young, male effeminate as the future "manly man" of Athenian politics, Aristophanes *Knights* 417–426, 483–485, 878–880; Plato *Symposium* 192a; Saïd 1996:286–289.

their male disguise, insofar as it obscures, but cannot wholly suppress, their femininity, does not lessen but enhances their allure and persuasiveness.[89]

We learn more from a riddle joke posed by one of Praxagora's co-conspirators:

Woman 1:

(*with mirror*) Praxagora, my sweet. Come look at how ridiculous this getup is!

Praxagora:

Why so ridiculous?

Woman 1:

It's as if someone had tied a beard to a lightly braised cuttlefish!

Aristophanes *Assemblywomen* 124–127

Why, one wonders, would a bearded woman remind herself of a lightly braised cuttlefish? "Because," explains the scholiast, "cuttlefish are white." That is, women, indoor creatures that they are, cannot easily pass for deeply tanned men. But these women have, in fact, worked hard on their tans (63–65). Still, all they can show for it is the complexion of "pasty-faced cobblers," which is to say, male effeminates.[90]

Yet this image of women, particularly *bearded* women, as cuttlefish, in context evokes associations extending well beyond coloration. Exemplars of guile, cuttlefish when threatened are described as using their ink to cloud not just the water around them but the wits of predators.[91] Breeding pairs entwine their prey-snaring tentacles — "tresses" (*plokoi*) extending from their mouths — in a kiss-like embrace confusing backwards and forwards, male and female, self and other.[92] Women disguised as men can, therefore, be regarded as cuttlefish as much for their fake beards as for their ambiguous coloration. Thus

---

[89] Rothwell 1990:89. Feminine/effeminate sexual allure equals *peithô*-power: Rothwell 1990:88–89, 98–100.

[90] Aristophanes *Assemblywomen* 385–387, 432; Sommerstein 1998:143, 175.

[91] Hiding in its ink, as opposed to emitting ink merely out of fear, like the octopus or squid, the cuttlefish is the "most mischievous" (*panourgotaton*) of soft sea creatures: Aristotle *Historia animalium* 621b28–622a1. The cuttlefish as *dolomêtis*: Oppian 2.120; cf. 1.312–313, 3.156. See further Detienne and Vernant 1978:159–161 with notes.

[92] Mating: Detienne and Vernant 1978:160. Hair-like tentacles to snare prey: Oppian *Haleutica* 2.121–3 (*hôste plokoi*); Detienne and Vernant 1978:159 and 173n173.

Woman 1, by comparing her bearded self to the tentacular, chameleon-like, deviously elusive, ambiguously gendered cuttlefish,[93] encapsulates all the visual and verbal cunning Praxagora and her cohorts will mobilize against the city's men.[94] "Fish," including cuttlefish, "seduces and conquers. It functions like the forces of persuasion, or the allure of a hetaera, or the magical power of charms."[95]

But so, too, does Praxagora, whose *peithô* Aristophanes illustrates through a clever variation on the ship-of-state metaphor. Dead in the water (109), Athens is a ship ineptly manned by its citizen crew. That stands in contrastive proximity to Praxagora's equation of femininity/effeminacy with eloquence, which is to say, with the ability to lead (111–114; see above). But this metaphor is also made to play off the image of women as sexually submissive "rowed ships." Thus women will, as both skippers and steerage, embody for Athenian males a beguilingly passive-aggressive variety of leadership.[96] As for Praxagora herself, she shows a side more overtly feminine and sexual than does Lysistrata.[97] But her intention to "advance against" the men she would lead (*proskinêsomai*, 256) also suggests a take-charge approach to sexual congress (*kinein* = *binein*), as does her knowledge of strokes (*kroumatôn*, 257) and wrestling moves (*exankôniô*, "I'll elbow them," 259) effective against male "intrusions" of a simultaneously discursive and sexual character (*hupokrouôsi*, 256; cf. 588). Equating, therefore, sexual aggression with the unruly give-and-take of the assembly,[98] these strokes and counterstrokes highlight a male-aggressive element to Praxagora's assembly rhetoric.

Men succumbing to her *peithô* will, then, have been worsted on their own turf.[99] Indeed, they will resemble the Commissioner, the politically and

---

[93] Ability to take on background coloring: Aristotle *Historia animalium* 622a11–13. Play on "cuttlefish" as prostitute's name: Antiphanes 27.1–4 *PCG* with notes; Davidson 1997:10. According to certain older traditions, the cuttlefish was the last of Thetis' magical transformations before Peleus was able to pin her down and win her hand: Detienne and Vernant 1978:158–159.

[94] Byl 1982:35.

[95] Davidson 1997:10.

[96] Woman 1 had to spend the night being "rowed" (sexually) by her Salaminian husband (37–39); see Sommerstein 1998:141. Ship-of-state imagery in *Assemblywomen*: Rothwell 1990:48–49. Erotics of gynaecocratic *peithô*: Rothwell 1990:46–60 et passim.

[97] Lysistrata's *iunx* (her "sex appeal," *Lysistrata* 1110) resides in the first instance in her leadership qualities. Praxagora, by contrast, is overtly sexual: Rothwell 1990:88–90.

[98] *Hupokrouein* can mean "to interrupt" a speaker (cf. Aristophanes *Acharnians* 38; Pseudo-Plato *Eryxias* 395e). *Krouein* and compounds figure prominently as sexual double-entendres (hetero- and homoerotic) at various points in Aristophanes *Assemblywomen*: Taaffe 1993; Rothwell 1990:49–51, 88–89.

[99] If men come "knocking," Praxagora will "thrust back" (*proskinêsomai*, trans. Sommerstein): Aristophanes *Assemblywomen* 256. Issues of vocabulary: Henderson 1991:153, 171.

intellectually bankrupt official whom Lysistrata & Co. dress down as a woman and then a corpse (*Lysistrata* 530–538, 599–607). Or, closer to home, they will resemble Blepyrus, Praxagora's husband. Needing to relieve himself, he goes outside in his wife's gown and slippers while she, wearing his clothes, sneaks off to revolutionize Athenian politics (*Assemblywomen* 311–326). If, as Lauren Taaffe maintains, this or any instance of theatrical cross-dressing needs to be approached from the perspective of theater as "a system of signs and representations,"[100] then we must not overlook the ideological value of cross-dressing in a play as gendered and politicized as *Assemblywomen*.[101] Praxagora, by stealing her sleeping husband's clothes and covering his sleeping self with her own wrap, has virtually laid him out like corpse (535–538), that is, drained him of his masculine effectiveness in the public sphere, while she, insinuating herself into his discursive community, co-opts his political prerogatives.[102]

So Praxagora speaks and men listen, but do we ever get a sense that she wins acceptance into their discourse community? To a limited degree, yes: her arguments make sense to Chremes and Blepyrus (436–453), ordinary folk with man-on-the-street attitudes. To that extent, she speaks their language, she is "one of the boys." But gynaecocracy, the proposal she pushes in the assembly, does not go unopposed. Farmers, reports Chremes, grumbled and booed at it, to which Blepyrus responds that they, the farmers, were only using their brains.[103]

But Praxagora has not come to the Pnyx unprepared. In case her proposal falls flat, she packs the assembly with like-minded women ready to vote as required (cf. 434). At the same time, she understands that part of the challenge will be not to let the discourse take its *own* course. Thus her rehearsal speech culminates with the following, rather unusual, request:

> And so, gentlemen, let's just hand the city over to these women, and let's not blather on about it. Let's not even try to learn what they intend to do. Let's just *let them rule*.
>
> Aristophanes *Assemblywomen* 229–232 (my emphasis)

---

[100] Taaffe 1991:92.

[101] Cross-dressing in *Assemblywomen*: Taaffe 1991; Rothwell 1990:97–99

[102] See Dorati 1998:51; Taaffe 1993:113. McGlew and Rothwell point out that Blepyrus has been, Demos-like, revived when he reappears onstage with a girl on either arm. Cf. Aristophanes *Knights* finale; see McGlew 2002:198–199; Rothwell 1990:57–59. But this is still a virtually disfranchised Blepyrus.

[103] Aristophanes *Assemblywomen* 432–433. Farmers are conventionally regarded as upholders of tradition: Sommerstein 1998:178; Carter 1986:76–98. Farmer-hoplites as civic symbols: Hanson 1995. As masculine symbols: Winkler 1990:45–70.

Praxagora does, to be sure, want voters to consider all the benefits women have to offer (232–238). But she discourages deliberation, disparaged as so much "blather" (*mê perilalômen*; cf. LSJ s.v. λαλέω), the same term already used twice to disparage women's speech generally, and men's pre-assembly chatter specifically, as inconsequential.[104] The alternative? "Let's just let them rule" (*all' haplôi tropôi / eômen arkhein*). This jussive formulation, one recalling Clytemnestra's plea to a resistant Agamemnon,

> Oh, do give in (*pithou*). *You're* the winner if you willingly yield to me!
>
> Aeschylus *Agamemnon* 943[105]

coaxingly seeks to nudge Praxagora's male audience into compliance. Heading off attempts to meet her arguments head on, Praxagora maneuvers men into accepting as leaders women whose aversion to change, and whose connection to past traditions (*arkhaion nomon*, 'ancient custom,' 215–229), suggest a matriarchal version of Bakhtin's "word of the fathers."[106]

On the other hand, if Praxagora really means for Athenians to forego debate on this or any issue, then her message contrasts sharply with the sort of advice the evidence would lead us to expect: that decision makers, including assemblymen, should resist being persuaded *not* to think for themselves.[107] Of course, Praxagora puts her *peithô* in the service of a noble cause: to curb the pleonectic, stasiastic tendencies of the *dêmos*. Still, under the circumstances, that entails curbs on *isêgoria*, not just the freedom to speak out on matters of state, but an expression of the individual citizen's stake in the political order.[108]

And so gynaecocracy, a return to tradition that *breaks* with tradition, is duly enacted. Praxagora, though, continues to worry about male resistance, this time, to the novelty of the system — communalism — she will soon have to propound (583–585). But maybe she worries too much: "Our chief virtue? To ignore tradition!" announces a neighbor grandly (586–587; cf. 218–220). If male impulsiveness, their obsession with novelty and their cavalier disregard of "the old things," proves fortuitous for Praxagora, later in the play, it rubs

---

[104] Aristophanes *Assemblywomen* 120, 129; Taaffe 1993:116.

[105] A damaged line, but I translate the standard reconstruction. Clytemnestra seeks, of course, to induce Agamemnon to seal his fate by hubristically stepping upon the luxurious carpet she has laid out for him. Here and elsewhere in *Agamemnon*, Clytemnestra's rhetoric targets male "resistance motivated by suspicion"; see Bers 1994a:184.

[106] Bakhtin 1981:342.

[107] Cf. Thucydides 3.38.4, 7 (deliberative *logos* as spectator sport); 2.40.2–3. See also p. 51 above.

[108] Cf. Herodotus 5.78.

a pair of speakers the wrong way. Complains a Skeptic, Athenian men no sooner pass decrees than they rescind them. His interlocutor agrees, adding only that henceforth men will have no such opportunity (812–831). Fickleness like that seems to share something with the kind of short-term memory deficit worrying the Chorus Leader just before the final scene. Thus he urges judges not to behave like "confounded call girls" (*kakais hetairais*), who only remember — *mnêmên ekhousi* — their latest customers. When voting the winner, they must, rather, "keep it all in mind" (*panta tauta . . . memnêmenous*), that is, remember the *Assemblywomen*, though it was first on the bill.[109]

I cite that exhortation along with other evidence to suggest memory and cognitive connectedness — to past, present, and future — as themes operative in our play. Thus when Praxagora complains of the assembly's fickleness (199–200) and the city's passion for novelty (218–220), when she praises women's constancy and traditionalism (214–218, 221–228), when various speakers address similar issues in relation to the decision making of the city's men (139, 229–232, 586–587, 812–829, 1155–1162), it all sounds of a piece with an "old saw" alluded to by a Blepyrus remarking on the women's legislative coup: "However mindless (*anoêt'*) or foolish (*môra*) our deliberations (*bouleusômetha*), everything always turns out for the best."[110]

Further reflection on that old saw, specifically, its "backstory," will further reveal its resonance with themes of gendered political memory in our play. According to one source, Blepyrus' proverb derives from a myth telling of how Poseidon, embittered at losing out to Athena in the contest for the city, cursed the city's citizens with poor deliberative skills (*kakôs bouleuesthai*), a curse canceled out when Athena blessed their deliberations, however bad, with favorable outcome (scholium to *Assemblywomen* 473; cf. scholia to *Clouds* 587–589). On one level, that myth seems to fly in the face of other accounts, not just those pertaining to the high value Athenians placed on deliberative *logos*,[111] but also the story, examined earlier, of how Poseidon and Athena, despite their quarrel, were able to let bygones be bygones with a little help from Lethe, "Lady Oblivion." By contrast, the myth evoked by Blepyrus perpetuates that quarrel. Poseidon, god of disturbance on land and sea and ever the sore loser, unrelentingly undermines Athenian efforts to deliberate wisely, only to be foiled at every turn by Athena's providential interventions.

---

[109] Aristophanes *Assemblywomen* 1155–1162, on which Sommerstein 1998:237; Ussher 1973:233–234, 1158–1159.

[110] Aristophanes *Assemblywomen* 473–475; cf. *Clouds* 587–589; Eupolis 219 *PCG*; see Wankel 1976:1111.

[111] See p. 69n93 above.

Yet we note, too, deeper connections. The quarrel that gave birth to Athens also gave birth to disruptive and constructive dynamics within the discourses of the city.

Thus I would suggest that *Assemblywomen* does not so much enact a parody of the Amnesty of 403 as it does explore issues lying at the Amnesty's heart, specifically, the benefits and hidden costs of maneuvering around cognitions dissonant with the aim of solidifying civic bonds. We see this in persuasive strategies pursued by Praxagora: both those to control the discourse (229–232), and those of a distractive character. For in advertising communalism's gastric and phallic attractions, she manages to draw attention away from dissonance between gynaecocracy's democratic and counter-democratic sides. Acutely aware of context and atmosphere as a way to modulate and diffuse dispute, Praxagora therefore angles her pitch toward her interlocutors' baser appetites, and reassures them that no one, not even women, though now the leadership elite, will enjoy special perks (627–629). Bonds are affirmed, dissonant cognitions glossed over. Democracy will henceforth equate with a big party. Praxagora does not, then, simply trust in *logos*, rational discourse, to make the case for communalizing property. As in *Lysistrata*, as in the Periclean Funeral Oration, so, too, in *Assemblywomen*, something extra seems needed to push through a plan that, though it offers tangible benefits, requires citizens to transcend differences and give something up.

We see now more clearly the overall design of the New Athens. A utopian dream within the here-and-now, its delights beckon like Sappho's sacred grove — apple trees, gurgling stream, wafting incense, roses, "shimmering foliage" from which sleep descends (fr. 2). So, too, in the pleasure dome decreed by Praxagora, a kind of sleep descends. Is this a good thing? It depends on whom you ask.

Elenchus

In the first of two scenes putting Praxagora's revolution to the test, we encounter a Neighbor lining up his things as if for a Panathenaic procession. That was the parade forming the highpoint of the Panathenaia, a festival bringing citizens and foreign residents together to honor Athena, the city's protector (730–745). One gathers that this Neighbor's "parade," like its model, expresses civic unity: all Athenians, unless they wish to defy the new regime, will likewise be "marching" their belongings to the central collection point. Only now, these parades celebrate a city whose greatness derives not, as before, from empire but from sharing at home.[112] Note that this Neighbor's parade, unlike its Panathenaic counterpart, is headed not for the Acropolis but for the Agora. Once a venue for contentious wheeling and dealing, it is where Praxagora plans to hold a feast to inaugurate her reforms.

Enter an unnamed man whom we, with Ober, shall dub the "Skeptic."[113] This Skeptic, treating his Neighbor as mouthpiece for official policy, subjects Praxagora's policies to a quasi-Socratic interrogation, what in Plato we would call an elenchus. Why, wonders the Skeptic, would any citizen surrender his property until he can be sure others will do likewise (769–772)? Well, it is the law (758–763). But, notes the Skeptic, Athenians cannot be relied upon to obey their own enactments (797–798) or even to leave them on the books for very long (812–829). Given the likely impermanence of this one, indeed, given the national preference for taking over giving (777–783), the Skeptic would rather not be caught looking stupid: "Me acquiesce to confiscation? An accursed wretch of a man (*anêr*) would I then be, and a sucker to boot" (746–747). From his blinkered perspective, the new order threatens more than his property; it threatens his manhood (cf. LSJ s.v. ἀνήρ IV.).

No surprise, then, that our Skeptic takes issue not just with communalism, but with the very notion of women's rule. Told that men will no longer have the chance to rescind this or any policy,

Neighbor:

Look, friend, times have changed. Then we ruled; now women do.

Aristophanes Assemblywomen 830–831

the Skeptic responds with the following, rather startling, outburst:

Skeptic:

Rest assured I'll keep an eye out for them. No, they'll not piss on me (*mê katourêsôsi mou*), so help me Poseidon! (*nê ton Poseidô*)

Aristophanes Assemblywomen 831–832

---

[112] For the neighbor's "parade" as quasi-Panathenaic: Sommerstein 1998:203–205; Ussher 1973: 178–180. The Panathenaic procession as an expression of the "the united power and glory of Athens": Parke 1977:37. Panathenaea: Parker 1996:89–92; Parke 1977:33–50.

[113] Ober 1998:122–155. Sommerstein calls him "Dissident"; in the transmitted text, he has no name: Sommerstein 1998:206; Sommerstein 1984:316 and n21.

Projecting, as he does, a deeply paranoid antisociality, this counter-revolutionary is probably not meant by the playwright to earn our sympathy. Yet his misogyny manifests what can only be described as bias deeply ingrained in Greek culture of the time. Democritus, the fifth-century BCE philosopher, is said to have written that "to be ruled by a woman would be extreme *hubris* for a man" (fr. 111 D-K). Aristophanes' Skeptic seems to have something similar in mind. Sommerstein explains "piss on me" as "treat me (sc. and all men) with arrogant contempt, in revenge for the way men have so long treated them" — gynaecocracy, in other words, as a kind of *hubris* avenging the *hubris* of patriarchy (the Neighbor's "Then we ruled").[114] This Skeptic seems, then, to respond to women's rule much as men do to a supposedly gynaecocratic *coup* in *Lysistrata*. Only here, it is specifically confiscation that the Skeptic feels threatened by (cf. 746–747).

We have seen that our Skeptic responds to gynaecocratic communalism with paranoid misogyny. That mindset extends, I would suggest, even to the oaths he swears. Having already sworn by Poseidon that he will never surrender his property (748), in the outburst just quoted, he swears as if naming Poseidon an ally in some war of the sexes.[115] He does not, of course, allude directly to any such war the god himself has waged, by which I mean Poseidon's famous quarrel with Athena. Still, under the circumstances, the aggressiveness of the Skeptic's oath *mnêsikakei*, it brings bad feelings into the cognitive foreground. That is, it projects precisely the sort of negativity gynaecocratic communalism needs to overcome if it is to work, indeed, was intended to address in the first place. Juxtaposed with Thucydides' description of attitudes typical of *stasis*, this Skeptic's overall attitude — his deep mistrust combined with his determination not to let others get the better of him — can be seen as stasiastic:

> Factional splits took shape, ones driven mostly by mutual mistrust. For no spoken word was forceful enough, nor any oath fearful enough, to resolve differences. Counting on the hopelessness of a secure settlement, no one felt he could trust his enemy; everyone plotted how to come out on top by administering harm before falling victim to it.

Thucydides 3.83.1–2

---

[114] See Sommerstein 1998:210. Hubristic excretion: Demosthenes 54.4; Sommerstein 1998:195; Fisher 1992:50 and n45.

[115] Aristophanes *Assemblywomen* 832. Swearing by Poseidon can carry a contextually relevant point: Aristophanes *Clouds* 83 (in relation to horses, Poseidon's gift); Aristophanes *Birds* 1614 (Poseidon speaking); *Assemblywomen* 339; *Lysistrata* 403; *Thesmophoriazusae* 86 (tension between the sexes). Oaths in Aristophanes: Dillon 1995.

I cite the passage from Thucydides to suggest affinities between, on the one hand, the attitudes and behavior of Aristophanes' Skeptic, on the other hand, the hyper-proactive selfishness of *stasis* as described by the historian. But they are not exactly alike. What sets this Skeptic apart is the paradox that consensus and conformity, not factionalism, provoke his own hyper-proactive and contrarian conduct.

To get a better sense of that, we should look at the following exchange, in which the Skeptic doggedly refuses to be swayed either by the Neighbor's assurances or by his threats:

Skeptic:

I know these guys. No sooner do they pass a resolution than they turn around and renounce it.

Neighbor:

They'll bring their stuff, friend.

Skeptic:

And if they don't, then what?

Neighbor:

Don't worry, they will.

Skeptic:

And if they don't, then what?

Neighbor:

We'll fight them.

Skeptic:

And if there are more of them, then what?

Neighbor:

I'll just go away and leave it be.

Skeptic:

And if they sell your stuff, then what?

Chapter Four

Neighbor:

Blast you!

Skeptic:

And if I do get blasted, then what?

Neighbor:

You'll be doing us a favor.

Aristophanes *Assemblywomen* 797–804

Pestered by the Skeptic with visions of non-compliance, the Neighbor invokes the coercive power of the state, the "We" to whom the Neighbor refers. But what if, as the Skeptic says, the noncompliant element will enjoy a numerical edge? Indeed, what if the whole operation goes awry, and an unspecified, unsupervised, unscrupulous "they" commandeer the goods? A silly question, perhaps, especially in view of the evident groundswell of compliance (805–806; cf. 771–774). Yet the question cannot simply be made to go away. If the point of communalization and related policy (amalgamation of housing, of families) is, ultimately, to bring Athenians together into a close-knit, harmonious whole, then what does it mean that implementation of that policy might, in however many cases, produce resistance, cheating, ill-will, fighting? Of course, to the Neighbor, the question is moot: all around them, team spirit prevails. But that spirit of cooperation, *sine qua non* for Praxagora's plan to succeed, also represents her plan's implicit goal. Yet if concord relies at every turn on concord, that necessarily implies a hurdle, discord, to be surmounted at every turn, too. *Homonoia* and *stasis*, diametrical opposites, would seem, then, to go hand in hand.

These problematics of communalism, though nowhere mentioned by the Skeptic, are nevertheless modeled by his behavior and attitudes. Utterly reckless of legislation, a freeloader (872–876) musing over the possibility that "they" — really, "skeptics" like himself — might commandeer and sell off communalized property for personal profit,[116] he encapsulates all that was wrong with the old Athens and all that threatens the new. But he also insists on subjecting communalism to a thorough cross-examination before he will acquiesce (746–755), a course the women earlier sought to head off (229–232, 433–434). That cross-examination, however unimpressive, nevertheless hear-

---

[116] Aristophanes *Assemblywomen* 802. Sommerstein 1998:208 points out likely resonances with the sale of exiled democrats' goods in 404/3.

kens back to a right once a pillar of the democratic franchise: *isêgoria*, the right of free speech. That right will, though, have nowhere to go under a regime as reliant as this one on *homonoia*, the "same-thinking" manifested by the Neighbor and others compliant with communalism, though eschewed by nonconformists like the Skeptic.[117]

Which is not to say that we are supposed to cheer for the Skeptic or what he represents. But he does help us see the double-voiced character of a revolution providing for a "shared life" (*koinê diaita*) of peace and plenty, though at the expense of free speech and an individual citizen's title to his own property, an "entitlement" cherished under the restored democracy, though an entitlement citizens must now forget. Our play, then, in no way presents an unambiguously *pro* or *contra* viewpoint vis-à-vis gynaecocratic communalism or its corollary, the privileging of consensus over debate. As things often do in the real world, it pulls at us from different directions.

Tug of War

That brings us to the second scene in which the play's action seems to interrogate the New Athens. Praxagora, we recall, has, in addition to other communalistic reforms, decreed the sharing of sexual partners. No longer will individuals, men *or* women, wrangle for dates. All will have to wait their turn, seniors to the front of the line (613–634). What if some citizens, too impatient to cue up, look to the commercial sector? Too bad for them: Praxagora will, as she puts it, put all the "whores" (*pornas*) out of business (718–719).

Into the breach rush elderly citizen-women, who eagerly assume the trappings, as well as partners (cf. 719–724), of the *pornai* Praxagora sacks. Note that in classical Greek culture, *porneia* (from *pornê/pornos*, "whore") emphasized commoditization, asymmetry, and above all, publicity, that in contrast to *Hetärentum* (*hetaira*, 'companion,' 'courtesan'), a pricier, less impersonal type of prostitution. For the *pornê*'s sphere of operations included streets, doorways, windows, rooftops — the sort of place thought unsuitable for respectable women to occupy for very long.[118] It is, then, a sign of changing times for

---

[117] Sommerstein's points against the Skeptic (1984:319–320) are well taken, but the Skeptic's distrust of having to surrender his property could well have resonated with Athenians who had experience or knowledge of confiscation under the Thirty.

[118] *Porneia* generally: Kurke 1997; Halperin 1990:88–112. Publicity: Theophrastus *Characters* 28.3; Graham 1998; Davidson 1997:78–83; Cohen 1991:148. Cf. Aristophanes *Thesmophoriazusae* 798–799 on the embarrassment of respectable women caught peeking out their windows; Lycurgus 40. For this scene (*Assemblywomen* 877–1111): Sommerstein 1998:214.

us to find elderly citizen-women playing, to all appearances, the *pornê* as they stand outdoors, decked-out and hoping to be noticed (877–937; 1072). And so they are, by a young man who, intent on sleeping with his young girlfriend, labels two of his elderly admirers *kasalbades* (1106), a synonym for *pornê*, though more contemptuous.[119]

As for the girlfriend, she, too, exploits newfound freedom. Showing herself to her lover from an upper window of her house, she joins him in the typical sort of lover's lament sung "at the locked door" (a *paraklausithuron*; cf. 962–963). But that door belongs not to a *hetaira*, a pricy prostitute, as would have been typical for such a song at this time. It is the door of a respectable citizen Girl. And so in a duet rich in sexual reference, one emphasizing the Girl's parity with her male lover, each begs the other to join her/him in her/his bed.[120]

Alas, it is not to be. Fought over by his elderly admirers, Epigenes falls victim to a sexual tug of war,[121] a curious variation on the hurly-burly normally associated with amorous young men. Two declarations summarize young Epigenes' predicament, the first from the young man himself. Longing to sleep with his girlfriend, he exclaims that he, a "free man" (*eleutherôi*), cannot abide the thought of having to service the needs of old women first (938–941). He has not, it would seem, yet reconciled himself to what he still reads as untoward interference with his civic and sexual autonomy.

The second declaration comes from Old Woman 2. Parodying the sort of speech an aggrieved husband would make when inflicting licit revenge on his wife's lover (cf. Lysias 1.26), she solemnly declares, "Not I but the law (*ho nomos*) drags you off!"[122] In so declaring, Woman 2, or rather, *nomos* — "law" — in effect rapes the young man. Thus she/it inflicts counter-*hubris* upon a youth hubristically refusing to submit to rules intended to level the sexual playing field,[123] rules sanctioning violence to prevent something

---

[119] *Kasalbas = pornê*: Pollux 7.202; Sommerstein 1998:232; Henderson 1991:212–213.

[120] Aristophanes *Assemblywomen* 952–975. See Sommerstein 1998:221; Taaffe 1993:125, 189n43; Olson 1988. Paraclausithyron seems to have been an established genre by Aristophanes' time. Alcaeus fr. 374 Lobel-Page may come from such a song; cf. Euripides *Cyclops* 502.

[121] I borrow Sommerstein's term: 1998:214. Cf. Aristophanes *Assemblywomen* 1017–1020, 1074–1088.

[122] Aristophanes *Assemblywomen* 1055–1056. The citing/quoting of law(s)/decree(s) in *Assemblywomen*: 944–945, 1015–1020, 1049–1051; Ober 1998:122–155; Sens 1991:32–37. Legal self-help combined with declarations like the Old Woman's: Lysias 1.26; Aristotle *Constitution of the Athenians* 57.3; Fisher 1998:78–80; Sens 1991:30–106.

[123] Epigenes as hubristic, the Old-Comic stereotype of the hubristic young man, youth as hubristic generally: Fisher 1992:97–99; Rothwell 1990:71–72; Sommerstein 1984:320–321.

worse: social chaos stemming from a strictly laissez-faire policy regarding sexuality.[124]

But law as rapist? That and more as citizen-women, failing to agree over legal points (1077–1078), instigate a miniature *stasis* and seem poised to subject Epigenes to a Pentheus-like dismemberment.[125] What if, though, this represents a kind of poetic justice for a youth who, like youths in other comedies, flouts the rules and fails to give his elders their due?[126] Perhaps, then, Epigenes will have come across no more sympathetically to audiences than the very unsympathetic Skeptic from earlier in the play.[127] Still, as in that earlier scene, so too here, the goings on suggest stress points within Praxagorean communalism.[128] Absent the "fair empire" (Aristophanes *Knights* 1111) Athens once possessed, the good life will come not from external acquisition but from redistribution.[129] Thus the "give" of communalism entails a "take" generating resistance from skeptics and dissensus among the amorous. Desire turns inward, the system feeds on itself.

Perhaps, though, we are over reacting, as unpleasantness gives way to festivity and fun in the play's final scene.[130] That feast, to which the chorus and all the play's admirers, whether audience or judges, have been invited (1141–1143), effectively collapses two victories into one: the victory of communalism and a nearly unanimous vote for Aristophanes' play.[131] Of course, we do not actually know yet how the festival judges will vote, but no matter: "We shall dine ... as if for victory" (*deipnêsomen ... hôs epi nikêi*, 1181–1182). If we can *think* ourselves the victors, if we can somehow contrive not to hear dissenting voices, then victory, naturally, will be ours.[132]

---

[124] In Aristophanes *Assemblywomen*, rape and *hubris* are suggested by use of the verb *helkein*, "drag off": 1020, 1037, 1050, etc. Likewise the youth's cry for help: 1053–1054. See generally Fisher 1998:79, 95n39; Fisher 1992:96, 104–109, 267–268; Cohen 1991:177–179; Sens 1991:78–81.

[125] "You'll pull me apart!" Aristophanes *Assemblywomen* 1076; cf. Euripides *Bacchae* 1125–1136. I thank Gerald Kadish for pointing out the parallel.

[126] The natural comparison is to sophistically-educated, parent-beating Pheidippides in Aristophanes *Clouds* and to the father-beater in *Birds*.

[127] Rothwell 1990:71–72; Sommerstein 1984:320–321.

[128] Critics tend not to take this dismemberment overly seriously, nor should we. Still, the fact that it represents visual-verbal horsing around does not preclude its symbolic value.

[129] Cf. Saïd 1996:296–299.

[130] Aristophanes *Assemblywomen* 1112–1183; cf. 834–852. For the question of whether this is a mirage-feast, Sommerstein 1998:236, 239; Sommerstein 1984:322–323. Real or mirage, this feast celebrates what is, at best, an equivocal salvation for Athens.

[131] Cf. Aristophanes *Assemblywomen* 1157. Sommerstein 1998:239 distinguishes Praxagora's feast from the producer's cast party. I am not, however, so sure such a distinction is clearly made; cf. *Assemblywomen* 581–587 (the audience's response to Praxagora's plan matters); 1141–1142 (invitation of audience and judges favorable to the play).

[132] Cf. the performative future in curse formulas: Faraone 1995. This sort of wishful speaking-thinking is typical for the closing lines of comedy: Sommerstein 1998:239–240.

Concordia discors

Assemblywomen, it seems safe to say, is about no one thing. But again and again, the play returns to the same, basic theme: how to regain prosperity and banish strife under the post-403 reality. One part of that reality, loss of empire, drastically altered the political climate. Once, empire and democracy existed in a tight nexus. But with the loss of empire came the loss of that external Other validating the power of the *dêmos* and deflecting its more aggressive energies.[133] Absent that, where could Athenians turn?

In 404, against themselves. Though it is hard to know if Thucydides' description of *stasis* as a Panhellenic phenomenon reflects the historian's experience of the Athenian *stasis* of 404,[134] narratives of the latter do at least echo key elements of the historian's overall scheme, especially in the matter of a *polis* devouring itself from the inside.[135] But with the restoration of democracy came the need to think the city whole again. Hence a reconciliation bolstered by a willed act of forgetting. That remedy haunts *Assemblywomen* like an *idée fixe*. As the city struggled to quell divisive thoughts, Aristophanes could not help but notice struggle internal to same-thinking, the city's saving grace, taken to the extreme: how it must forever resist resistance and dissent with dissent. In so doing, *Assemblywomen* does not stand alone. Other narratives, those dealing with the Sicilian Debate and the rush to judgment of the generals at Arginusae, likewise focus on the capacity for democratic deliberation to give way to a tyranny of consensus.[136] But apart from tyranny itself, no system of governing was immune. So, for instance, Xenophon reveals how the oligarchs of 404, perpetrators of outrage upon outrage, dealt with the mounting opposition. Finding strength in unity, they felt safe enough until one of their own, fed up with the indiscriminate killing, broke ranks. Branding Theramenes a traitor, Critias and his cronies dealt with him accordingly (*Hellenica* 2.3.14–51).

Of course, that is not Praxagora's style. Rather, she devises, as we have seen, a "poetics" of same-thinking, a concretized reification of discourse dubbed "centripetal" by Bakhtin. Yet *Assemblywomen* dramatizes no totalizing victory for the pleasure dome Praxagora decrees. Rather, it dramatizes *concordia discors*, that plane along which same- and different-thinking forever

---

[133] Cf. Rosen 1997 on the personification of empire as love-object.

[134] See Wolpert 2002b:145n1 with references.

[135] Cf. Loraux 2002; Loraux 1995:37 on *stasis* as figurative cannibalism.

[136] Sicilian debate (415 BCE): p. 18 above. Condemnation of the generals (406): Xenophon *Hellenica* 1.7.8–35; Aristotle *Constitution of the Athenians* 34.1; Plato *Apology* 32b.

grapple and world-views collide. In our play, those world-views correspond, roughly speaking, to male and female, though scenes like the one where elderly women man-handle a youth mix it up. Still, in *Assemblywomen*, the playwright "sees" gender from a vantage point squarely within the mindsets of his time and place. But his seeing also reflects an ambivalence, a double-voicedness, informing the play's every scene, especially where women are concerned. Finding themselves the butt of the usual misogyny, these women, in remaking Athens after their own image, create as many problems as they solve. In so doing, they play to the prejudices of Aristophanes' audience. But *Assemblywomen* nowhere spells out the failure of Praxagora's revolution. On the contrary, it poses a question itself revolutionary for 390s Athens: whether human nature committed the *dêmos*, the play's notional audience and dramatic subject, to an immutable destiny of patriarchal politics.[137]

But what about prospects for same-thinking and free speech under the restored democracy? What does *Assemblywomen* have to say about that? Surely not that freedom equates with anarchy, or consensus with tyranny; that kind of paranoia we find modeled by the likes of Aristophanes' Commissioner and Skeptic. So if *Assemblywomen does* send a message, perhaps it is this: that dialogue cannot happen outside of community, but efforts to *impose* community must always *undercut* dialogue. For the values we share will not always harmonize. But to value harmony above all else may not always be the best idea.

---

[137] Ober 1998:122–155.

5

SATYR, LOVER, TEACHER, PIMP
SOCRATES AND HIS MANY MASKS

W HAT WAS THE MOST AMAZING THING about Socrates? If we trust Alcibiades, it was that no one living or dead could compare to him. Any number of remarkable individuals shared with Socrates a trait or two, yet none could match that singular "strangeness" (*atopia*) of his (Plato *Symposium* 221c–d). What, then, made Socrates so different? Evidently no single thing, but one idiosyncrasy clearly ranked high on the list. We are told that Socrates was an *erastês*, a "lover": of Alcibiades, of philosophy, and so on. Hence for the authors of Socratic literature[1] a theme: *erôs* as expression or summation of Socrates' extraordinary nature. Take, for instance, Plato's *First Alcibiades*. There, Socrates, indifferent to his beloved's outward beauty, loves what no one else does: Alcibiades' *soul*. That view of Socratic *erôs* as *philia* — "affection" or "friendship" — at its best and most intense finds wide resonance in Socratic literature. This *erôs* aims high: on the improvement of others, on wisdom, on immortality. In Plato's *Symposium*, it is, to quote, Charles Kahn, "resolutely rationalistic."[2]

But what kind of *erôs* is "resolutely rationalistic"? Perhaps an *erôs* indifferent to physical beauty[3] — *erôs*, then, as the highest expression not just of *philia* but of *sôphrosunê*, 'self-control,' a notion that finds expression in Plato and Xenophon.[4] Still, we have our assurances that Socrates really did feel

---

[1] Plato, Xenophon, Antisthenes, Aeschines Socraticus, et al. — third-century prose-authors writing about Socrates, his circle, and related topics. See *SSR*.

[2] Kahn 1992:592, which see *passim*. Newell 2000 contrasts the Platonic Socrates' transcendental *erôs* with *thumos*, a lower-order possessiveness. Cf. Ober 1998:198 on a "philosophy-loving (ergo strictly rational . . .)" Socrates in Plato's *Gorgias*. Contrast Vlastos 1987:90–93: Socratic *erôs* (limited tolerance of sensual pleasure, non-transcendental) versus Platonic (a non-physical divine rage). Socratic *erôs* as desire to improve others (*Bessermachen*): Döring 1984; Ehlers 1966. Socrates' critique of non-philosophic *erôs* in Plato's *Lysis*: Nightingale 1993:114–116.

[3] E.g. Plato *Symposium* 210b–c, 216d, 222a–b; Xenophon *Memorabilia* 4.1.2.

[4] Plato *Symposium* 188d, 196c; *Laws* 711d; Xenophon *Symposium* 1.10.

the allure of physical beauty, male and female.[5] Further, in Plato's *Phaedrus*, Socrates expatiates not once but twice (237d–241d, 244a–257b) on an *erôs* that is anything but "resolutely rationalistic," indeed, on *erôs* as a form of madness (241a, 245b–c). Yet this madness, if reined in, that is, if diverted from the objects of physical lust, can be ridden like a chariot to realms of transcendent truth (244a–257b) — which brings us right back to *sôphrosunê*, albeit on a higher plane.

We have, then, discovered a curious property of Socratic *erôs*: though often treated as a defining feature of Socrates' inimitable self, its boundaries shift. Even within a single text like Xenophon's *Symposium*, one juxtaposing Socrates' advocacy of spiritual *erôs* with Socrates the pimp, Socratic *erôs* presents no simple account of itself; even within a single passage, Socrates can be described as both attracted to, and unmoved by, physical beauty.[6] Perhaps, then, what we need is sensitivity to irony and playful invention, a way to resolve seeming contradiction within our texts. But if our sources for Socrates' *erôs* are literary sources (rather than, say, interviews, questionnaires, or the like), should we privilege this or that representation as more true to life, more "Socratic," than the next? Should we not treat them all as fictions, as *masks*?

In what follows, we shall do just that as we examine Socrates and his several masks: how they offer us a model of the dialogical self as a boundary phenomenon, a negotiation between self and other. To see how that works, it will help to illustrate the logic underlying the self-other distinction with a thought experiment testing Socrates' supposed simplicity and purity. From that will emerge how the very notion of a simple Socrates generates its own *heteros logos*, its own alternative account.

The Socrates Question

"Know thyself" — so commands the Delphic oracle, but what is it to know oneself? For Socrates in Plato's *Phaedrus*, it is to know what sort of creature he is: whether a beast more complex and fiery than the monster Typhon,[7] or a simpler being partaking of a divine and mild nature (229e–230a). But

---

[5] Vlastos 1987:88 cites Plato *Protagoras* 309a; *Gorgias* 481d; *Charmides* 155c–e; *Meno* 76c; Xenophon *Symposium* 8.2. See also Dover 1989:154–155. Heteroerotic interests: Aristoxenus fr. 54a.15–16, 54b.12; Xenophon *Memorabilia* 3.11.3.

[6] Plato *Symposium* 216d–e, on which Vlastos 1987:90.

[7] Polycephelous, serpentine, fiery, cacophonous Typhoeus/Typhon: Tsifakis 2003:94–95; Gantz 1993:48–51.

are we to suppose that Socrates would ever identify with the Typhon-like convolutions — the tortured logic and specious speechifying — Socrates targets throughout the dialogue? So the question begins to look rhetorical: opposing Socratic simplicity to thinking and teaching consistently contested by the sage in the *Phaedrus* and elsewhere, it highlights the Socrates we know and love against the backdrop of his "Other," his anti-self.[8]

Yet to keep self and other distinct, and the self pure, turns out to be less simple than might at first appear. For Derrida, to posit such distinctions necessarily casts otherness, all that lies outside the genuine article (in the present instance, the authentic self), in the role of contagion, an enemy-at-the-gates to be held at bay — a view Derrida deconstructs as utopian myth, a solipsistic nowhere.[9] But how does Socrates feel about it? It is curious that Plato's Socrates, though seemingly more sanguine than Derrida about prospects for inner purity, at least acknowledges the main hurdle to achieving such a goal: the problem posed by borders themselves. Thus in the dialogue's closing lines, Socrates prays that the gods will, among other things, grant him a fair interior (*kalôi*), an exterior to match, and the good sense to place a premium on wisdom, not gold. He prays, in other words, to be a philosopher through and through, though in so praying, seems to treat his interior as closer to his authentic self than his exterior; it is "me" (*moi*) as opposed to "what I have outside."[10] Yet in laying claim to that outside, does not Socrates acknowledge some element of himself extending beyond his inner essence, which is to say, some element of his outside mixing with himself? What, then, if Socrates' outer self really did fail to match the inner Socrates — if, say, Socrates were to present the appearance of a sophist or rhetorician while remaining true to philosophy internally? That is no idle question. In the *Phaedrus*, Socrates plays the sophist with consummate skill and considerable ambivalence. How deep, then, do we need to go for the pretense to end? Where does the outer edge of Socrates' authentic, inner self lie?

To find out, it will help to try a simple thought experiment, one to test the implications of the pure and simple self Socrates envisions for himself in the *Phaedrus*. To conceptualize that as simply as possible, we need to imagine Socrates as something set off and nothing more — something set off from what

---

[8] Socrates will portray sophists and rhetoricians as highly versatile with "comparisons and disguises" with which to spin truth, facts, etc.: Plato *Phaedrus* 261c–e. Cf. *Republic* 382e, god as "a thing simple and true" (*haploun kai alêthes*).

[9] Derrida 1981:100–104.

[10] Plato *Phaedrus* 279b–c. Cf. Socrates as lover of Alcibiades himself (his soul), not "what is yours" (physical beauty): Plato *First Alcibiades* 131e.

he is not. On paper, that would look like a demarcation, preferably circular (it offers the fewest linear features), showing the limit of Socrates' pure and undifferentiated self, the limit beyond which Socrates' Other begins. But to say that Socrates represents a bounded entity already recognizes elemental complexity in him: *Socrates as a product of his relationship to his Other.*[11]

We can think of it this way: If Socrates could somehow detach himself from his outer boundaries, shrink a little so as to lose touch with his outside, he will have lost touch with what confirms him as a unique and separate being. In a sense, he will have ceased to be. Thus his relationship to what is outside him, to his Other, counts; at a basic level, it engenders him. We can, then, speak of Socrates as an entity in a dynamic relationship with its environment, as a *Gestalt*.[12] But that carries with it an important corollary: Socrates the *Gestalt* as a term (Socrates) within the binary (Socrates ~ Not-Socrates) expressing Socrates the *Gestalt*. Let me restate that. For Socrates to *be* he must be something *set off*. But that internalizes his being-set-off, his being apart, within his being, what makes him what he is. And that, in turn, will set off a rippling effect locating Socrates not wholly apart from, but in a dynamic relationship with, his surroundings. Socrates still lies at the center of it all, but he no longer possesses a determinate edge.

Important is the social-cognitive dimension to all this. Thus to understand the self-other relation, even at its most elemental, we must do so perspectivally, viewing things from the inside, as if that self were ourselves. But wherever we look, we look out; even reflexive viewing, our looking into a mirror, is looking at something outside ourselves.[13] But never fear: what defines us, what gives us value and meaning, comes from the outside, from external subjects and objects, entities that, in one way or another, matter to us. Self-knowledge becomes, then, an exploration of the self-other connection, the self not as a flat picture but as a bas-relief bulging out into the world.[14] Conversely, pure introspection, self-centered and detached from its environment, *can* give rise to despair: "In relation to myself, I am profoundly *cold*, even in the act of self-preservation."[15] Thus our search for the "real" Socrates

---

[11] Cf. the "first" or "primary distinction" and Spencer-Brown's logic of distinctions: Neuman 2003:89–98.

[12] Gestalt here in the sense of perceptions from which the mind produces progressively more organized formations: Neuman 2003:100; Brandist 2002b:533–536; Brandist 2002a:21–22; Holquist 1990:14–39; Vološinov 1986:29–30.

[13] Mirroring: Neuman 2004.

[14] Bakhtin 1990:30. Cf. Holquist 1990:18 on Bakhtin on dialogical consciousness ("In dialogism, the very capacity to have consciousness is based on otherness"); Neuman 2003:143–156.

[15] Bakhtin 1990:51; more generally 4–59; Neuman 2004:61–62.

reveals not static limits but dynamic, shifting surfaces, a self located somewhere between Self and Other.[16] Like Vološinov's utterance, Socrates absorbs and processes within himself other voices, other realities, to which his outer being, that which others see and hear, responds. Thus even if we were to grant him a simple essence, still, that essence could not be abstracted from its environment *and still be itself.*

What does that have to do with *Socrates*, specifically, his literary portrait? Let me suggest, a great deal. Vlastos sees in Socrates' penchant for self-deprecation what he calls "complex irony," where "what is stated both is and isn't what is meant."[17] Take the argument, "Socrates is beautiful," a notion underpinning Socrates' part in the beauty contest Xenophon relates (*Symposium* 5). Such a claim makes sense insofar as it refers to the *utility* of various body parts: protruding eyes the better to see with, broad nostrils the better to smell with, and so on. But it is also absurd with respect to the *visual impression* left by a Socrates whose body violates the norms of harmonious proportion as the Greeks understood them. One could argue that irony here resides in equivocation: competing senses of the term "beauty." But one could also argue that we are dealing with complex framing: ugliness as *frame* for beauty and *vice versa.* Thus the "uglier" Socrates' eyes (the more they protrude), the more "beautiful" (the more functional) his peripheral vision, as in the extreme case of a crab. But that further involves multiple, yet connected, levels of analysis, as each side to Socrates' complex self shapes and defines its opposite. And it is in that space between self and other, the simple and the complex, that the literary Socrates as a meaningful self begins to take shape.

Which brings us to what is, perhaps, the best known image, simultaneously a mirror and a foil, associated with Socrates: the image of him as satyr or silen, an image exploring Socrates as a kind of boundary phenomenon. One ought, though, to proceed in proper sequence: from the somatic to the symbolic. That Socrates physically looked the part is treated as common knowledge by Plato and Xenophon.[18] But one hesitates to judge this book by its cover. For is it not ludicrous to think of Socrates, that paragon of restraint, as an inveterate boozer and sexual predator, a human counterpart to satyrs and silens, creatures "considered the antithesis of *sophrosyne*, the ideal of moderation and sober self-control"?[19]

---

[16] Cf. Neuman 2003:102–104.

[17] Vlastos 1987:86.

[18] Plato *Symposium* 215b; Xenophon *Symposium* 4.19, 5.7.

[19] Padgett 2003:27. Satyrs and silens (anthropoid often with equine features, sex- and drink-addicted) mediate culture and nature, the human and the Dionysian: Isler Kerényi 2004; Padgett 2003; Lissarrague 1993.

If so, satyr-Socrates will represent no more than a casing hiding the true Socrates within. And so he does in Plato's *Symposium*, where Alcibiades compares his erstwhile lover to a silen-figurine like those sold by herm carvers.[20] Open them up and you will find miniature gods; open up Socrates and you will find god-like temperance, wisdom, and beauty (215a–b, 216d–217a). Yet this shell Socrates carries about with him, not just his physical appearance, but the libidinous incontinence he is said to affect combined with the satyr-like absurdity of his analogies, not to mention the insincerity of his self-deprecation[21] — all that, though only skin-deep, still defines the dialogical self that is Socrates interacting with his world.

But how detached from this skin is the inner Socrates? Curiously, as Alcibiades elaborates upon his sage-versus-silen contrast, we find that the grotesque exterior begins to infiltrate the exquisite interior. Thus Alcibiades, labeling Socrates a *hubristês* (215b; cf. 175e, 219c, 221e), that is, a perpetrator of outrage, describes how the music of Socrates' *logos*, like the music of the satyr Marsyas, leaves those who listen dumbstruck and powerless. Yet Socrates' hubristically bewitching *logos* cannot originate from his outer, supposedly libidinous self. Because it compels Alcibiades to feel so ashamed of his shallow ambitions that he turns his attention to the really important things (read "soul"), Socrates' *logos*, however violent and satyr-like, must issue from, and express, his inner essence: his soul (215b–216c). But when we penetrate the corporeal exterior to explore the inner being, we still find features of Socrates' hubristic and satyr-like skin (*saturou . . . hubristou doran*, 221e): those hackneyed analogies, which on closer inspection, reveal a unique kind of sense, *but which, even when we go deep, are still there* (221d–222a).

But Socratic *hubris*? Of course, Alcibiades indulges in paradox: to implicate as exemplary a being as god-like Socrates in a kind of *hubris* confuses surface and depth, the good with the bad.[22] Paradox continues as Alcibiades turns to the subject of *erôs*: Socrates' for him and his for Socrates. Thus Socrates, only *posing* as an *erastês*, turns out to be the *paidika* — the "darling" or beloved — of his disciples (216d–e, 217c, 222a–b; cf. Xenophon *Memorabilia* 4.1.2). He has not fallen in love with them; rather, they have with him. That conceit — a thinker-teacher's students and adherents as his "lovers" (*erastai*) — is a commonplace among the Socratics.[23] Here, though, that conceit finds concrete expression

---

[20] Alcibiades' speech as praise oratory (encomium): North 1994; Nightingale 1993:123–127.

[21] Plato *Symposium* 216c–217a, 221e; cf. 175e; Plato *Republic* 337a, for which Vlastos 1987:81; Gooch 1985.

[22] Cf. Neuman 2003:105–106 on Deleuze 1990:9.

[23] Antisthenes fr. 99 *SSR*; Xenophon *Symposium* 8.4; Plato *Phaedrus* 257b; *Symposium* 173b; *Protagoras* 317d; Edmonds 2000; Kahn 1992:587–588; Halperin 1986.

as Alcibiades, obsessed not just with Socrates' philosophy but with the very man, presents the symptoms of the love-besotted suitor as he yearns to play the passive partner in a sexual encounter with his beloved.[24] But Socrates will not trade wisdom for sex, nor gratify Alcibiades' lusts at all (217a–219e). So Socrates' *hubris* was to have refrained from *hubris*.[25] But what kind of *hubris* is that? It is, of course, *hubris* as mask. Like Socrates' satyr-skin, it expresses something profound about the man, but at the surface. To quote Deleuze, "What is most deep is the skin."[26]

Consideration of the Socrates question as handled by Stilpo, the fourth-century BCE leader of the Megarian school, reveals further aspects — dialogical ones — to this problematic of Socrates' supposed simplicity and singularity. According to Stilpo (or his school), things whose discourses differ must themselves be different (*hôn hoi logoi heteroi, tauta hetera estin*), and difference entails separation (*ta hetera kekhôristhai allêlôn*). Imagine that you and I are talking. If what I am saying differs in any way from what you are saying, even the slightest bit, then necessarily we are talking about two, disparate things.[27] To most of us, as to ancient critics (including Simplicius, our source), Stilpo's insistence on the radically monological character of things (the exclusive connection of each thing to one *logos* and one alone) will seem an almost laughable sophistry. Imagine further that you and I are talking about *Socrates* — different aspects of him, you, his educational attainments (Socrates as *mousikos*), I, his light-skinned complexion (Socrates as *leukos*). Are we not, then, saying different things about one and the same thing? Stilpo says "No," though with a twist. Since your *logos* differs from mine, we are necessarily talking about different things — though in either case, *that thing is Socrates*. Hence a paradox: Socrates, the man of multiple discourses, as a "self split-off from himself" (*autos hautou kekhôrismenos*, 30 SSR).[28]

That paradox rises above the level of parlor trick if we think of it in relation to *dialogue*: different *logoi* ostensibly focused on a common object of thought. Thus Stilpo's paradox forces us to ask whether we, as speakers

---

[24] Reversal in Alcibiades' *erôs* for Socrates: Wohl 2002:161–169; Edmonds 2000:272–277.

[25] Edmonds 2000:275. Gagarin 1977 attributes Socrates' failure as teacher of Alcibiades to Socrates' *hubris*, his antisociality generally and refusal to consummate his *erôs* for Alcibiades. For Socrates' *hubris* here, also North 1994:94–98.

[26] Deleuze 1990:10.

[27] That appears to be a corollary of the dictum that no subject can validly carry a predicate other than itself, e.g. horses are horses and running is running, but horses are not running (Stilpo 29 SSR).

[28] Cf. Stoic use of paradox as linguistic thought-experiment: Chrysippus in Diogenes Laertius 7.187; Brunschwig and Lloyd 2000:357–358, 382–383 on Megarians and Stoics; Deleuze 1990:8–9.

asserting different things about Socrates, can really share between us one and the same *vision*. Put that way, the answer still seems to be "no": no two of us envisions precisely the same Socrates. But what else are we talking about if not Socrates? And what else drives our dialogue if not the belief, the hope, that there is a graspable reality out there, an authentic Socrates transcending our individual constructions of him? But can dialogue ever bring us to that longed-for common ground if truly it is to remain dialogue, speech that enacts difference?

Perhaps not, yet still we want it to. "Eros is an issue of boundaries. He exists because certain boundaries do."[29] Contemplating Socrates, we find ourselves at the edge, cut off from that singular and extraordinary being who, if we could but grasp him, would yield up an account of himself to silence all others. "The moment of desire is one that defies proper edge, being a compound of opposites forced together at pressure."[30] Attraction and separation operate simultaneously: the nearer we get, the more frustrated we feel.

We are now ready to venture an answer to the question with which we began, the question Plato's Socrates asks about himself: whether he, Socrates, is a simple or complex creature (*Phaedrus* 229e–230a; see above). At first glance, that appeared rhetorical: what else could Plato have meant but that his protagonist embodies a moral and intellectual purity to which Typhon's snaky coils offer a telling contrast? But the prayer closing the *Phaedrus*, distinguishing, as it does, between an inner and an outer self, hints at complications more fully developed in Alcibiades' notion of Socrates as hybrid, a god in satyr's skin. Alcibiades' conflicted response to Socrates, his *erôs* and panic, a terrified fascination (Plato *Symposium* 215b–216c), would seem, then, to make Socrates out to be, if not a Typhon, then at least *some* kind of monster. Yet how much store should we set by Alcibiades' evidence? Perhaps not much if, as Vlastos remarks, Alcibiades can do no better than paint for us "the picture of a man who lives behind a screen — a mysterious, enigmatic figure, a man nobody knows."[31] But Alcibiades nowhere claims the last word in matters Socratic. Struggling to convey his *experience* of Socrates, of Socrates' dialogical self, he vividly conveys his struggle to process the conflicting data Socrates presents.

We shall, in a sense, inherit that struggle when we examine *erôs* as index to Socrates' dynamic relationship with his world. As we shall see, that *erôs*

---

[29] Carson 1986:30. Cf. Diotima in Plato *Symposium* 202a, 203e on *erôs* as *metaxu*, "a median between contraries" (Gagarin 1977:27).

[30] Carson 1986:30.

[31] Vlastos 1987:90; cf. Plato *Symposium* cf. 216c–d.

pushes in two directions at once: away and toward. Presenting Socrates as the ideal lover, it lifts him up and out from our midst. Yet it also stresses Socrates' zeal to bridge separation. Taken to extremes, it suggests Socrates' *atopia*, his utter disconnection from the ordinary.[32] Yet in that form, it can show him engaging other speakers at close quarters as he strives to bring them around to his own worldview. So we need to be patient with this dialogically engaged, if at times infuriatingly ironic Socrates. We need to give him a chance to show us how he struggles to make a difference with those likely to make a difference in the city. Yet we need also to acknowledge those moments when Socrates' teaching yearns not for the pluralistic discourses of free debate, but for the normative discourses of philosophical idealism.

Socratic Maenadism in Aeschines Socraticus

Aeschines of Sphettus, called "Socraticus" ("of the Socratic circle") to distinguish him from Aeschines the orator, may not be a household name today, but in antiquity he ranked in the forefront of Socratic authors. None of his works survives entire, but one yielding extensive fragments is the *Alcibiades*, in which Socrates strives to dissuade the title character from entering public life without first getting the knowledge he needs, not just in politics and military strategy, but in moral wisdom (*aretê*) — an education Socrates seems determined to offer the young man.[33] Judging from the remains, Socrates has his work cut out for him. Arrogant and irreverent (cf. 45–46 *SSR*), yet keen to make his mark in the assembly (cf. 42 *SSR*), Alcibiades will not gladly sit still for instruction. But matters are complicated by certain deficiencies on Socrates' part. Claiming not to possess any technical expertise from which a youth in Alcibiades' condition could benefit (53.4–5 *SSR*), Socrates reflects on the one thing he *can* count on, his *erôs*:

> In consequence of the desire (*erôs*) which I happened to feel for Alcibiades, I had undergone an experience no different from a bacchant's. For indeed, whenever they are possessed by the god (*epeidan entheoi genôntai*), they are able to draw milk and honey from sources that others cannot even draw water from. As for myself,

---

[32] Socrates' *atopia* ('nowhere-ness', 'strangeness'): Plato *Symposium* 175a, 215a; 221d. Eide 1996 understands Socratic *atopia* in the scientific-mathematical sense of "'illogical', 'inconsistent', 'contradictory'" (60); cf. Kofman 1998:18–21.

[33] Aeschines Socraticus and his *Alcibiades*: *SSR* vol. 3 pp. 605–610 (VI A 41–54), vol. 4 pp. 585–591; Giannantoni 1997; Kahn 1994; Joyal 1993; Ehlers 1966; Taylor 1934:10–19; Dittmar 1912.

though I knew nothing beneficial to teach anyone, still, I thought that by being with Alcibiades, I could, because of my *erôs* (*dia to eran*), improve him.

Aeschines Socraticus 53.22–27 *SSR*

Erôs, then, as catalyst of miracles, but how? And what can it mean that Socrates, in becoming the teacher he wants to, must take on the persona of a bacchant (*bakkhê*), whose very name could in ancient sources serve as a byword for a dangerous loss of self-control? Past scholarship, superimposing Socrates' ostensibly sober self on his bacchic mask, has denied that Socrates here associates himself with *mania*, the divine rage regularly associated with bacchants and maenads.[34] But unless we lay the mask on the *outside*, how can we pay the image its due? Framing Socrates' pedagogy *within* his maenadic persona, I shall argue that Socrates' mask draws him out of his normal self and locates him closer to his dialogical other. But possession by *erôs*, Socrates' "Dionysus" and the inspiration for his intuitive teaching, carries with it evaluative two-sidedness. Thus as Socratic apologetic, Aeschines' *Alcibiades* makes the case for Socrates' good intentions and heroic efforts on behalf of his beloved pupil. Yet Socrates' maenadism problematizes the risks Socrates takes and the impression his pedagogy will likely make.

First, structure and theme. Aeschines' *Alcibiades*, like Plato's *Republic* or Xenophon's *Symposium*, presents us with "narrated drama."[35] A narrator, here, Socrates, reports a conversation, here, Socrates' with Alcibiades, held at some point in the dramatic past. To the outer, narrative frame belongs the coda, quoted earlier, in which Socrates struggles to express the feelings that impelled him to try to help Alcibiades, and why he felt that he could. In the process, our speaker slips in a seemingly extravagant comparison: Socrates as bacchant. But rather than try to filter out surplus resonance, we should instead let the whole image say its piece, even at the risk of allowing a bacchic "madness" to place its stamp on Socrates' exercise in intervention.

More in a moment on that madness. For now, let us consider two motifs, very important in Socratic literature, introduced into Aeschines'

---

[34] "Maenad" (*mainas*) and "bacchant" (*bakkhê*): female worshippers of Dionysus, god of wine and madness. "Maenadism": the mental state and demeanor of maenads-bacchants. Non-manic Socrates in Aeschines Socraticus: Kahn 1994:104; Vlastos 1987:91n42; Ehlers 1966:22; contrast Taylor 1934:14–15.

[35] Taylor 1934:9.

coda: (a) Socrates' disavowal of knowledge and the ability to teach it,[36] and (b) Socrates as benefactor of those he kept company with.[37] Merging those two themes, Aeschines in effect acknowledges a dilemma: what business has a pedagogically challenged teacher like Socrates to try to teach those whom he would help? How, in other words, can he know that his teaching will not fall short of the mark, how can he be sure it will not, somehow, corrupt pupils, *if all Socrates knows is that he does not know?*[38] Elsewhere, the admission of ignorance becomes for Socrates the beginning of wisdom. Elsewhere, too, we need to take Socrates' disclaimers with a grain of salt. Here, though, Socrates' admission of ignorance has to be taken seriously, else his reliance on inspiration makes little sense.

So one might say that Socrates would have to be mad to take up such a challenge, though in Socrates' case, madness — bacchic *erôs* — empowers. But *how* does it empower? Since we do not have the whole *Alcibiades*, conjecture becomes unavoidable, yet conjecture aided by parallels has led to broad agreement that Socrates' *erôs* is quite simply the desire to do another good. In contrast to an acquired art (*tekhnê*), this "divine dispensation" (*theia moira*) operates like a physical reflex (53.4–7, 10–15 *SSR*). Thus when Alcibiades triggers *erôs* in Socrates, it compels and enables good teaching from the older man, a self-fulfilling desire. That lesson — *erôs* as catalyst of *Bessermachen*, 'moral improvement'[39] — appears meant to trickle down to Alcibiades, who desperately needs to have his selfish ambitions refocused on whatever good he can do his city. Else Alcibiades must, like Themistocles, the role-model he both envies and despises, suffer disfranchisement and exile.[40]

Still, the question remains: How can Socrates be so sure he has handled it right? I would suggest that he does *not* feel altogether sure, which is where the bacchant image with its multiple resonances fits in. That image Aeschines seems to have borrowed from Plato's *Ion*,[41] where Socrates argues that poets

---

[36] Plato *Apology* 19d–e; *Menexenus* 236a; *Symposium* 175d–e, 177d–e (*erôs* his sole expertise), 216d; *Laches* 186c; Xenophon *Memorabilia* 1.2.3, 1.2.7–8. Socrates acknowledges-boasts of his reputation for teaching: Xenophon *Apology* 21.

[37] Kahn 1994:92–94, 101–102; Döring 1984; Gaiser 1969; Ehlers 1966:10–25, 85–95; Gaiser 1959:92–95.

[38] Untaught in virtue, Socrates does not teach it: Plato *Laches* 186b–c. Diotima Socrates' teacher in *erôs*: Plato *Symposium* 201d–212c. Aspasia in rhetoric, matchmaking: Plato *Menexenus* 235e–236a; Xenophon *Memorabilia* 2.6.36; *Oeconomicus* 3.14. See Morrison 1994:198–203.

[39] *Bessermachen*: Ehlers 1966, aspects of whose views are picked up by Giannantoni 1997:362–363; Kahn 1994; Joyal 1993; Döring 1984:17–25.

[40] Aeschines Socraticus 46, 49, 50.3–5, 50.32–41 *SSR*. According to Döring 1984:20–21n11, the specific charge against Themistocles will have been that of aiding the Persian foe.

[41] Kahn 1994:103–106; Kahn 1992:590; Ehlers 1966:22 and n30 with bibliography.

and performers, inasmuch as they lack technical expertise, must rely on inspiration — really, divine possession (*enthousiazein*, 533c–536d). Hence in Plato's *Ion* power comparable to that of bacchants who, while literally out of their minds (*aphrones*), draw, as in Aeschines' *Alcibiades*, milk and honey from unwonted sources.[42] But those similarities highlight an important contrast: in Plato, a *not*-Socrates, Ion, "channels" the divine; in Aeschines, it is none other than the philosopher himself. Thus Aeschines privileges his hero's "divine dispensation" (*theia moira*, 53.5 *SSR*) in ways that Plato does not (*theia moira*, 534c). Both authors detach skill (*tekhnê*) from inspiration, but Plato presents the latter as something of a crutch, Aeschines, as an asset.[43]

What else will Plato's and Aeschines' bacchant image have betokened? More explicit in Plato than in Aeschines is the rapturous transport — in the *Ion*, being *ekphrôn* 'out of one's mind', elsewhere called *ekstasis* — characteristic of the bacchant or maenad in her element.[44] Though Aeschines does not mention that condition by either name, he does, like Plato, speak of the bacchant as *entheos*, as possessed or inspired by the god, in our sources, a condition concomitant with *ekstasis*, even to the point that terms like *ekstasis* and *enthousiasmos* 'possession' often cover the same territory.[45] In surviving fragments of Aeschines' *Alcibiades*, Socrates does not exactly dwell at length on possession *per se*, but we see its reflection in Socrates' "divine dispensation" (*theia moira*), his *erôs* functioning like an involuntary reflex outside his control. That is, to the extent that his *erôs*, his "Dionysus," is in him and works through him, to that extent at least, *Socrates' rational self is inoperative*.[46] That may not present us with all the classic symptoms of clinical *mania*,[47] but it does not have to. In stating that his condition was "no different from a bacchant's," Socrates invites us to view that condition as a kind of possession, *a kind of madness*.[48]

And any such madness will have carried with it polarizing potential. Discussing ecstatic possession and related states, Albert Henrichs notes how they can elicit sharply divergent reactions, positive and negative, from observers, whether ancient or modern. Thus for someone on the outside,

---

[42] Plato *Ion* 534a, for which Murray 1996:112–125. For poetic madness, cf. Plato *Phaedrus* 245a.

[43] Plato's ambivalence about *mania*-inspiration: Murray 1996:10–12.

[44] Plato *Ion* 534b; see Murray 1996:118.

[45] Henrichs 1994:37.

[46] Aeschines Socraticus 53.4–7, 10–15, 22–27 *SSR*. Cf. *theia moira* in Plato *Ion*.

[47] Clinical *mania*-possession: Aretaeus *De causis et signis acutorum morborum* book 2 1.6.11 (*entheos . . . maniê*); Henrichs 1994:34–35.

[48] Cf. Taylor 1934:14–15.

"ecstasy" is often the disparaging term for an anomalous religious condition, while from the standpoint of participants, the experience of ecstasy, though still something out of the ordinary, has rather to do with an anticipated departure from the profane realm . . . to a higher level of consciousness.[49]

For students of the ancient sources, the *locus classicus* will be Euripides' *Bacchae*, where the world in and around Thebes is divided into those who empathize and identify with the maenadism of the city's women and those who do not.[50] Socrates, then, in declaring his maenadism, challenges others to declare their stance vis-à-vis it and what it stands for in Aeschines' dialogue: Socrates' teaching.

What of the psychological-subjective dimension to this "outsidedness"? Simply put, when the god is in us/with us (when we are *entheoi*, when we are in *ekstasis*), that fundamentally involves the relocation of our "state" (*stasis*), our being, to our *outside* (*ek*).[51] So too, in a sense, do masks. Prominent in Dionysian cult and art, masks are not simply things to hide behind. Fixing the image of a different self to our outsides, they draw us outside ourselves; they free us to exist outside the normal ambit of our lives. But when, as in scenes depicted on "Lenaea" vases (masks and god's attire set up as cult images), the disguise is not worn, but in and of itself embodies the god,[52] then the circuit of imitation brings us back again and again to the surface. For god as mask collapses image and original, surface and depth, into a single image-reality, "the concrete embodiment of the power of Dionysus," who seizes possession of us by looking us straight in the eye — through his mask.[53] Similar can be said of bacchants and maenads. Though they went unmasked, their altered state showed itself like a mask at the surface.[54] But maenads can themselves mask. Thus in poetry, tragedy especially, a maenadic "mask of words" ("So-and-so rages like a bacchant") will at times superimpose a transformative Dionysianism upon a character.[55] Just so in Aeschines' *Alcibiades*, Socrates'

---

[49] Henrichs 1994:36 (my translation); see generally 35–38.

[50] Cf. Demosthenes 18.259–260, for which Wankel 1976:1132–1134.

[51] Murray 1996:118; Henrichs 1994:37.

[52] Cf. Dionysus mask-faces: Tarquinia, Museo Nazionale, RC 1804; François Vase, Florence, Museo Archeologico 4209. See Isler Kerényi 2001:89; Csapo 1997:255–258; Seaford 1996:39, 186; Henrichs 1993:36–39.

[53] Csapo 1997:257–258.

[54] Insensitivity to cutting, piercing, cold, fire; the visual impression left by their demeanor, visage, clothing, accoutrements: Seaford 1996:32–38, 186, 222; Bremmer 1984:268–273.

[55] E.g. *Iliad* 22.460; Euripides *Hippolytus* 550–551. See Schlesier 1993:94–97 et passim.

mask of words invests him with a bacchic persona, and his teaching, with a special kind of power.

That power can be clarified with reference to Deleuze's "simulacrum," a concept developed partly in response to Plato's notion of the phantasm, the copy of a copy with no firm connection to an original at the end of the chain of imitation. Only in Deleuze, a "Dionysian machinery" assigns positive value to these simulacra. Like masks, they generate meaning on their own and draw power from the *difference* between themselves and the "realities" over which they are fitted.[56] And that, at least at a very basic level, seems to describe what is happening in our dialogue's final sentences, where Socrates, to illustrate his case, pictures himself a wonder-working bacchant possessed by *erôs*. In several respects, this "mask" fits him poorly. He, a man, assumes a feminine persona; he, a proponent and teacher of *epistêmê*, rational knowledge, disavows any such of his own; he, in the throws of bacchic *erôs*, seeks to rein in the wayward ambitions of his young friend. Yet this mask, the source of his power, is *the very thing that he has undergone* (53.23–24 SSR). A "bacchant" now, he "plays his other":[57] he has stepped outside his normal self and has embodied himself on the outside, closer to his dialogical other, but closer, too, to his anti-self, what he is not. As such, it responds not to his *intention* to make Alcibiades better but to his desire, his *erôs*, to do so, *something over which Socrates as autonomous subject has absolutely no control*. Like blood drawn to the body's surface by the cold, Socrates' *erôs* expresses the interpenetration of inside and outside, of action and passion.

I have said that Socrates' bacchant's mask responds not to intention but to desire. But we cannot simply ignore intention. Rather, we should view it, at least in the present instance, as indistinguishable from expression, and Socrates' teaching, as rhetoric merging the two. For Socrates is, for the moment at least, all show. But so are his examples, interventions meant both to open up and to narrow the world of possibilities facing his pupil[58] — exercises, one might say, in masking, and as such, ambivalent, like Socrates' bacchant's mask. We see this especially in Socrates' eulogy of Themistocles (50 SSR), a speech designed to leverage Alcibiades' envy and ambition to maximum effect with minimal damage (cf. 49, 51 SSR). Thus Socrates, while praising Themistocles for winning favor with both Greeks *and* their bitter enemy, the Persian king ("such was the superiority of his intellect"), delicately sidesteps

---

[56] Reversing Plato's deprivileging of copies, images of images, etc.: Deleuze 1990:253–279.

[57] For the phrase and the concept, Zeitlin 1996.

[58] Cf. Rushton 2002 on Deleuze on faces.

the whole issue of Themistocles' role in letting the Persians escape back to Asia. According to Herodotus, Themistocles, falsely taking credit for the idea (cornered in Europe, the retreating Persians might have put up a stout resistance and prevailed), did so in order to ingratiate himself with the Persian king, should Themistocles ever find himself in need of refuge abroad.[59] And need one he would, though Socrates, in discussing Themistocles' exile, judiciously airbrushes the general's "Medizing," all the aid and comfort he ended up providing to the Persian enemy, out of the scene.[60] For Socrates stresses instead Themistocles' great good fortune even in exile (50.32–35 *SSR*). Yet Themistocles' disfranchisement and expulsion cannot but betoken what Athens finally thought of its native son, or illustrate the depths to which Themistocles' fortunes sank as a result of his imperfect wisdom.[61]

As to the effect Socrates' words have over their intended target, overcome, Alcibiades collapses in Socrates' lap and weeps (46.9–15; 51.6–7, 17–18; 52 *SSR*). But does that signify a breakthrough on Alcibiades' part? Possibly, though it may only signify how mortified Alcibiades is by how far short of his role model he has fallen — so much so that, in having failed in the care of himself, he has so far risen no higher than the vulgar herd, as Socrates seems to imply (50.41–43 *SSR*; cf. 51.1–13 *SSR* = Aristeides 3.576–577). True, Alcibiades now desires *aretê* (*virtutem*: 52 *SSR* = Cicero *Tusculan Disputations* 3.32.77–78), but the surviving fragments provide no clear indication whether that will be that higher sort of moral wisdom (*aretê*) Socrates cares about, or the kind of "manly excellence" (*aretê*) Alcibiades envies in Themistocles. At all events, Themistocles, in offering Alcibiades this simulacrum of greatness achieved through a mix of wisdom and cunning, of achievement both enviable and surpassable, offers the young man a seductive glimpse into his future. It is the persona Alcibiades will himself someday assume.

And that provides a connection to the dialogue's ambivalent ending, where Socrates' mask fuses image, Socrates' maenadism, with message, Socrates' intuitive, *erôs*-driven pedagogy — *erôs* that, like an involuntary reflex, remains outside Socrates' control. But is *Socrates* out of control? In Socrates' case, maenadism will itself be a symptom of something else: *erôs*.

---

[59] Herodotus 8.103–109. For spin in Socrates' speech, cf. Aristeides 3.576–577 (= Aeschines Socraticus 51.1–13 *SSR*) on praise, censure modulated with a view to damage control vis-à-vis Alcibiades. Themistocles has a mixed reception in the historiographical tradition, e.g. Herodotus 8.108–112; Thucydides 1.135–138; Plutarch *Themistocles*.

[60] Unmentioned in the text, but noted by Kahn 1994:93 n19; Döring 1984:20–21n11.

[61] Aeschines Socraticus 50.38–41 *SSR*, cf. 48; Ehlers 1966:15.

And in tragedy, that in combination with the maenadic can turn out, well, tragic.[62] But does it here?

Earlier, we saw how, in our sources, maenadism and associated states can have a polarizing effect, exciting in onlookers either identification with, or rejection of, what they see. It is, then, interesting to note that Socrates, who as teacher impersonates a bacchant, senses polarizing potential in his teaching. For the lesson he seeks to get across to Alcibiades is one that, he fears, both Alcibiades and the public at large will take the wrong way: that human fortune hinges on the success or failure of human beings to attain wisdom, thereby to gain control over their lives. That lesson, Socrates imagines, will run afoul of anyone who superstitiously privileges *tukhê*, fortune as god-directed causation, above all else. Those who think like that will likely charge Socrates with atheism. But only let them try: Socrates will sooner convict *them* of atheism than they *him*.[63]

Socrates seems at this point to be getting unnecessarily exercised: no one yet is talking about an impiety trial. But that bit of foreshadowing (Socrates will be tried, convicted, and executed for impiety in 399 BCE) conveys Socrates' own misgivings that, to those outside his circle, even perhaps to an ambivalent Alcibiades, his pedagogy must come across as impious rationalism. Note the element of masking, its power both to reveal and to conceal. To Socrates' critics, this "mask," his sophist's persona, projects a dangerous sort of "madness," the kind of madness that Strepsiades, fed up with Socrates' teaching, seeks to incinerate in Aristophanes' *Clouds* (1476–1509). Still, as Socrates sees it, his critics have got it all wrong. Failing to apprehend what this mask "really" projects, they miss his deeply felt religiosity, not to mention the *irrational* source of his teaching: his *erôs* to improve others. But even there, Socrates' zeal to help destabilizes. Daunted by Alcibiades' nearly incorrigible arrogance, Socrates tries to get through to the youth by means of a role-model whose triumphs and failures prefigure those of Socrates' pupil.

Has, then, Socrates' knowledge deficit got the better of him? Xenophon, that unflagging advocate for his one-time teacher, concedes in passing that the philosopher would have done well to teach prudence (*sôphronein*) first, then politics, to his "companions" (*Memorabilia* 1.2.17) — a curious admission,

---

[62] Schlesier 1993:99, 108–112 on Phaedra in Euripides *Hippolytus*.

[63] Aeschines Socraticus 50.43–50 *SSR*. Tyche 'Fortune' figures as personification starting with Hesiod (*Theogony* 360), as cult figure perhaps as early as mid sixth century BCE (Smyrna); Tyche and Agathe Tyche ("Good Fortune") in Athenian cult from at least 392/1 BCE: Hamdorf 1964:37–39, 97–100.

since it hints that Socrates, even if he did nothing actively to inflame Critias' or Alcibiades' wayward ambitions, could at least have done more to curb them. In Aeschines, Socrates definitely makes the effort, but like a bacchant, he draws on dry wells. For the trick to work, it would take a miracle.

Philosophy versus Demerasty in Plato's *Gorgias*

Plato's *Gorgias*, named for one of the great sophist-rhetoricians of the fifth and early fourth centuries BCE, plays like a three-act drama. After a brief overture, Act One has Socrates dispute the title character's contention that to lead effectively, a city's leaders need only master the art of persuasion. The next act pits Socrates against Polus, a rhetorician promoting rhetoric as the path to power and happiness. But the previous two acts are only warm-ups for the third, in which Callicles, a demagogue on the make (515a), champions nature and the cause of the stronger over convention and the cause of the weaker. Callicles can see a role for Socrates' philosophy — as a child's plaything. Eventually, though, everyone has to grow up. And so the man of affairs, the only kind of "real" man, must cast toys aside and master the art of speaking, both to get ahead and to guard his rear.[64]

That side to the dialogue's argument, the side concerning the morality of rhetoric — rhetoric's value in the larger scheme of things — has been explored elsewhere.[65] It will not concern us here. What will is the reverse: the rhetoric of morality, especially as that concerns Socrates' presentation of the moralist's case for philosophy. For just when Socrates reveals the full measure of his uncompromising dissatisfaction with the kindred arts of rhetoric and sophistic, he begins, we shall see, to package his moralism for a resistant audience. In the process, that audience — Callicles — labels Socrates a sophist, by which he means a manipulator of argument and meaning, an identification that, if on target, would hoist Socrates on his own petard. But rather than evaluate the accuracy of Callicles' characterization, we shall explore how the dialogue's third act conveys the *sense* of Socrates as anti-sophistic sophist — how, in other words, a kind of rhetoric frames Socrates' uncompromising moralism, and how that moralism frames Socrates' turn toward the rhetorical. My reading will be dialogical, but I shall not follow the

---

[64] Speakers in the dialogue: Dodds 1959:6–17.

[65] See e.g. Newell 2000:9–41; Nichols 1998:1–24; Gentzler 1995; Dodds 1959:1–17. See the review of scholarship in Zappen 2004:120–124. Related is Ober 1998:190–213 on the inadequacy of philosophy to make a difference under rhetorocratic democracy.

suggestion that Socrates' role in the *Gorgias* instances a free-wheeling, carnivalesque, pluralistic contribution to the discursive climate.[66] Rather, what will emerge is "Socrates" as a forward stance dialogically, a position from which to mount an assault on Callicles' ideological space.

Let us begin at the dialogue's turning point, where Callicles feels he can no longer sit on the sidelines as Socrates, summing up positions he has charted out in conversation with Gorgias and Polus, combines two arguments: (1) that rhetoric, a spurious kind of persuasion analogous to the confectioner's art, serves no useful purpose in a well-run state; and (2) that it is better to suffer than to do harm. Argument (1) Socrates qualifies tongue-in-cheek with (2): rhetoric serves a valid purpose only when used to procure just and salutary punishment for ourselves or our friends, or to "harm" enemies by saving them from same (480a–481b). Which is to say, rhetoric is justified only when used altruistically, which is never.

Unable to keep quiet any longer, Callicles turns to Chaerephon and Socrates to ask if the latter could be serious (481b–c). From the standpoint of self-interest and conventional wisdom, enemies richly deserve any suffering that comes their way, our friends, none. That accords with the "help friends, harm enemies" ethic, the golden rule of traditional Greek morality.[67] So, for instance, Gorgias earlier stipulated that rhetoric, a weapon of verbal combat, *not* be used against family and friends (447a, 456c–457a), against whom Socrates *would* deploy rhetoric, provided they deserve it. Hence what Polus terms the "strangeness" of Socrates' arguments (*atopa*, 473a, 480e), which fly in the face of an egocentrism most everyone sympathizes with (471c–d, 473e–474b, 481b–c). But Socrates presses the argument to its (il)logical extreme by commending punishment helpful to our friends and ourselves, and deprecating punishment helpful to our enemies. That deviously re-subscribes to the conventional wisdom, but contradicts it too: Socrates would withhold suffering from those who, in the view of the many, deserve it.

To that, Socrates can only have expected an incredulous reception, which, as we have seen, is just what he gets. Iakovos Vasiliou calls that "reverse irony": shock listeners into perplexity ("You can't be serious!?"); whet their interest and leave them impatient to get to the bottom of it.[68] It can, then, be regarded as a rhetorical "hook." Whether or not Socrates himself would class

---

[66] Early Plato, including *Gorgias*, as carnivalized dialogue: Zappen 2004:12–15, 45–66, 117–140; Bakhtin 1984a:109–112, 132–133; Bakhtin 1981:24–26.

[67] See p. 57 above.

[68] Vasiliou 2002:227–229.

that with rhetoric or sophistic (practically identical from Socrates' perspective), it holds an ironic mask in front of the speaker's serious message.

But it also risks *alienating* listeners, who can be expected to chafe at the feeling of being put on, of being asked to entertain a seemingly ludicrous suggestion.[69] Now, I am not suggesting that moralism is itself ludicrous, only that here, Socratic irony underscores what Polus takes to be the thinker's *atopia*, an attitudinal-ideological "Nowheresville" deeply at odds with conventional wisdom. Hence an incredulous Callicles' sudden entry into the discussion.[70] Were Socrates serious, he would, comments Callicles, turn all human life completely upside down (481b–c).

Aware that he is losing his audience, Socrates tries to reconnect:

> It has occurred to me that you and I, even as we speak, are in the throes of one and the same passion. For the two us feel *erôs*, each for a different pair of beloveds: you for the Athenian *dêmos* and for Demos son of Pyrilampes; I for Alcibiades, son of Cleinias, and for Philosophy.

> Plato *Gorgias* 481d

Why bring up eros? Comments Dodds, "Socrates is trying to find common ground to make Callicles understand his passion for truth."[71] In proposing that it is better to suffer than to do harm, Socrates challenges conventional wisdom, and in so doing, signals his disconnection from society, present company included. Yet in so doing, Socrates merely echoes his beloved philosophy; with that, surely a lover like Callicles can sympathize. For, as Socrates has just finished explaining, there can be no communication without shared consciousness:

> Callicles, what if there were no single emotion human beings shared — not exactly the same for each person, but basically the same? What if each of us instead felt something unique to each and foreign to the others? To explain to someone else what it was that one felt would not, in that case, be easy.

> Plato *Gorgias* 481c–d

---

[69] Cf. *eirôneia* 'prevarication' as irksome: Plato *Republic* 337a; Aristotle *Nichomachean Ethics* 1108a21–23; Theophrastus *Characters* 1.1–2. See Vasiliou 2002; Michelini 1998b:51–52; Vlastos 1987:80–83.

[70] *Atopia* 'strangeness,' 'absurdity,' 'inconsistency' and irony in Plato's *Gorgias*: Turner 1993.

[71] Dodds 1959:261; cf. Ober 1998:197–198.

Again, quoting Dodds, "Communication is possible only on the basis of some community of experience. . . ."[72] Here, Socrates addresses an important aspect of the sociality of language: shared consciousness (Socrates speaks of shared emotion, but that can be generalized to shared experience, values, etc.) as basis for shared speech. We see, then, Socrates at work trying to forge with Callicles that first link in Vološinov's ideological chain. If love is more than a word to each, then "I love" or "you love" becomes more than information. It becomes, potentially, at least, a moment of identification, of social bonding.

But how alike are Socrates and Callicles in their *erôs*? They both love; they feel substantially the same emotion. Still, if not the substance, then the *sense* of their *erôs* differs — "sense," that is, both in the French sense of "direction" (*sens*) and in Deleuze's sense of the event or surface effect that an utterance presents. We can think of sense as that chariot passing through one's lips when one says "chariot," not a meaning, not a syntactical or logical operator, but a *happening*.[73] I would extend that in the direction of the social to say that sense represents not the intention conveyed by an utterance or expression, but the impression it leaves at its outermost edge, its event horizon. Yair Neuman illustrates with the sentence, "I love you." Whatever the truth-value of that sentence, however we analyze its syntax, semantics, or logic, it is an *event*, one that happens, as we have seen, between lover and beloved, a "happening" located in — or rather, on — the utterance itself.[74] But there is more. If something happens when I say, "I love you," still, we cannot say that that something will always be the same. We are, then, concerned with the *sense* of love, not its unitary meaning, but its surface orientation, its *spin*.

Let me illustrate with Plato's *First Alcibiades*,[75] where Socrates makes much of the exceptional character of his *erôs* for the title character. Yet it is the *sense*, not the essence, of his *erôs* that is exceptional. On one level, *erôs* is no more than a word. But when Socrates says, "I love" (*erô, philô*), something very special happens. Thus Socrates, doggedly following Alcibiades around, as Alcibiades puts it, "harassing me" (*enokhleis me*, 104d), exhibits overtly erotic behavior. Nothing special there: so have plenty of others.[76] Yet Socrates' *erôs*, love not of body but of soul, sets Socrates apart from rivals (131c–e). In pedagogical terms, that translates as mentoring; for a budding statesman like Alcibiades, Socrates' attentions model how to lead. But so does the wrong-

---

[72] Dodds 1959:261; cf. Rocco 1995–1996:369.

[73] Chrysippus in Diogenes Laertius 7.187, on which Deleuze 1990:8.

[74] Sense: Deleuze 1990. The sense of "I love you": Neuman 2004:63; pp. 50–51 above.

[75] Questions of authenticity will not concern us here. Pro-authenticity: Denyer 2001:14–26.

[76] Plato *First Alcibiades* 103a. Erotic harassing-following: Aeschines 1.139; Dover 1989:48, 54–57.

way *erôs* of demagogic *dêmos*-lovers (*dêmerastai*) whose ranks, Socrates fears, Alcibiades may join (132a). Socialized into the city's values and eager to please, the demagogue receives upon himself the imprint of the *dêmos'* moral stupidity, which he then imprints right back on the *dêmos*.[77] Compare that to Socrates' right-way approach: along the vertical axis, a properly top-down pederasty, pedagogy, and politics channeling goodness on high to those below (105d–106a, 106c–d, 118c–d, 132b, 134b–c, 135b); along the horizontal, a spiritually uplifting dialogue, *erastês* to *erastês*, producing mutual benefit (132d–133c, 135d–e). Thus to alter the sense, the directionality, of *erôs* is to reappraise its objects: on the one hand, "real" beauty and knowledge, on the other hand, simulacra of same, an *erôs* that, for Socrates, at least, will feel as if it is headed the wrong way.

And that will help us understand how the sense of Socrates' *erôs* differs from Callicles' in the *Gorgias*. Just to review, when I say, "X loves," the meaning of "loves" does not vary with the identity of X. Still, when I say, "Callicles loves" and "Socrates loves," different things happen. Though Callicles identifies with those seeking to *dominate*, not be dominated by, the many (483b–484c, 491e–492c), his *erôs*, whether for the Athenian *dêmos* or for Demos Pyrilampes' son, forces him to conform to *their* erratic will (481d–482b, 512e–513c, 521b). A slave to his urges, he might as well be living the life of a "bugger" (*kinaidos*, cf. 494e). With that contrast Socrates' right-way *erôs*: a slave only to his beloved philosophy, his message never varies because neither does hers (cf. 482a–b). There is a dialogical dimension to all this. Discourse as frank speech (*parrhêsia*) free from the taint of demeaning self-compromise earns Socrates' admiration.[78] But when a verbal transaction involves self-assimilation to listeners unworthy of emulation by reason of their inconstancy, then it will not receive the philosopher's nod. Viewed through the lens of *philia* 'friendship,' 'affection', such discourse translates as *kolakeia* 'flattery';[79] through the lens of *erôs*, as buggery.[80]

Socrates does not, of course, come out and accuse Callicles of being a *kolax*-bugger outright, but Socrates' arguments are not hard to follow, and Callicles reacts accordingly (521b, 494e). As for his being cast as *dêmos*-lover (481d, 513c), he cannot have found it much to his liking. Callicles despises "the

---

[77] Plato *First Alcibiades* 110d–112d, 120a–b. Cf. demagogues dazed and brainwashed by the crowd's uproar: Plato *Republic* 492b–c, on which Denyer 2001:139, 226

[78] E.g., Plato *Gorgias* 487a; see Monoson 1994:161–165.

[79] Sophistic and rhetoric as branches of *kolakeia* (along with cookery, cosmetics, poetic entertainment): Plato *Gorgias* 463a–467a; cf. 501c–503a, 513d, 521b.

[80] Cf. Ober 1998:197–206.

many," in other words, the *dêmos*, for their natural weaknesses, and regards it as scandalous that the system permits sons of the elite to be brainwashed into the slave mentality holding them and their fathers back (483b–484c). In point of ideology, Socrates and Callicles are closer than one might think; for both, popular sovereignty leaves much to be desired, only Callicles refuses to face his complicity in a system he detests, whereas Socrates has nothing to be ashamed of. Hence Socrates' use of the demerast characterization: fraught with all sorts of negative connotations, it is meant to shame Callicles into reconsidering his position.

If there is no right-way demerasty, then what takes it place? For Socrates, that will be *erôs* for philosophy (481d–482a). Only from philosophy could Socrates have gained the political expertise (*tekhnê*, 521d; cf. 500b–d) that he opposes to rhetoric, its simulacrum (*eidôlon*, 463d); only through knowledge of justice, implicitly, a gift of philosophy, can one become an orator "the right way" (*orthôs*, 508c). At no point does Socrates actually state that he intends to convert Callicles to philosophy. Still, Socrates and Callicles seem to recognize that their debate will necessarily oppose the competing claims of philosophy and practical rhetoric (484c–486d, 487e–488a, 500c). But Callicles also offers Socrates an opportunity not to be missed: to win over so worthy an opponent "will demonstrate these convictions," those held by Socrates, "to be true" (486e). Framed as it is by Socrates' passionate devotion to his mistress, this desire for a meeting of minds, though it may not itself qualify as *erôs* in the strictest sense, carries the stamp of the erotic.

That meeting of minds we can reasonably expect to be conducted according to principles of fairness, courtesy, and cooperation enunciated by Socrates, observed in discussion with Gorgias,[81] and reaffirmed in conversation with Callicles (505e–506a). Socrates hopes, of course, not just to converse but to convert. Still, simply to defeat his "opponent" will not do; he must, as Socrates puts it, bring his interlocutor to "bear witness" in Socrates' behalf (472b–c). How do things go? Along the way, Socrates extends to Callicles courtesies extended to Gorgias[82] and presents the more cogent case, as Callicles himself intimates at one point.[83] Still, Socrates also engages in captious argument, as when he presses Callicles to admit that "To the more intelligent should go the larger share," Callicles claim, equates with "to the shoemaker should go more shoes" and similar absurdities (490d–e).

---

[81] Plato *Gorgias* 453c, 454c, 457c–458b, 472b–c; Nichols 1998:136; Gentzler 1995:25–27.

[82] E.g. the chance to clarify one's position: Plato *Gorgias* 489d–e. See Gentzler 1995:33–34.

[83] Ambivalently at Plato *Gorgias* 513c; see Ober 1989:190–213.

This tendentious side to Socrates' discourse comes to the fore not least when Socrates, having professed his love for philosophy, then proceeds to "frontload" it into his arguments with a view to biasing discussion in his favor. What do I mean by "frontloading"? When subject matter exerting its own field of force ("Let us consider beauty / God / truth") is put up for debate, as philosophy is in Plato's *Gorgias*, then it can take an act of will to approach it dispassionately. At that point, the grounding of discussion can begin to resemble the effort to impose a shared consciousness: discussants will either be drawn to the premise like a magnet or will just as automatically resist. To all appearances, dialogue proceeds as it should, yet all on its own, the discursive focus imposes a "center-seeking" (centripetal) dynamic, or else so polarizes dialogue as to end it.

In the *Gorgias*, frontloading happens during Socrates' opening speech to Callicles, specifically, when he challenges his interlocutor to refute not *his* word but that of his beloved *philosophy* (482a–b), which becomes thereby both a focus of discussion and a party to debate. In so doing, Socrates risks alienating Callicles, for whom, as Socrates well knows, philosophy holds little appeal (487c–d). Still, Socrates goes ahead anyway to illustrate how this lady-love of his offers him a privileged subjectivity within society, a subjectivity wedded to and derived from a higher and unvarying source of authority. Out of sync with the rest of humanity, Socrates will, at least, be in sync with himself, all thanks to his beloved philosophy (cf. 482b–c). That shifts the burden of argument upon Callicles. If Socrates fails to convince Callicles, Socrates will be none the worse for wear. If, however, Callicles fails to convince Socrates, Callicles, ever the slave to his fickle beloveds, must find himself at variance with himself. Philosophy, by contrast, never changes her tune because she does not have to. The logic is compelling, if circular. To all intents and purposes, philosophy's constancy marks both the starting point and goal of Socrates' reasoning. Does Callicles notice? I should say he does. Quoting Euripides, Callicles supposes that Socrates behaves no differently from the common run of humanity: he validates his personal strengths and preferences by presenting them as if naturally superior to the alternative (484e–485a).

To be fair, Callicles defends egocentricism and *Realpolitik* no less tendentiously. Charging Socrates with a kind of ivory-tower naïveté, he warns his "friend" to get with the program or suffer the consequences (482c–486d). Conceding philosophy's charms, he belittles them. For Callicles characterizes philosophy as a childish pursuit, a toy to be discarded by grown-ups (484c–486a). Thus for Callicles to be won over to philosophy would, at least from his perspective, amount to surrendering his manhood — not his masculinity *per se*, but all that entitles him, a free and fully grown man of quality (a *kalos k'agathos*, 484d), to pursue his ambitions. Yet *each* of our two discussants impugns the other's manhood: Callicles when he faults Socrates for refusing to grow up and learn the techniques of judicial self-defense, Socrates when he implies that Callicles stoops to *kolakeia*, even *kinaidia*, in courting his beloveds as he does.

Why does Socrates go at it this way? Gyl Gentzler, addressing the sophistic side to Socrates' cross-examination of Callicles, provides an interesting explanation. By demonstrating competence in what he rejects (viz. sophistic rhetoric), the philosopher proves that his preference represents an informed choice. And by giving Callicles a taste of his own medicine, Socrates demonstrates its ineffectiveness and lays the groundwork for a more genuinely "Socratic" exchange later on.[84]

But that also implies an element of calculation and distance in Socrates' self-presentation, as if in playing his "other" (the sophist-rhetorician) he does not really mean it. To that view I would suggest an alternative: that Socrates' "pitch," the case he makes for his beloved philosophy, cannot as *manifestation*, as Socrates' presentation of his discursive "I,"[85] be so easily parsed as a momentary pose foreign to whatever "reality" the philosopher embodies. Rather, Callicles, by stepping back from his and Socrates' discussion, effectively draws out Socrates the contentious arguer latent within Socrates the true believer. Projecting his dialogical self outside the ambit of the courteously dispassionate debater, Socrates grows "violent" (*biaios*, Callicles at 505d). No playacting version of himself, but the real McCoy, he takes up a forward position from which to mount a frontal assault on his interlocutor. *Erôs* can, then, be said to express the dual character of Socrates' attachment to philosophy: on the one hand, the absence of any vulgar or impure motivation; on the other hand, a commitment so complete as to rule out any real chance at dialogue. That introduces a coercive dynamic into the discourse. Unwilling to yield so much as an inch, Socrates leaves Callicles little choice but to submit or quit.

Does, then, dialogue in Plato's *Gorgias* fail, either by fault of the speaking characters, or else through flaws intrinsic to dialogue itself? What is difficult to understand is why, if the debate between Socrates and Callicles actually goes nowhere, Gorgias and the other bystanders remain raptly attentive (cf. 497b, 506a). So a kind of chemistry develops between the two men as each brushes up against the other's abrasive obduracy.[86] Dodds points out how the

---

[84] Gentzler 1995:42 et passim.
[85] See p. 85 above.
[86] Cf. Dodds 1959:16–17.

periodic recycling of themes in the dialogue combines with an intensifying seriousness and depth to produce an "ascending spiral," a "dynamic movement, from the superficial to the fundamental."[87] This strange version of the love-dance by which lovers ascend the cognitive-existential ladder in Plato's *Phaedrus, Symposium,* and *First Alcibiades* may not do much for either Socrates or Callicles, but it does for us who watch from the sidelines. Among other things, it suggests that no simplistic scheme will explain dialogue in the real world; that missteps and disconnects, aggression and frustration, inevitably figure into the process.

Socratic Pandering in Xenophon's *Symposium*

"But the way I see it, we should remember men of quality not just for their serious accomplishments, but also for the things they have done in a more playful mood." So begins Xenophon's *Symposium,* a dialogue dramatizing a drinking party notable for the wit and wisdom evinced by the *kaloi k'agathoi,* the "men of quality," in attendance. But Xenophon tests limits when he has Socrates masquerade as that most immoderate, inconstant, and self-compromised of characters: a pimp. For how can this mask, one that, if taken at "face" value, expresses everything disreputable, confirm Socrates as a *kalos k'agathos*? As we shall see, Xenophon's *Symposium* shows Socrates "playing his other," his anti-self, as a way of negotiating relationships with *dialogical* others. Because a mask, pimping distances the man behind it from skills that notoriously drew to him the likes of Critias and Alcibiades, Socrates' two most infamous pupils. Yet this mask also reveals the networker — the "pimp" — in Socrates, and therefore his ability to reach out and compromise with a paradoxical kind of grace.

Bragging Rights

Composed probably in the 360s, Xenophon's *Symposium* purports to reenact a drinking party (a *sumposion*) honoring Autolycus son of Lycon for his Panathenaic boxing victory in 422.[88] There to lend the festivities cachet is Socrates (1.4), who urges the assembled company to take care of their own amusement, so as not to be outdone by the paid performers, persons of inferior quality (3.2). And so it is that Callias, the party's host, suggests a game

---

[87] Dodds 1959:3–4.
[88] Date of composition, dramatic date, occasion: Huß 1999:71–73.

of show-and-tell: participants will take turns stating, then proving, whatever each takes special pride in (3.3, 4.1).

What do these guests and their host take pride in? Antisthenes, a poor man, boasts of his "wealth," meaning his poverty, because it easily supports his frugal life-style (3.8, 4.34–45). Charmides, likewise impecunious, wears poverty as a badge of honor: it frees him from care (3.9, 4.30). We can think of that in terms of mask and sense. Thus Antisthenes and Charmides don the mask of the *eudaimôn*, the man fortunate in his material situation, not to *conceal* their poverty but to reveal their sense of it, the ways in which each has reconciled himself to his situation.

But in so doing, they obviously decline to play Callias' game straight. That is, they avoid the kind of unambiguous self-aggrandizement that, for instance, Gorgias models in Plato's like-named dialogue (449a). But so do most of Xenophon's other players. Thus Hermogenes, showing off his piety, at first boasts only of his "friends" (*philoi*, 3.14), later revealed to be the gods. Yet he represents those "friendships" as a kind of cheap flattery: powerful protectors, the gods dispense favor cheaply in return for praise (4.49). Similar can be said of low characters whose "boasts" speak frankly of their disreputable professions (3.11, 4.50, 4.55). Even Autolycus, whose victory would seem to provide obvious bragging rights, will take credit only for having a good father (3.12–13).

One gathers that for most players, playing it straight will not do, not at this party,[89] but why not? Straight talk, *parrhêsia*, though admirable in its own way (cf. above on Plato *Gorgias* 487a), could be objectionable talk. To fail to modulate one's message appropriately, to allow, in other words, one's "manifestation" to become overtly intrusive, could be to fail to take into consideration one's listeners' sensitivities, and therefore to risk alienating them.[90] Plutarch observes that praise wittily (*meta paidias*) couched as abuse can be more agreeable than its straightforward counterpart (*Moralia* 632d–e, on Xenophon *Symposium* 4.61–64). So, too, *self*-praise becomes more palatable if mingled with self-censure (*Moralia* 543f–544d). The name of the game will, then, be not simply to parade one's talents, but to do so *engagingly*, to explain what sets one apart, but *without setting oneself apart* — to flatter oneself without alienating others.

---

[89] Niceratus seems to be the only player whose boast, expertise in Homer, plays it straight. For that, he is gently teased: Xenophon *Symposium* 3.5–6, 4.6–9.

[90] See Michelini 1998b:53–56.

Pimping

But Socrates trumps them all when he proclaims *mastropeia*, 'pimping,' his special skill (3.10). That claim raises a laugh — what could be more ludicrous than the thought of Socrates plying so disreputable (*adoxôi*, 4.56) a trade? The aura of sexual passivity and foreign origins, both prejudicial to the honorable standing of any citizen male, could be said to have hung about the profession.[91] As for what *mastropoi* actually did, first and foremost, they hunted down customers for sex-providers, a function reflected in the etymology of their name.[92] In that capacity, they could be associated with a predatory type of cunning, as could the prostitutes they worked for.[93] Diphilus shows us *mastropoi* playing the role of go-betweens helping arrange a sex party (42.22 *PCG*); that suggests overlap between the business of the *mastropos*, a "seller's agent," and that of the *proagôgos*, a "buyer's agent" whose job was, in the narrow sense, to procure sex-providers for clients (Xenophon *Symposium* 4.61; Theopompus 115 F 227 *FGrH*; Plutarch *Moralia* 632e).

Socrates, then, in boasting of his pimping, "plays his other," at least insofar as this pimp's mask of his ill fits the civic-masculine dignity elsewhere associated with him.[94] But has Socrates never actually plied the trade? Apparently he has not, though he thinks he "could make a lot of money, should I choose to practice the art" (3.10; cf. 4.61). Yet at no point does he flatly deny ever having pimped. Indeed, by admitting that he intends to hand the business over to his friend Antisthenes (4.61), Socrates' playacting implicitly embraces pimping as a biographical fact. Yet Socrates still plays coy. However deep — or shallow — his past involvement, he intends to leave that life behind. How do others understand his pimping? Antisthenes teasingly addresses Socrates as a pimp who pimps *himself* (*mastrope sautou*, 8.5); Callias, whom Socrates encourages to enter politics, takes that encouragement as a hint that Socrates intends to pimp for *him*, and to the whole city, no less (*me ... mastropeuseis pros tên polin*, 8.42).

---

[91] Cf. stereotyping of the brothel keeper (foreign born, sexually passive) in Herodas' second mime; the *kollopsi mastropois* in Diphilus 42.22 *PCG* (*kollops* = sexually passive, Henderson 1991:212–213). Sexual passivity as highly prejudicial public "fact": Winkler 1990:45–70.

[92] See Chantraine s.v. μαίομαι, whence μαστροπός.

[93] A *mastropos* who "wheedled" a speaker (*teleôs m' hupêlthen,*): Epicrates 8 *PCG*. *Mastropoi* "entangling" men in the "nets" of the women they represent: Theophilus fr. 11 *PCG*; cf. Lucian *Toxaris* 13. Predatory *hetairai*: p. 60n62 above.

[94] Military service: Plato *Symposium* 219e–221c; *Laches* 181a–b. Cf. his council service: Plato *Apology* 32b–c.

We shall need to keep in mind Socrates' ambivalence toward this art, one that he can speak of in both literal and figurative terms, both boast about and hold at arm's length; it will prove important to how he defines himself. For the moment, though, it will help to place Socrates' pimping in context: to consider how it fits into the larger profile of all that he is good at. Thus when Socrates assimilates his friend's matchmaking — teacher-pupil pairings and conversation partnerings — to sexual procurement (4.61–64), what Socrates leaves out is that he, too, excels at just that sort of thing.[95] What makes Socrates so good at it? From Aspasia, matchmaker *par excellence*, Socrates has learned the value of truth in advertising: that misrepresentation can produce unhappy results (*Memorabilia* 2.6.36). But sincerity does not, evidently, preclude a flair for spin, as when Socrates expertly reconciles men down on their luck to arrangements that, while intended to provide for their material needs, also carry social stigma.[96]

But it is in the art of coaching others in the art of friendship that Socrates' expertise most closely approximates a pimp's. This skill, which Socrates likens to hunting and enchantment (Xenophon *Memorabilia* 2.6.8–13, 2.6.28–35, 3.11.6–17), involves a crucial element of seeming "good" (*agathos*) based ideally on being it (2.6.39). So when Socrates treats Theodote, a courtesan renowned for her beauty, to a lesson in "friend-hunting" (3.11.10), his expertise impresses her enough that she offers him a job "hunting" — pimping — right on the spot.[97] At no point in the narrative are terms like "pimp" or "prostitute" (*hetaira*) used, but the obvious luxury of Theodote's establishment and retinue (3.11.2–5), combined with the narrator's coyly suggestive explanation that Theodote "was one to keep company with anyone who would 'persuade' her" (3.11.1), leave little doubt as to the nature of her business or the fees she commands — or the value to her of a good pimp (3.11.9).[98]

As to the "moral" of this last episode, William Johnson points out that Socrates' interview with a prostitute, by exposing the tricks of the trade, "immunizes" friends listening in.[99] But I would suggest that the episode does

[95] Socratic "matchmaking": Xenophon *Memorabilia* 1.6.14, 2.2–10, 3.11; Plato *Laches* 180c–d; Aeschines Socraticus *Aspasia* (59–72 SSR), for which Ehlers 1966:35–43.

[96] Xenophon *Memorabilia* 2.7–10, on which Scholtz 1996:82–83; Osborne 1990:96–98; Millett 1989:33.

[97] Xenophon *Memorabilia* 3.11.15. Cf. pederastic courtship as "hunting": Barringer 2001:85–89; Dover 1989:87.

[98] Fee schedules for Hetärentum in comparison to *porneia*: Davidson 1997:194–200.

[99] Johnson 2005:199.

more than that. In defining Theodote's profession in terms of her indiscriminate choice of "companions" or "friends" and the monetary incentive for doing so, Xenophon allows us to draw parallels between prostitution and sophistic, which, like prostitution, involves a service provider's willingness to share indiscriminately with anyone who can come up with the cash, not with a select group whom he will befriend.[100] And so, suggests Socrates, the sophist might as well be trading, like a *pornos* (a male prostitute) or, one might add, like Theodote, on his looks (Xenophon *Memorabilia* 1.6.13; cf. 1.2.5–8). That parallel can be extended along predictable lines. Thus sophists, like courtesans and the pimps working for them, "hunt" for wealthy young clients (Xenophon *On Hunting with Dogs* 13.9; cf. Plato *Sophist* 223a–b). Indeed, Love himself (the god Eros), an *adikos sophistês* or "devious sophist," by getting one of his victims into trouble, teaches the man lessons in love and the soul — perhaps, lessons in getting oneself out of a sticky situation — in a roundabout sort of way (Araspas in Xenophon *Cyropaedia* 6.1.41).

I am emphasizing these parallels specifically to argue that Socrates, through what Plato's Socrates might have termed a "pleasant turn" (*Phaedrus* 257d–e), deviously masquerades at being pimp to acknowledge with plausible deniability the potential for his pedagogy to supply what a sophist offers. To see that, we need ourselves to play along with Socrates' play-acting: we need to ask how, *when we view Socrates with his mask on*, it alters our sense of what Socrates does. Thus we note how this masquerade brings to light Socrates' expertise in "love magic" (*philtra, epôidai*), expertise that makes Socrates popular with "girlfriends" (*philai*), which is to say, with pupils like Apollodorus, Antisthenes, and others (Xenophon *Memorabilia* 3.11.16–17). Socrates seems here to be associating himself with a type, the sorceress dealing in love potions and *pharmaka*, whose activities placed her at the margins of society.[101] Figuratively (mis)representing his teaching in this way, Socrates presents it in a paradoxically transgressive light. Yet Socrates, still speaking tongue-in-cheek, deals in just the sort of magic (*philia*-arousing *epôidai*) that won the Athenian people over to Themistocles and Pericles (2.6.12–14) and enabled Cyrus to command the willing obedience of entire nations[102] — "magic," in

---

[100] See Blank 1985.

[101] Cf. Medea, Nino, and Theoris (scholia Demosthenes 19.495; 25.41). See Dillon 2002:104, 169–178, 324n203, 343nn221, 224.

[102] Subjects' "desire" (*epithumia*) to "gratify" (*kharizesthai*) Cyrus: Xenophon *Cyropaedia* 1.1.5 (note also rule by fear). Rulers should "cast a spell" (*katagoêteuein*): 8.1.40. *Erôs* and rulership in *Cyropaedia*: Rubin 1989.

other words, conventionally associated not just with sexual seduction but with persuasion generally and sophistic in particular.[103]

But Socrates as sophist? Is that not precisely the thing Xenophon takes great pains to refute?[104] Still, Socrates need not have *been* a sophist for pupils to feel they could get from him what they might otherwise have sought from his "other." So, for instance, Critias and Alcibiades are said to have gone to Socrates for instruction in effective speaking and politicking (*genesthai an hikanôtatô legein te kai prattein*, Xenophon *Memorabilia* 1.2.15), the sort of thing that might have marked Socrates a genuine sophist had he taught only that and nothing else (cf. 1.2.31, 48). Yet Xenophon's Socrates, though the very model of the anti-sophist, by no means discounts the importance to leaders of learning how to speak (cf. 3.3.11). As for Socrates' own skills, he offered, Xenophon tells us, the example of one who "in argument . . . could do what he liked with any disputant" (1.2.14, Loeb trans.). Imitated but misapplied by a pupil like Alcibiades (1.2.39–46), that more or less translates as eristic, the art of competitive debate and verbal entrapment, reportedly a specialty of Protagoras, sophist extraordinaire.[105]

Taking stock, we have so far been exploring Socrates' pimping on two levels: as a serio-comic way to think about Socrates' skill at negotiating the complexities of social networking; as Xenophon's spin on his erstwhile mentor's unique sort of pedagogy, a way, in other words, for Xenophon to negotiate the fit between the principled if versatile philosopher he champions, and the sophist attacked in polemics that preoccupy the first book of the *Memorabilia*. In either case, Socrates' pimp's mask says something important about its wearer, namely, that Socrates, for all his uncompromising idealism, recognized the importance of surface as interface between inner and outer being. We see that, among other places, in the philosopher's conversation with Pistias the armorer. There, Socrates establishes that the well-proportioned breastplate follows no absolute rule, but adapts itself to the shape and needs of the one inside; it is all a matter of fit (Xenophon *Memorabilia* 3.10.9–15). Similar can be said of painting and sculpture, where outer form manifests inner character and feeling (*êthos* and *pathos*, 3.10.1–8). Those principles can be extended

---

[103] Magic, technologies of persuasion, sophistic: Aeschylus *Eumenides* 81–82; Eupolis *Demes* fr. 102 PCG; Gorgias *Helen*; Plato *Euthydemus* 288b; Romilly 1975:3–43; Segal 1962.

[104] Xenophon contra Socrates as professional teacher of practical rhetoric et sim.: *Memorabilia* 1.2, 1.5.4, 1.5.6–1.6.15; Blank 1985; Classen 1984. Cf. anti-sophistic broadside: *On Hunting with Dogs* 13.

[105] Protagoras testimonia 1, 3, 21, fr. 6 D-K. Cf. Pericles' "we used to go in for that kind of cleverness" (*esophizometha*): Xenophon *Memorabilia* 1.2.46. See Gentzler 1995:18–23; O'Connor 1994:156–158.

outward toward the observer, and so they are in Socrates' pimping lecture (3.11.7–14), where the impression — visual, verbal, and so on — one leaves on others, though it originates from within oneself, from one's soul, is articulated at, and emanates from, the surface. As for whether it does so to the better-ment of all concerned, that depends on how well it negotiates the fit between inner and outer being; there can be no one-size-fits-all good.[106] Socrates, then, in lecturing the *hetaira*, offers more than an antidote to the *hetaira*'s charms. He offers a lesson in how to project a self well-adapted to mediating the self-other divide.

And so does he in Xenophon's *Symposium*, where Socrates defines pimping (*mastropou ergon*) as the art of rendering clients *areskontes*, 'agreeable' (4.57). Combining the functions of cosmetician and coach, pimps concern themselves with hair, clothes, facial expressions, utterance, all that bears upon "agree-ableness," which is to say, sex appeal.[107] But Socrates shows himself principally concerned with utterance: modest versus shameful, hostile versus friendly (4.58). Thus "any pimp worth his salt will teach (*didaskoi an*) only those utter-ances conducive to agreeableness (*toutôn ... ta sumpheronta eis to areskein*)" (4.59). Lest we miss the point, Socrates adds that the perfect pimp will offer instruction with a view to rendering clients pleasing *to the entire city* (*holêi têi polei areskontas*); anyone who can do that deserves a high fee (4.60). For "pimp," read, then, "sophist"; for our pimp's clients, politicians in training.

But does Socrates actually pimp in the *Symposium*? As we shall soon see, he does toward the end of his speech on love. Yet that speech contains some distinctly un-pimp-like talk. Focused on a more mature man's *erôs* for a younger man or adolescent (i.e. on pederasty), it champions love focused on the love-object's inner beauty as basis for enduring affection. As elsewhere, so too here, that leaves little scope for carnal desire, what Socrates calls Pandemian or "vulgar" love, which, if consummated, can, he tells us, do the younger man harm.[108] As to the financial end of things, money can purchase sex, but not affection (8.21). And with that, pimp Socrates, speaking frankly now of the sham he evidently thinks Pandemian love to be, seems to have left his pimp's persona far behind.

Still, like a pair of bookends, evocations of Socratic pandering frame that speech: on the one hand, where Antisthenes, professing love for Socrates,

---

[106] Cf. Xenophon *Memorabilia* 3.1.6, 3.8, *Symposium* 5.3–6.

[107] Training of prostitutes: Demosthenes 59.18; Hamel 2003:25–26, 168n32.

[108] Cf. Euripides fr. 388 Nauck; Plato *Symposium* 180c–185c; *First Alcibiades* 131c–e; Xenophon *Spartan Constitution* 2.13; see Huß 1999:32–34, 355–437, 451–455.

mischievously suggests his beloved pimps himself (*mastrope sautou*) by playing hard to get (8.4–5), on the other, where Callias divines from Socrates' love speech that this supposed pimp intends to pimp for him (8.42). Why would Callias think that? Having offered various reflections on Ouranian love, Socrates shifts from the general to the particular when he takes up the question of how so excellent and worthy a youth as Autolycus ought to be courted. How else but for the *erastês* to prove himself a worthy partner to his beloved's endeavors (8.37–38)? Taking his cue from the fame Autolycus will win in the public eye, Callias must likewise make a name for himself — something, we gather, that Callias has yet to do. But Callias, unlike Autolycus, will pursue fame not in war or sport but in politics. Callias needs, then, to gain the necessary knowledge:

> If, then, you would prove yourself agreeable (*areskein*) to the lad, you should consider the types of knowledge that equipped Themistocles for the freeing of Greece, or what it was that Pericles had learned that made him the perfect statesman in the eyes of his countrymen (*kratistos edokei*). But you should also consider how Solon's philosophy established for his city such excellent (*kratistous*) laws, or how Spartan training confers on Spartans the aspect of great commanders (*kratistoi dokousin hêgemones einai*).

> Xenophon *Symposium* 8.39

The word *kratistos* 'excellent', 'best', used three times in the preceding passage, has already been used by Socrates to describe the suitor who will "best" guide Autolycus on the path to glory (8.38). But Socrates speaks here in terms not just of being, but of *seeming* to be, best (*kratistos*). Thus it was in seeming (*edokei*) to be the best counselor of the *dêmos* that Pericles' political expertise proved of value to him. So, too, Spartans profit from their rigorous training by seeming (*dokousin*) to be great commanders. Does that mean that Callias, in cultivating the appearance of excellence, can afford to neglect its substance? Not exactly. Elsewhere in Xenophon (*Memorabilia* 2.6.39; *Cyropaedia* 1.6.22), the reality of virtue offers the best route to the appearance of it, and nothing in Socrates' *Symposium* speech contradicts that.[109]

Still, unless Callias can leverage appearances, he will fail in his bid for glory and for Autolycus, too. Socrates' focus accordingly shifts as he touts what campaign managers today would refer to as Callias' "positives." Callias comes from noble stock and holds a prestigious priesthood; he has one of the

---

[109] Cf. Xenophon *Symposium* 8.43. Civic virtue in Xenophon: Seager 2001.

most attractive bodies in town, though a body ready to endure hardship. This is not Socrates speaking through his wine, this comes from the heart. Both he and the city have never ceased to be lovers, *sunerastai*, of such men — men of a noble nature, men ambitious to excel in virtue. Men, in other words, like Callias (8.40–41).

Autolycus' gaze is by now riveted on Callias, and Callias' on Autolycus, though the older man does manage a response to Socrates' effusions: "So I suppose, then, you'll pimp me to the city? That way as a politician I'll never cease being agreeable to it" (8.42). Or, for that matter, to Autolycus. "Agreeable" here translates the adjective *arestos*, cognate with the verb *areskein*, used by Socrates to describe both the agreeableness of prostitutes decked out by their *mastropoi*, and the agreeableness Socrates seeks to instill in his host to make him a more attractive *erastês* to Autolycus.

Using, then, Autolycus as bait to inflame Callias' hitherto dormant ambitions, Socrates plays the pimp with consummate skill on multiple levels. In so doing, he would appear to offer a kind of validation for Critobulus' belief in the power of physical attraction — of Pandemian love — to spur lovers on to deeds of distinction to impress their beloveds (3.7, 4.15–16). Now, Critobulus may not possess the wisdom of a Socrates. But he does, at least, recognize the role of appearances, a general's good looks, where leadership and command are concerned (4.16). That leadership model receives fuller treatment in Xenophon's *Cyropaedia*, where Cyrus seems particularly attuned to the value of appearances and what can only be called "sex appeal" to a monarch like Cyrus.[110]

I would suggest that Xenophon's picture of barbarian absolutism in the *Cyropaedia* frees that work to express more bluntly what receives careful packaging — heavy doses of *paidia* mixed with *spoudê* — in Xenophon's *Symposium*, namely, that only through surface manifestation, whether verbal or visual, can inner meaning, the "soul," enter the give-and-take of social reality and thus make a difference.[111] Given the extraordinary character of Callias' get-together, a before-the-fact second chance for victims and perpetrators of *stasis* to get along,[112] Socrates' pimping, the very picture of agreeableness and

---

[110] See p. 139n102 above. No unalloyed eulogy to Cyrus (Johnson 2005; Rubin 1989), the *Cyropaedia* still expresses amazement at the quasi-erotic obedience commanded by the king.

[111] Cf. Vološinov 1986:19: "Social psychology in fact is not located anywhere within (in the "souls" of communicating subjects) but entirely and completely without — in the word, the gesture, the act."

[112] Callias' drinking party brings Charmides, loyal adherent of oligarchy in 404/3, together with Niceratus and Autolycus, both victims of that oligarchy. Lycon, Autolycus' father, will join the prosecution of Socrates in 399. See further Huß 1999:38–49.

sociality, conveys that message with special poignancy for a post-403 audience. Yet the Pandemian side to Socratic *erôs* carries ambivalence as well. Rallying citizens around leaders "groomed" to inspire *erôs* for community and consensus (Socrates on *sunerastai*, 8.41), it enacts Pandemos the unifier, who, though suppressed in Xenophon's text, would seem to have emerged into public consciousness at least by the time of Xenophon's writing.[113] But it also enacts Pandemos the Prostitute, sponsor of carnal love and, by devious routes, of all the "love magic" that went into making Pericles great, or at least seem that way.

And so when Socrates has finished with his lecture on love, Lycon, Autolycus' father and Socrates' future prosecutor, will pay the sage that highest of tributes: he will pronounce him a *kalos k'agathos*, a "man of quality." But note how Lycon expresses that not in terms of core essence but of outward appearance: "By Hera, Socrates, you certainly do appear to me a person of quality!" (*kalos ge k'agathos dokeis moi anthrôpos*, 9.1). One senses in those words genuine appreciation, but also recognition of the role of surfaces, of seeming, and with that, maybe a hint of doubt.

---

[113] See pp. 16–17 above.

6

CONCLUSIONS

RHETORIC, AESTHETICS, ETHICS, POLITICS — one might think that only one of those four directly concerns how things *should* be versus how they *are*. Still, as in Aristotle, so too in Bakhtin, ethics casts its net wide. Thus for the Russian thinker, poetics and aesthetics count as moral sciences concerned not just with the laws of form, but with an artist's responsibility to art and life. We can think of that as the ethical side to Bakhtin's dialogism. If all utterance is socially embedded, then none of it is immune to another's evaluation. *Otvetstvennost'* — answerability or responsibility — becomes, then, more than an aspect of human language. It becomes the very thing that gives meaning to human existence. Taken in context, it becomes the thinker's response to Stalinism, a centripetal discourse that believed itself answerable to none, and would stop at nothing to silence dissent.[1]

Yet Bakhtin, committed though he was to this many-voiced, center-fleeing vision of social discourse, arguably did not always think and write in tune with himself. In his writings, dialogue explains the linguistic side to human sociality; it supplies a framework for understanding literary creation. Yet it represents discourse not just as it is, but as it ought to be. Thus dialogue, simultaneously a tool of analysis and a defining ideal, points to fault-lines within approaches to which we apply the label "dialogical." For if a concept as value-laden as that provides the road-map for scholarly investigation, then does not the discourse of scholarship fall prey to a normativity Bakhtin himself might well have called "centripetal"? Is not scholarship so guided being guided not simply by theory, but by ideology?

I have been talking just now about Bakhtin. But one can surely say that about any discourse — intellectual, political, artistic, social — grounded in

---

[1] Responsibility-answerability (*otvetstvennost'*), the focus of early essays ("Toward a Philosophy of the Act," "Art and Answerability": Bakhtin 1990:1–3; Morson and Emerson 1990:68–74), remained fundamental to Bakhtin's thought from beginning to end.

the sorts of commonalities, Vološinov's ideological chain, without which no sharing of ideas can happen. How, then, to free our discourse from limits imposed by its ideological grounding? One way, perhaps the only way: to intervene with a system of rules to make sure that no single vision predominates. But if our study of dialogue has revealed anything, it is that all such interventions, seeking, as they do, to shape social discourse to fit some preconceived notion of what discourse should be all about, inevitably carry the earmarks of ideology. We need, then, to be realists. Rather than approach dialogue as a neat balancing act, we need to face the fact that individual voices will always seek power over others; that countervailing power derives only from a shared commitment to discursive freedom; that any shared commitment, no matter how benign, carries the potential to tyrannize over individual or group consciousness. For dialogue takes place in the space between perfect harmony and perfect chaos, the former, a featureless soundscape with nothing to listen for, the latter, mere noise drowning out whatever music there might be. Caught between those extremes, dialogue feels the tug of both: I speak to prove that I am one of you, I speak to assert my individuality. Driving dialogue will, then, be its attraction to either or both poles, a life-force insofar as it propels our sociality, a destructive force if it comes too close to consummation.

BIBLIOGRAPHY

Adams, J. N. 1982. *The Latin Sexual Vocabulary*. London.

Alexiou, M. 1974. *The Ritual Lament in Greek Tradition*. Cambridge.

Althusser, L. 1972. *Lenin and Philosophy, and Other Essays*. New York.

———. 1977. *Reading Capital*. Translated by Ben Brewster, ed. 2. London.

———. 1979. *For Marx*. Translated by Ben Brewster. London.

Ameling, W. 1981. "Komödie und Politik zwischen Kratinos und Aristophanes: Das Beispiel Perikles." *Quaderni catanesi di studi classici e medievali* 3:383–424.

Anderson, C. A. 1995. *Athena's Epithets: Their Structural Significance in Plays of Aristophanes*. Beiträge zur Altertumskunde; Bd. 67. Stuttgart.

Andrewes, A. 1978. "The Opposition to Perikles." *Journal of Hellenic Studies* 98:1–8.

Atkinson, J. E. 1992. "Curbing the Comedians: Cleon versus Aristophanes and Syracosius' Decree." *Classical Quarterly* 42:56–64.

Austin, J. L. 1975. *How to Do Things with Words*, ed. 2. Cambridge, Mass.

Badian, E. 1992. "Thucydides on Rendering Speeches." *Athenaeum* 80 [70]:187–190.

Bakhtin, M. M. 1981. *The Dialogic Imagination: Four Essays*. University of Texas Press Slavic Series no. 1. Translated by Caryl Emerson and Michael Holquist. Austin.

———. 1984a. *Problems of Dostoevsky's Poetics*. Theory and History of Literature, v. 8. Translated by Caryl Emerson. Minneapolis.

———. 1984b. *Rabelais and his World*. Translated by Hélène Iswolsky, ed. 1st Midland book. Bloomington.

———. 1986. *Speech Genres and Other Late Essays*. University of Texas Press Slavic Series, no. 8. Translated by Vern W. McGee. Austin.

———. 1990. *Art and Answerability: Early Philosophical Essays*. University of Texas Press Slavic Series, no. 9. Translated by Vadim Liapunov and Kenneth Brostrom, ed. 1. Austin.

Bakhtin, M. M., and P. N. Medvedev. 1985. *The Formal Method in Literary Scholarship: A Critical Introduction to Sociological Poetics*. Translated by Albert J. Wehrle. Cambridge, Mass.

Balot, R. K. 2001. *Greed and Injustice in Classical Athens*. Princeton.

Barringer, J. M. 2001. *The Hunt in Ancient Greece*. Baltimore.

Bassi, K. 1998. *Acting Like Men: Gender, Drama, and Nostalgia in Ancient Greece*. Ann Arbor.

Bell, M., and M. Gardiner. 1998. *Bakhtin and the Human Sciences: No Last Words*. Theory, Culture & Society. London.

Belloni, L., V. Citti, et al., eds. 1999. *Dalla lirica al teatro: nel ricordo di Mario Untersteiner (1899-1999), atti del convegno internazionale di studio, Trento-Rovereto, febbraio 1999*. Labirinti 43. Trento.

Ben, N. v. d. 1986. "Hymn to Aphrodite 36–291." *Mnemosyne* 39:1–41.

Bers, V. 1994a. "Tragedy and Rhetoric." In Worthington 1994:176–195.

———. 1994b. "Κοσμίως λέγειν." Paper presented at the "Onstage Offstage Conference", Yale University, New Haven, Conn.

———. 1997. *Speech In Speech: Studies in Incorporated Oratio Recta in Attic Drama and Oratory*. Lanham, Md.

Beta, S. 1999. "La 'parola inutile' nella commedia antica." *Quaderni urbinati di cultura classica* N. S. no. 63:49–66.

Billig, M. 1996. *Arguing and Thinking: A Rhetorical Approach to Social Psychology*, ed. 2. Cambridge and New York.

Blank, D. L. 1985. "Socratics versus Sophists on Payment for Teaching." *Classical Antiquity* 4:1–49.

Blundell, M. W. 1989. *Helping Friends and Harming Enemies: A Study in Sophocles and Greek Ethics*. New York.

Boedeker, D. D., and K. A. Raaflaub, eds. 1998. *Democracy, Empire, and the Arts in Fifth-Century Athens*. Cambridge, Mass.

Boegehold, A. L., and A. C. Scafuro, eds. 1994. *Athenian Identity and Civic Ideology*. Baltimore.

Bonnamour, J., and H. Delavault, eds. 1979. *Aristophane, Les femmes et la cité*. Les Cahiers de Fontenay, XVII. Fontenay aux Roses.

Brandist, C. 1996. "Gramsci, Bakhtin and the Semiotics of Hegemony." *New Left Review* 216:94–109.

———. 2002a. *The Bakhtin Circle: Philosophy, Culture and Politics*. London.

———. 2002b. "Two Routes To Concreteness" in the Work of the Bakhtin Circle." *Journal of the History of Ideas* 63:521–537.

———. 2004. "Voloshinov's Dilemma: On the Philosophical Roots of the Dialogic Theory of the Utterance." In Brandist et al. 2004:97–124.

Brandist, C., D. Shepherd, et al., eds. 2004. *The Bakhtin Circle: In the Master's Absence*. New York.

Brandist, C., and G. Tikhanov, eds. 2000. *Materializing Bakhtin: the Bakhtin Circle and Social Theory*. New York.

Branham, R. B. 2005. *The Bakhtin Circle and Ancient Narrative*. Ancient Narrative. Supplementum 3. Groningen.

Braund, D. 1994. "The Luxuries of Athenian Democracy." *Greece & Rome* 41:41–48.

Bremer, J. M. 2000. "The Amazons in the Imagination of the Greeks." *Acta Antiqua Academiae Scientiarum Hungaricae* 40:51–59.

Bremmer, J. N. 1984. "Greek Maenadism Reconsidered." *Zeitschrift für Papyrologie und Epigraphik* 55:276–286.

Brock, R. W. 1986. "The Double Plot in Aristophanes' *Knights*." *Greek, Roman and Byzantine Studies* 27:15–27.

Brunschwig, J., and G. E. R. Lloyd, eds. 2000. *Greek Thought*. Translated by Catherine Porter et al. Cambridge, Mass.

Burckhardt, A. 1924. *Spuren der athenischen Volksrede in der alten Komödie*. Basel.

Buxton, R. G. A. 1982. *Persuasion in Greek Tragedy: A Study of Peithō*. Cambridge.

Byl, S. 1982. "La mètis des femmes dans l'Assemblée des femmes d'Aristophane." *Revue belge de philologie et d'histoire* 60:33–40.

Calame, C. 1999. *The Poetics of Eros in Ancient Greece*. Translated by Janet Lloyd. Princeton.

Carpenter, T. H., and C. A. Faraone, eds. 1993. *Masks of Dionysus*. Myth and Poetics. Ithaca.

Carson, A. 1986. *Eros the Bittersweet: An Essay*. Princeton.

Carter, L. B. 1986. *The Quiet Athenian*. Oxford.

Cartledge, P., E. E. Cohen, et al. 2002. *Money, Labour and Land: Approaches to the Economies of Ancient Greece*. London.

Cartledge, P., P. Millett, et al. 1990. *Nomos: Essays in Athenian Law, Politics, and Society*. New York.

Cartledge, P. A., and F. D. Harvey. 1985. *Crux: Essays Presented to G.E.M. de Ste. Croix on His 75th Birthday*. History of Political Thought; v. 6, issue 1/2. London.

Christ, M. R. 1992. "Ostracism, Sycophancy, and Deception of the Demos: [Arist.] *Ath. Pol.* 43.5." *Classical Quarterly* 42:336–346.

———. 2006. *The Bad Citizen in Classical Athens*. Cambridge.

Classen, C. J. 1984. "Xenophons Darstellung der Sophistik und der Sophisten." *Hermes* 112:154–167.

Cobb-Stevens, V. 1985. "Opposites, Reversals, and Ambiguities: The Unsettled World of Theognis." In Nagy 1985:159–175.

Cohen, D. 1991. *Law, Sexuality and Society: The Enforcement of Morals in Classical Athens*. Cambridge.

Connor, W. R. 1971. *The New Politicians of Fifth-Century Athens.* Princeton.

———. 1985. "The Razing of the House in Greek Society." *Transactions of the American Philological Association* 115:79–102.

Cornford, F. M. 1907. *Thucydides Mythistoricus.* London.

Crane, G. 1992. "The Fear and Pursuit of Risk: Corinth on Athens, Sparta and the Peloponnesians (Thucydides 1.68–71, 120–121)." *Transactions of the American Philological Association* 122:227–256.

———. 1998. *Thucydides and the Ancient Simplicity: The Limits of Political Realism.* Berkeley.

Csapo, E. 1997. "Riding the Phallus for Dionysus: Iconology, Ritual, and Gender-Role De/construction." *Phoenix* 51:253–295, ill.

David, E. 1984. *Aristophanes and Athenian Society of the Early Fourth Century B.C.* Mnemosyne, Bibliotheca Classica Batava. Supplementum 81. Leiden.

Davidson, J. N. 1997. *Courtesans & Fishcakes: The Consuming Passions of Classical Athens.* New York.

Deleuze, G. 1990. *The Logic of Sense.* European Perspectives. Translated by Mark Lester with Charles Stivale. New York.

Dentith, S. 1995. *Bakhtinian Thought: An Introductory Reader.* Critical Readers in Theory and Practice. London.

Denyer, N. 2001. *Plato. Alcibiades.* Cambridge Greek and Latin Classics. Cambridge.

Derrida, J. 1981. *Dissemination.* Translated by Barbara Johnson. Chicago.

———. 1982. *Margins of Philosophy.* Translated by Alan Bass. Chicago.

———. 1991. *A Derrida Reader: Between the Blinds.* New York.

Detienne, M., and J.-P. Vernant. 1978. *Cunning Intelligence in Greek Culture and Society.* Translated by Janet Lloyd. Hassocks.

Dettenhofer, M. H. 1999. "Praxagoras Programm: eine politische Deutung von Aristophanes' *Ekklesiazusai* als Beitrag zur inneren Geschichte Athens im 4. Jahrhundert v. Chr." *Klio* 81:95–111.

DeVoto, J. G. 1992. "The Theban Sacred Band." *The Ancient World* 23:3–19.

Dillon, M. 1995. "By Gods, Tongues, and Dogs: The Use of Oaths in Aristophanic Comedy." *Greece & Rome* 42:135–151.

Dillon, M. P. J. 1999. "Post-nuptial Sacrifices on Kos (Segre, ED 178) and Ancient Greek Marriage Rites." *Zeitschrift für Papyrologie und Epigraphik* 124:63–80.

———. 2002. *Girls and Women in Classical Greek Religion.* London.

Dittmar, H. 1912. *Aischines von Sphettos, Studien zur Literaturgeschichte der Sokratiker; Untersuchungen und Fragmente.* Philologische Untersuchungen 21. Berlin.

Dobrov, G. W., ed. 1997. *The City as Comedy: Society and Representation in Athenian Drama*. Chapel Hill, N.C.

Dodds, E. R. 1959. *Plato. Gorgias: A Revised Text with Introduction and Commentary*. Oxford.

Dorati, M. 1998. "Lisistrata e la tessitura." *Quaderni urbinati di cultura classica* N. S. 58:41–56.

———. 1999. "Acqua e fuoco nella *Lisistrata*." *Quaderni urbinati di cultura classica* N. S. 63:79–86.

Döring, K. 1984. "Der Sokrates des Aischines von Sphettos und die Frage nach dem historischen Sokrates." *Hermes* 112:16–30.

Dorjahn, A. P. 1946. *Political Forgiveness in Old Athens; the Amnesty of 403 B. C.* Northwestern Studies in the Humanities no. 13. Evanston, Il.

Dougherty, C., and L. Kurke, eds. 1998. *Cultural Poetics in Archaic Greece: Cult, Performance, Politics*. New York.

Dover, K. J. 1968. *Lysias and the Corpus Lysiacum*. Sather Classical Lectures, v. 39. Berkeley.

———. 1972. *Aristophanic Comedy*. Berkeley.

———. 1974. *Greek Popular Morality in the Time of Plato and Aristotle*, ed. 2. Berkeley.

———. 1975. "The Freedom of the Intellectual in Greek Society." *Talanta* 7:24–54.

———. 1989. *Greek Homosexuality*, ed. 2. Cambridge, Mass.

Easterling, P. E., ed. 1997. *The Cambridge Companion to Greek Tragedy*. Cambridge.

Edmonds, R. G., III. 2000. "Socrates the Beautiful: Role Reversal and Midwifery in Plato's *Symposium*." *Transactions of the American Philological Association* 130:261–285.

Edmunds, L. 1987. *Cleon, Knights, and Aristophanes' Politics*. Lanham, Maryland.

———. 2001. *Intertextuality and the Reading of Roman Poetry*. Baltimore.

Ehlers, B. 1966. *Eine vorplatonische Deutung des sokratischen Eros. Der Dialog Aspasia des Sokratikers Aischines*. Zetemata: Monographien zur klassischen Altertumswissenschaft, Heft 41. Munich.

Eide, T. 1996. "On Socrates' atopia." *Symbolae Osloenses* 71:59–67.

Fairweather, J. 1981. *Seneca the Elder*. Cambridge.

Faraone, C. A. 1995. "The 'Performative Future' in Three Hellenistic Incantations and Theocritus' Second *Idyll*." *Classical Philology* 90:1–15.

———. 1996. "Taking the 'Nestor's Cup Inscription' Seriously: Erotic Magic and Conditional Curses in the Earliest Inscribed Hexameters." *Classical Antiquity* 15:77–112.

Fehling, D. 1988. "Phallische Demonstration." In Siems 1988:282–323.

Fisher, N. R. E. 1992. *Hybris: A Study in the Values of Honour and Shame in Ancient Greece.* Warminster, England.

———. 1998. "Violence, Masculinity, and the Law in Athens." In Foxhall 1998:68–97.

Fitzgerald, J. T., ed. 1996. *Friendship, Flattery, and Frankness of Speech: Studies on Friendship in the New Testament World.* Leiden.

Flashar, H. 1969. *Der Epitaphios des Perikles; Seine Funktion im Geschichtswerk des Thukydides.* Sitzungsberichte der Heidelberger Akademie der Wissenschaften. Philosophisch-Historiche Klasse. Jahrg. 1969, 1. Abhandlung. Heidlberg.

Foley, H. P. 1981a. "The Conception of Women in Athenian Drama." In Foley 1981b:127–168.

———. 1981b. *Reflections of Women in Antiquity.* New York.

———. 1982. "The Female Intruder Reconsidered: Women in Aristophanes, *Lysistrata* and *Ecclesiazusae.*" *Classical Philology* 77:1–21.

Forde, S. 1989. *The Ambition to Rule: Alcibiades and the Politics of Imperialism in Thucydides.* Ithaca.

Forrest, W. G. 1975. "An Athenian Generation Gap." *Yale Classical Studies* 24:37–52.

Foucault, M. 1990. *The History of Sexuality. Volume 2. The Use of Pleasure.* Translated by Robert Hurley. New York.

Fowler, R. L. 1996. "How the *Lysistrata* Works." *Échos du monde classique* 40:245–249.

Foxhall, L. 2002. "Accesses to Resources in Classical Greece: The Egalitarianism of the Polis in Practice." In Cartledge et al. 2002:209–220.

Foxhall, L., and J. B. Salmon. 1998. *When Men Were Men: Masculinity, Power and Identity in Classical Antiquity.* Leicester-Nottingham Studies in Ancient History, 8. London.

Frangeskou, V. 1999. "Tradition and Originality in Some Attic Funeral Orations." *Classical World* 92:315–336.

Funke, P. 1980. *Homónoia und arché: Athen und die griechische Staatenwelt vom Ende des peloponnesischen Krieges bis zum Königsfrieden (404/3-387/6 v. Chr.).* Wiesbaden.

Furley, W. D. 1996. *Andokides and the Herms: A Study in Fifth-Century Athenian Religion.* Bulletin of the Institute of Classical Studies. Supplement 65. London.

Gagarin, M. 1977. "Socrates' Hybris and Alcibiades' Failure." *Phoenix* 31:22–37.

Gaiser, K. 1959. *Protreptik und Pärenese bei Platon; Untersuchungen zur Form des Platonischen Dialogs.* Tübinger Beiträge zur Altertumwissenschaft, Heft 40. Stuttgart.

———. 1969. Review of Barbara Ehlers, *Eine vorplatonische Deutung der sokratischen Eros.* (Munich 1966). *Archiv für Geschichte der Philosophie* 51:200–209.

Gantz, T. 1993. *Early Greek Myth: A Guide to Literary and Artistic Sources.* Baltimore.

Gardiner, M. 1992. *The Dialogics of Critique: M. M. Bakhtin and the Theory of Ideology.* London.

Garrity, T. F. 1998. "Thucydides 1.22.1: Content and Form in the Speeches." *American Journal of Philology* 119:361–384.

Gehrke, H.-J. 1985. *Stasis: Untersuchungen zu den inneren Kriegen in den griechischen Staaten des 5. und 4. Jahrhunderts v. Chr.* Munich.

Gentzler, J. 1995. "The Sophistic Cross-Examination of Callicles in the *Gorgias.*" *Ancient Philosophy* 15:17–43.

Giannantoni, G. 1997. "L'*Alcibiade* di Eschine e la letteratura socratica su Alcibiade." In Giannantoni and Narcy 1997:349–373.

Giannantoni, G., and M. Narcy, eds. 1997. *Lezioni socratiche.* Naples.

Gomme, A. W., A. Andrewes, et al. 1970–1981. *A Historical Commentary on Thucydides.* Oxford.

Gooch, P. W. 1985. "Socrates: Devious or Divine?" *Greece & Rome* 32:32–41.

Graham, Alexander J. 1998. "The Woman at the Window: Observations on the 'Stele from the Harbour' of Thasos." *Journal of Hellenic Studies* 118:22–40.

Hall, E. 1993. "Political and Cosmic Turbulence in Euripides' *Orestes.*" In Sommerstein et al. 1993:263–285.

———. 1997. "The Sociology of Athenian Tragedy." In Easterling 1997:294–309.

Halperin, D. M. 1986. "Plato and Erotic Reciprocity." *Classical Antiquity* 5:60–80.

———. 1990. *One Hundred Years of Homosexuality and Other Essays on Greek Love.* New York.

Hamdorf, F. W. 1964. *Griechische Kultpersonifikationen der vorhellenistischen Zeit.* Mainz.

Hamel, D. 1998. *Athenian Generals: Military Authority in the Classical Period.* Mnemosyne, bibliotheca classica Batava. Supplementum 182. Leiden.

———. 2003. *Trying Neaira: The True Story of a Courtesan's Scandalous Life in Ancient Greece.* New Haven.

Hansen, M. H. 1987. *The Athenian Assembly in the Age of Demosthenes.* Oxford.

Hanson, V. D. 1995. *The Other Greeks: The Family Farm and the Agrarian Roots of Western Civilization*. New York.

Harris, E. M. 1992. "Pericles' Praise of Athenian Democracy (Thucydides 2.37.1)." *Harvard Studies in Classical Philology* 94:157–167.

Harvey, F. D. 1985. "Dona Ferentes: Some Aspects of Bribery in Greek Politics." In Cartledge and Harvey 1985:76–117.

Hedrick, C. W., Jr. 1999. "Democracy and the Athenian Epigraphical Habit." *Hesperia* 68:387–439.

Henderson, J. 1987. *Aristophanes. Lysistrata*. Oxford.

———. 1991. *The Maculate Muse: Obscene Language in Attic Comedy*, ed. 2. New York.

———. 1998. *Aristophanes. Acharnians. Knights*. Loeb Classical Library 178. Cambridge, Mass.

———. 2000. *Aristophanes. Birds. Lysistrata. Women at the Thesmophoria*. Loeb Classical Library 179. Cambridge, Mass.

———. 2002. *Aristophanes. Frogs. Assemblywomen. Wealth*. The Loeb Classical Library 180. Cambridge, Mass. and London.

Henrichs, A. 1993. " 'He Has a God in Him': Human and Divine in the Modern Conceptions of Dionysus." In Carpenter and Faraone 1993:13–43.

———. 1994. "Der rasende Gott: zur Psychologie des Dionysos und des Dionysischen in Mythos und Literatur." *Antike und Abendland* 40:31–58.

Henry, A. S. 1983. *Honours and Privileges in Athenian Decrees: The Principal Formulae of Athenian Honorary Decrees*. Subsidia epigraphica 10. Hildesheim.

Hesk, J. 2000. *Deception and Democracy in Classical Athens*. Cambridge.

Hess, W. H. 1963. "Studies in the *Ecclesiazusae* of Aristophanes." PhD dissertation, Princeton University, 1963.

Holquist, M. 1990. *Dialogism: Bakhtin and his World*. New Accents. London.

Homer, S. 2005. *Jacques Lacan*. Routledge Critical Thinkers. London.

Hornblower, S. 1991–. *A Commentary on Thucydides*. Oxford.

Hubbard, T. K. 1991. *The Mask of Comedy: Aristophanes and the Intertextual Parabasis*. Cornell Studies in Classical Philology, v. 51. Ithaca.

Huß, B. 1999. *Xenophons Symposion: Ein Kommentar*. Beitrage zur Altertumskunde, Bd. 125. Stuttgart.

Hussey, E. L. 1985. "Thucydidean History and Democritean Theory." In Cartledge and Harvey 1985:118–138.

Hutter, H. 1978. *Politics as Friendship: The Origins of Classical Notions of Politics in the Theory and Practice of Friendship*. Waterloo, Ontario.

Immerwahr, H. R. 1973. "Pathology of Power and the Speeches in Thucydides."
In Stadter 1973:16–31.

Isler Kerényi, C. 2001. *Dionysos nella Grecia arcaica: il conributo delle immagini.*
Filologia e critica 87. Pisa.

———. 2004. *Civilizing Violence: Satyrs on 6th-Century Greek Vases.* Orbis Biblicus
et Orientalis. Translated by Eric Charles de Sena. Göttingen.

Johnson, D. M. 2005. "Persians as Centaurs in Xenophon's *Cyropaedia.*"
Transactions of the American Philological Association 135:177–207.

Jordan, B. 1975. *The Athenian Navy in the Classical Period: A Study of Athenian
Naval Administration and Military Organization in Fifth and Fourth Centuries
B.C.* Berkeley.

Joyal, M. A. 1993. "The Conclusion of Aeschines' *Alcibiades.*" *Rheinisches
Museum* 136:263–268.

Kagan, D. 1975. "The Speeches in Thucydides and the Mytilenean Debate."
Yale Classical Studies 24:71–94.

Kahn, C. H. 1992. "Plato as a Socratic." *Studi italiani di filologia classica* 10:580–595.

———. 1994. "Aeschines on Socratic Eros." In Waerdt 1994:87–106.

Kalimtzis, K. 2000. *Aristotle on Political Enmity and Disease: An Inquiry into Stasis.*
SUNY Series in Ancient Greek Philosophy. Albany, N.Y.

Kallet, L. 1998. "Accounting for Culture in Fifth-Century Athens." In Boedeker
and Raaflaub 1998:43–58.

———. 2003. "*Demos Tyrannos*: Wealth, Power, and Economic Patronage."
In Morgan 2003:117–153.

Kambitsis, J. 1973. "'Ὄμματα Πειθοῦς." *Hellenica* 26:5–17.

Kofman, S. 1998. *Socrates: Fictions of a Philosopher.* Translated by
Catherine Porter. Ithaca, N.Y.

Konstan, D. 1993. "Friends and Lovers in Ancient Greece." *Syllecta
Classica* 4:1–12.

———. 1995. *Greek Comedy and Ideology.* New York.

———. 1996a. "Friendship, Frankness, and Flattery." In Fitzgerald 1996:7–19.

———. 1996b. "Greek Friendship." *American Journal of Philology* 117:71–94.

———. 1997. *Friendship in the Classical World.* Key Themes in Ancient History.
Cambridge.

Krentz, P. 1982. *The Thirty at Athens.* Ithaca.

Kurke, L. 1997. "Inventing the Hetaira: Sex, Politics, and Discursive Conflict
in Archaic Greece." *Classical Antiquity* 16:106–150.

Lakoff, G. 2006. "Staying the Course Right Over a Cliff." Op-Ed piece.
New York Times 27 October 2006, sec. A: 19.

Lakoff, G., and M. Johnson. 1980. *Metaphors We Live By.* Chicago.

Landfester, M. 1967. *Die Ritter des Aristophanes. Beobachtungen zur dramatischen Handlung und zum komischen Stil des Aristophanes.* Amsterdam.

Leitao, D. 2002. "The Legend of the Sacred Band." In Nussbaum 2002:143–167.

Lissarrague, F. 1993. "On the Wildness of Satyrs." In Carpenter and Faraone 1993:207–220.

Loraux, N. 1986. *The Invention of Athens: The Funeral Oration in the Classical City.* Translated by Alan Sheridan. Cambridge, Mass.

———. 1993. *The Children of Athena: Athenian Ideas about Citizenship and the Division Between the Sexes.* Translated by Caroline Levine. Princeton.

———. 1995. "Le Guerre civile grecque et la représentation anthropologique du monde à l'envers." *Revue de l'histoire des religions* 212:299–326.

———. 2002. *The Divided City: On Memory and Forgetting in Ancient Athens.* Translated by Corinne Pache and Jeff Fort. New York.

Ludwig, P. W. 2002. *Eros and Polis: Desire and Community in Greek Political Theory.* Cambridge.

MacDowell, D. M. 1971. *Aristophanes. Wasps.* Oxford.

Martin, R. P. 1987. "Fire on the Mountain: *Lysistrata* and The Lemnian Women." *Classical Antiquity* 6:78–105.

McGlew, J. F. 1993. *Tyranny and Political Culture in Ancient Greece.* Ithaca.

———. 2002. *Citizens on Stage: Comedy and Political Culture in the Athenian Democracy.* Ann Arbor.

Merkelbach, R. 1986. "Volksbeschluss aus Erythrai über den Bau eines Tempels der Aphrodite Pandemos." *Epigraphica Anatolica* 8:15–18.

Michelini, A. N. 1994. "Political Themes in Euripides' *Suppliants.*" *American Journal of Philology* 115:219–252.

———. 1998a. "Isocrates' Civic Invective: *Acharnians* and *On the Peace.*" *Transactions of the American Philological Association* 128:115–133.

———. 1998b. "ΠΟΛΛΗ ΑΓΡΟΙΚΙΑ: Rudeness and Irony in Plato's *Gorgias.*" *Classical Philology* 93:50–59.

Millett, P. 1989. "Patronage and its Avoidance in Classical Athens." In Wallace-Hadrill 1989:15–47.

Möllendorff, P. v. 1995. *Grundlagen einer Ästhetik der alten Komödie: Untersuchungen zu Aristophanes und Michail Bachtin.* Classica Monacensia Bd. 9. Tübingen.

Monoson, S. S. 1994. "Citizen as *Erastes*: Erotic Imagery and the Idea of Reciprocity in the Periclean Funeral Oration." *Political Theory* 22:253–76.

———. 2000. *Plato's Democratic Entanglements: Athenian Politics and the Practice of Philosophy.* Princeton.

Montag, W. 2003. *Louis Althusser.* Houndmills, England.

Morgan, K. A., ed. 2003. *Popular Tyranny: Sovereignty and its Discontents in Ancient Greece*. Austin.

Morrison, D. R. 1994. "Xenophon's Socrates as Teacher." In Waerdt 1994:181–208.

Morson, G. S., and C. Emerson. 1990. *Mikhail Bakhtin : Creation of a Prosaics*. Stanford, Calif.

Müller, H. M. 1980. *Erotische Motive in der griechischen Dichtung bis auf Euripides*. Hamburger philologischen Studien; Band 50. Hamburg.

Murphy, J. J. 2001. *Rhetoric in the Middle Ages: A History of the Rhetorical Theory from Saint Augustine to the Renaissance*. Tempe, Ariz.

Murray, O., ed. 1990. *Sympotica: A Symposium on the symposion*. Oxford.

Murray, P. 1996. *Plato on Poetry: Ion; Republic 376e-398b9; Republic 595-608b10*. Cambridge Greek and Latin Classics. Cambridge.

Nagy, G. 1985. "Theognis and Megara: A Poet's Vision of His City." In Nagy 1985:22–81.

Neil, R. A. 1901. *The Knights of Aristophanes*. Cambridge. Reprinted Hildesheim: 1966.

Neuman, Y. 2003. *Processes and Boundaries of the Mind: Extending the Limit Line*. Contemporary Systems Thinking. New York.

———. 2004. "Mirrors Mirrored: Is That All There Is?" *S.E.E.D. Journal (Semiotics, Evolution, Energy, and Development)* 4:58–69.

Neuman, Y., Z. Bekeman, et al. 2002. "Rhetoric as the Contextual Manipulation of Self and Non-Self." *Research on Language and Social Interaction* 35:93–112.

Neuman, Y., and I. Tabak. 2003. "Inconsistency as an Interactional Problem: A Lesson From Political Rhetoric." *Journal of Psycholinguistic Research* 32:251–267.

Newell, W. R. 2000. *Ruling Passion: The Erotics of Statecraft in Platonic Political Philosophy*. Lanham, Md.

Nichols, J. H., Jr. 1998. *Plato. Gorgias*. Ithaca and London.

Nightingale, A. W. 1993. "The Folly of Praise: Plato's Critique of Encomiastic Discourse in the *Lysis* and *Symposium*." *Classical Quarterly* 43:112–130.

North, H. F. 1994. " 'Opening Socrates': The Eikon of Alcibiades." *Illinois Classical Studies* 19:89–98.

Nussbaum, M. C., and J. Sihvola, eds. 2002. *The Sleep of Reason: Erotic Experience and Sexual Ethics in Ancient Greece and Rome*. Chicago.

O'Connor, D. K. 1994. "The Erotic Self-Sufficiency of Socrates: A Reading of Xenophon's *Memorabilia*." In Waerdt 1994:151–180.

O'Sullivan, N. 1992. *Alcidamas, Aristophanes and the Beginnings of Greek Stylistic Theory*. Hermes Einzelschriften, Heft 60. Stuttgart.

Ober, J. 1989. *Mass and Elite in Democratic Athens: Rhetoric, Ideology, and the Power of the People*. Princeton.

———. 1994. "Civic Ideology and Counterhegemonic Discourse: Thucydides on the Sicilian Debate." In Boegehold and Scafuro 1994:102–126.

———. 1996. *The Athenian Revolution: Essays on Ancient Greek Democracy and Political Theory*. Princeton.

———. 1998. *Political Dissent in Democratic Athens: Intellectual Critics of Popular Rule*. Princeton.

———. 2002. "Social Science History, Cultural History, and the Amnesty of 403." *Transactions of the American Philological Association* 132:127–137.

Olson, S. D. 1988. "The 'Love Duet' in Aristophanes' *Ecclesiazusae*." *Classical Quarterly* 38:328–330.

———. 2002. *Aristophanes. Acharnians*. Oxford.

Osborne, R. 1990. "Vexatious Litigation in Classical Athens: Sykophancy and the Sycophant." In Cartledge et al. 1990:83–102.

Ostwald, M. 1986. *From Popular Sovereignty to the Sovereignty of Law: Law, Society, and Politics in Fifth-Century Athens*. Berkeley.

———. 2000. *Oligarchia: The Development of a Constitutional Form in Ancient Greece*. Stuttgart.

Padgett, J. M. 2003. "Horse Men: Centaurs and Satyrs in Early Greek Art." In Padgett and Childs 2003:3–46.

Padgett, J. M., and W. A. P. Childs, eds. 2003. *The Centaur's Smile: The Human Animal in Early Greek Art*. New Haven.

Parke, H. W. 1977. *Festivals of the Athenians*. Aspects of Greek and Roman Life. London. Reprinted Ithaca: 1986.

Parker, R. 1996. *Athenian Religion: A History*. Oxford.

Parry, A. M. 1981. *Logos and Ergon in Thucydides*. Monographs in Classical Studies. New York.

Payne, M. 1997. *Reading Knowledge: An Introduction to Barthes, Foucault, and Althusser*. Cambridge, Mass.

Petrey, S. 1990. *Speech Acts and Literary Theory*. New York.

Pinney, G. F. 1984. "For the Heroes are at Hand." *Journal of Hellenic Studies* 104:181–183.

Pirenne-Delforge, V. 1994. *L'Aphrodite grecque: Contribution a l'étude de ses cultes et de sa personnalité dans le pantheon archaïque et classique*. Kernos Supplement 4. Athens.

Plaza, M. 2005. "The Limits of Polyphony: Dostoevsky to Petronius." In Branham 2005:193–225.

Pomeroy, S. B. 1975. *Goddesses, Whores, Wives, and Slaves: Women in Classical Antiquity.* New York.

———. 2002. *Spartan Women.* Oxford.

Price, J. J. 2001. *Thucydides and Internal War.* Cambridge.

Quillin, J. 2002. "Achieving Amnesty: The Role of Events, Institutions, and Ideas." *Transactions of the American Philological Association* 132:71–107.

Rechenauer, G. 1991. *Thukydides und die hippokratische Medizin: Naturwissenschaftliche Methodik als Modell für Geschichtsdeutung.* Spudasmata, Bd. 47. Hildesheim.

Reinders, P. 2001. *Demos Pyknites: Untersuchungen zur Darstellung des Demos in der Alten Komödie.* Drama: Beiträge zum antiken Drama und seiner Rezeption. Beihefte 15. M & P Schriftenreihe für Wissenschaft und Forschung. Stuttgart.

Rhodes, P. J. 1985. *The Athenian Boule,* ed. 2. Oxford.

Ribbeck, O. 1883. *Kolax. Eine ethologische Studie.* des IX. Bandes der Abhandlungen der philologisch-historischen Classe der Königl. Sächischen Gesellschaft der Wissenschaften, No. 1. Leipzig.

Riu, X. 1999. *Dionysism and Comedy.* Greek Studies. Lanham, Md.

Roberts, J. 1994. *Athens on Trial: The Antidemocratic Tradition in Western Thought.* Princeton.

Rocco, C. 1995–1996. "Liberating Discourse: The Politics of Truth in Plato's *Gorgias.*" *Interpretation* 23:361–385.

Rogers, B. B. 1910. *The Knights of Aristophanes.* London.

Roisman, J. 2005. *The Rhetoric of Manhood: Masculinity in the Attic Orators.* Berkeley.

Romilly, J. d. 1975. *Magic and Rhetoric in Ancient Greece.* The Carl Newell Jackson Lectures. Cambridge, Mass.

Rosellini, M. 1979. "*Lysistrata,* une mise en scène de la féminité." In Bonnamour and Delavault 1979:11–32.

Rosen, R. M. 1988. *Old Comedy and the Iambographic Tradition.* American Classical Studies 19. Atlanta.

———. 1997. "The Gendered Polis in Eupolis' *Cities.*" In Dobrov 1997:149–176.

Rosenbloom, D. 2004a. "*Ponêroi* vs. *Chrêstoi*: The Ostracism of Hyperbolos and the Struggle for Hegemony in Athens after the Death of Perikles, Part I." *Transactions of the American Philological Association* 134:55–105.

———. 2004b. "*Ponêroi* vs. *Chrêstoi*: The Ostracism of Hyperbolos and the Struggle for Hegemony in Athens after the Death of Perikles, Part II." *Transactions of the American Philological Association* 134:323–358.

Rosenzweig, R. 2004. *Worshipping Aphrodite: Art and Cult in Classical Athens.* Ann Arbor.

Rothwell, K. 1990. *Politics and Persuasion in Aristophanes' Eccleziazusae.* Mnemosyne, bibliotheca classica Batava. Supplementum 111. Leiden.

Rubin, L. G. 1989. "Love and Politics in Xenophon's *Cyropaedia*." *Interpretation* 16:391–413.

Rushton, R. 2002. "What Can a Face Do? On Deleuze and Faces." *Cultural Critique* 51:219–237.

Rusten, J. S. 1985. "Two Lives or Three? Pericles on the Athenian Character (Thuc. 2.40.12)." *Classical Quarterly* 35:14–19.

———. 1989. *Thucydides: The Peloponnesian War, Book II.* Cambridge Greek and Latin Classics. Cambridge.

Saïd, S. 1996. "*The Assembywomen*: Women, Economy, and Politics." In Segal 1996:282–313.

Sartori, F. 1999. " 'Rovesciare la democrazia' nell'ultimo Aristofane." In Belloni et al. 1999:141–158.

Saussure, d. 1986. *Course in General Linguistics.* Translated by Roy Harris, ed. 3. Chicago. Reprinted London: 1983.

Schauenberg, K. 1975. "*Eurumedōn eimi*." *Mitteilungen des Deutschen Archäologischen Instituts (Athen. Abt.)* 90:97–122.

Schiappa, E. 1992. "Response to Thomas Kent, 'On the Very Idea of a Discourse Community,' *CCC* 42 (December 1991), 425–45." *College Composition and Communication* 43:522–523.

———. 1999. *The Beginnings of Rhetorical Theory in Classical Greece.* New Haven.

Schlesier, R. 1993. "Mixtures of Masks: Maenads as Tragic Models." In Carpenter and Faraone 1993:89–114.

Scholtz, A. 1996. "Perfume from Peron's: The Politics of Pedicure in Anaxandrides Fragment 41 Kassel-Austin." *Illinois Classical Studies* 21:69–86.

———. 1997. "*Erastēs tou dēmou*: Erotic Imagery in Political Contexts in Thucydides and Aristophanes." PhD. diss., Yale University, 1997.

———. 2002/3. "Aphrodite Pandemos at Naukratis." *Greek, Roman and Byzantine Studies* 43:231–242.

———. 2004. "Friends, Lovers, Flatterers: Demophilic Courtship in Aristophanes' *Knights*." *Transactions of the American Philological Association* 134:263–293.

Schwartze, J. 1971. *Die Beurteilung des Perikles durch die attische Komödie.* Zetemata 51. Munich.

Scodel, R., ed. 1993. *Theater and Society in the Classical World.* Ann Arbor.

Seaford, R. 1996. *Euripides. Bacchae.* Warminster.

Seager, R. 2001. "Xenophon and Athenian Democratic Ideology." *Classical Quarterly* N. S. 51:385–397.

Segal, C. 1962. "Gorgias and the Psychology of the Logos." *Harvard Studies in Classical Philology* 66:99–155.

Segal, E., ed. 1996. *Oxford Readings in Aristophanes*. Oxford.

Sens, A. 1991. "Not I, but the Law: Juridical and Legislative Language in Aristophanes' *Ecclesiazusae*." PhD dissertation, Harvard University, 1991.

Shaw, M. 1975. "The Female Intruder: Women in Fifth-Century Drama." *Classical Philology* 70:255–266.

Shotter, J., and M. Billig. 1998. "A Bakhtinian Psychology: From Out of the Heads of Individuals and into the Dialogues between Them." In Bell and Gardiner 1998:13–29.

Shukman, A., ed. 1984. *Bakhtin School Papers*. Russian Poetics in Translation, v. 10. Oxford.

Sicking, C. M. J. 1995. "The General Purport of Pericles' Funeral Oration and Last Speech." *Hermes* 123:404–425.

Siems, A. K., ed. 1988. *Sexualität und Erotik in der Antike*. Wege der Forschung; Band 605. Darmstadt.

Smith, A. C. 1999. "Eurymedon and the Evolution of Political Personifications in the Early Classical Period." *Journal of Hellenic Studies* 119:128–141, pll. 8–11.

Sommerstein, A. H. 1981. *Aristophanes. Knights*. Warminster.

———. 1984. "Aristophanes and the Demon Poverty." *Classical Quarterly* 34:314–333.

———. 1986. "The Decree of Syrakosios." *Classical Quarterly* 36:101–108.

———. 1998. *Aristophanes. Ecclesiazusae*. Warminster.

Sommerstein, A. H., S. Halliwell, et al., eds. 1993. *Tragedy, Comedy, and the Polis. Papers from the Greek Drama Conference: Nottingham, 18-20 July 1990*. "Le Rane." Collana di studi e testi, 11. Bari.

Spence, I. G. 1990. "Pericles and the Defence of Attica during the Peloponnesian War." *Journal of Hellenic Studies* 110:91–109.

Stadter, P. A. 1989. *A Commentary on Plutarch's Pericles*. Chapel Hill.

———, ed. 1973. *The Speeches in Thucydides: A Collection of Original Studies with a Bibliography*. Chapel Hill.

Stone, I. F. 1988. *The Trial of Socrates*. Boston.

Taaffe, L. K. 1991. "The Illusion of Gender Disguise in Aristophanes' *Ecclesiazusae*." *Helios* 18:91–112.

———. 1993. *Aristophanes and Women*. London.

Taylor, A. E. 1934. *Philosophical Studies*. London. Reprinted New York: 1976.

Thornton, B. S. 1997. *Eros: The Myth of Ancient Greek Sexuality*. Boulder, Colo.

Tieman, W. 2002. " 'Cause' in History and the Amnesty at Athens: An Introduction." *Transactions of the American Philological Association* 132:63–69.

Todd, S. C. 2000. *Lysias*. The Oratory of Classical Greece, v. 2. Austin.

Too, Y. L. 1995. *The Rhetoric of Identity in Isocrates: Text, Power, Pedagogy*. Cambridge Classical Studies. Cambridge.

Tsifakis, D. 2003. " 'ΠΕΛΩΡΑ': Fabulous Creatures and/or Creatures of Death." In Padgett and Childs 2003:73–104.

Turner, J. S. 1993. "Atopia in Plato's *Gorgias*." *International Studies in Philosophy* 25:69–77.

Tylawsky, E. I. 2002. *Saturio's Inheritance: The Greek Ancestry of the Roman Comic Parasite*. Artists and Issues in the Theatre, v. 9. New York.

Ussher, R. G. 1973. *Aristophanes. Ecclesiazusae*. Oxford. Reprinted New Rochelle, N.Y.: 1986.

Vaio, J. 1973. "The Manipulation of Theme and Action in Aristophanes' *Lysistrata*." *Greek, Roman and Byzantine Studies* 14:369–380.

Vasiliou, I. 2002. "Socrates' Reverse Irony." *Classical Quarterly* 52:220–230.

Veligianni-Terzi, C. 1997. *Wertbegriffe in den attischen Ehrendekreten der klassischen Zeit*. Heidelberger althistorische Beiträge und epigraphische Studien, Bd. 25. Stuttgart.

Vlastos, G. 1987. "Socratic Irony." *Classical Quarterly* 37:79–96.

Vološinov, V. N. 1983. "Discourse in Life and Discourse in Poetry." In Shukman 1984:5–30.

———. 1986. *Marxism and the Philosophy of Language*. Cambridge, Mass.

Wade-Gery, H. T. 1958. *Essays in Greek History*. Oxford.

Waerdt, P. A. V., ed. 1994. *The Socratic Movement*. Ithaca.

Wallace-Hadrill, A. 1989. *Patronage in Ancient Society*. Leicester-Nottingham Studies in Ancient Society, v. 1. London.

Wankel, H. 1976. *Demosthenes: Rede für Ktesiphon Über den Kranz*. Wissenschaftliche Kommentare zu Griechischen und Lateinischen Schriftstellern. Heidelberg.

Weber, M. 1978. *Economy and Society: An Outline of Interpretive Sociology*. Translated by Ephraim Fischoff et al. Berkeley.

Weiss, M. 1998. "Erotica: On the Prehistory of Greek Desire." *Harvard Studies in Classical Philology* 98:31–61.

West, M. L. 1966. *Hesiod. Theogony*. Oxford.

———. 1978. *Hesiod. Works and Days*. Oxford.

Winkler, J. J. 1990. *The Constraints of Desire: The Anthropology of Sex and Gender in Ancient Greece.* New York.

———. 1991. "The Constraints of Eros." In Faraone, C.A. and D. Obbink, eds. 1991. *Magika Itiera: Ancient Greek Magic and Religion.* New York.

Winkler, J. J., and F. I. Zeitlin. 1990. *Nothing to Do with Dionysos? Athenian Drama in its Social Context.* Princeton.

Wohl, V. 2002. *Love among the Ruins: The Erotics of Democracy in Classical Athens.* Princeton.

Wolpert, A. 2002a. "Lysias 18 and Athenian Memory of Civil War." *Transactions of the American Philological Association* 132:109–126.

———. 2002b. *Remembering Defeat: Civil War and Civic Memory in Ancient Athens.* Baltimore.

Worman, N. B. 2002. *The Cast of Character: Style in Greek Literature.* Austin.

Worthington, I., ed. 1994. *Persuasion: Greek Rhetoric in Action.* London.

Yunis, H. 1996. *Taming Democracy: Models of Political Rhetoric in Classical Athens.* Rhetoric & Society. Ithaca.

Zappen, J. P. 2004. *The Rebirth of Dialogue: Bakhtin, Socrates, and the Rhetorical Tradition.* Albany.

Zastra, J. 1836. "De Aristophanis *Ecclesiazusarum* fabulae tempore atque consilio quaestiones selectae." Dissertation, Universität Breslau, 1836.

Zeitlin, F. 1988. "La politique d'Éros: Féminin et masculin dans les Suppliants d'Eschyle." *Métis* 3:231–259.

Zeitlin, F. I. 1996. *Playing the Other: Gender and Society in Classical Greek Literature.* Women in Culture and Society. Chicago.

Zimmermann, B. 1983. "Utopisches und Utopie in den Komödien des Aristophanes." *Würzburger Jahrbücher für die Altertumswissenschaft* 9, N.F.:57–77.

Ziolkowski, J. E. 1981. *Thucydides and the Tradition of Funeral Speeches at Athens.* Monographs in Classical Studies. New York.

INDEX

A

addressivity, 34, 85, 87
Aeschines Orator *Against Timarchus*
 (speech 1), 28–29, 58n58; *Against
 Ctesiphon* (speech 3), 49
Aeschines Socraticus, 111n1;
 Alcibiades 119–127
Aeschylus *Agamemnon*, 98;
 Eumenides, 17, 29n31;
 Suppliants, 17
aesthetics, 4–5, 145
affection, *see* love
Agyrrhius, 75
Alberic of Monte Cassino, 46n8
Alcibiades, 14, 18, 20, 49n21, 58, 73,
 111, 116–127, 129–131, 135, 140
Alcmaeon (Presocratic), 13–14
Althusser, L., 3–4, 7, 9
Amazons, 86–87
ambition, 2, 4, 14–15, 24n11, 27,
 29–30, 66–67, 91, 116, 121, 124,
 127, 133–134, 143
amnesty, 80–82, 100. *See also*
 forgetting

Andocides, 24, 49n22
Antiphon Orator, 23n5, 24
Antiphon Sophist, 57
Antisthenes, 111n1; fr. 132 *SSR*, 57
Aphrodite, 15–17, 88, 90; Aphrodite
 Hegemone, 16; Aphrodite
 Pandemos, 16–17, 90, 144,
 Aphrodite Ouranos, 16n68
apragmôn, apragmosunê, 63
architectonics, 6n21
archon eponymous, 78
aretê, see virtue
Aristogeiton, *see* Tyrannicides
Aristophanes, 59; *Acharnians*, 24n11,
 43, 56n47, 58n59; *Birds*, 92,
 107n126; *Assemblywomen*, 20,
 71–80, 89–92, 94–109; *Clouds*,
 92n79, 107n126, 126; *Frogs*, 65–66;
 Knights, 2–3, 20, 23–24, 43–47,
 51–70, 73, 75–76; *Lysistrata*, 18,
 20, 72, 79, 82–89, 90, 96–97, 102;
 Thesmophoriazusae, 62n74, 79,
 105n118; *Wasps*, 74; *Wealth*, 74
Aristophon, 65

Aristotle, 145;
Constitution of the Athenians, 78,
81; *Eudemian Ethics*, 16;
Historia animalium 95n91;
Nichomachean Ethics, 16, 49–50;
Politics, 36, 51, 78;
Rhetoric, 24, 25–26, 36, 40
Artemidorus, 13
Artemisia, 86–87
Aspasia, 62n74, 121n38, 138
assembly, 12, 17, 18, 19n78, 33,
40, 52–53, 55, 59n60, 64n83,
77, 84n53, 87, 94, 96–99, 119;
emergency assemblies, 71n2;
assembly pay, 75. *See also*
political oratory
Athena, 17, 81, 88–89; quarrel with
Poseidon, 81, 99–100, 102
atopos, atopia, 20, 111, 119, 128–129
Austin, J. L., 7, 50
author, authorship, 4–6, 9
axiôsis, 63–64

B

bacchants, *see* maenads
Bakhtin, M., 4–5, 7–9, 18–19, 24, 34,
40, 72, 91, 98, 108, 114n14, 145
Bateson, G., 85n57
Bers, V., 48n19, 50n26
Bessermachen, 111n2, 121
Billig, M., 79, 82
Boethius *In topica Ciceronis*, 46n8
boundary phenomena, 20, 112, 115
Brock, R., 2n3, 44n5, 62n72–73
bugger, buggery, *see* passivity, sexual
Bühler, K., 7

C

captatio benevolentiae, 37, 46, 55
carnival, carnivalesque, 8, 26, 69,
127–128
Carrol, L., 85
Carson, A., 118
castration, 86, 93
centrifugal discourse, 19, 91
centripetal discourse, 18–19, 40, 91,
108, 133, 145
Chrysippus, 117n28, 130
circumcision, 53
city, *see polis*
Clearchus of Soloi, 58
Cleon, 27n24, 43–45, 51n33, 61,
62–63, 68, 75
cognitive dissonance, 79
color, 49n24. *See also* spin
communalism, 71, 77–79, 89–91, 94,
98, 100–102, 105, 107
communism of love, 91
communism, *see* communalism;
communism of love
communitarianism, 15, 19, 78–79,
90–91, 94, 98, 100–102, 104–105,
107
concord, 5n18; civic, 16, 17–19,
20, 72–74, 78–79, 81, 103–105,
108–109, 144
concordia discors, 1, 4, 9, 19, 31, 73,
108–109
confiscation, 76–77, 101–102,
105n117. *See also* redistribution
consensus, *see* concord, civic
conspiracy, 73–75
contrary topics of common sense, 79
Cratinus, 14, 62n74, 69n95
Critias, 77, 108, 127, 135, 140
cuttlefish, 95–96
Cyrus, 139, 143

D

Darius, 2n5
de Man, P., 9n36
deception, 49, 54, 60, 63, 67, 76n25,
    95n91
deconstruction, 8–9, 113
Deleuze, 85, 117, 124, 130
Demades, *see* Pseudo-Demades,
demagogue, demagoguery, 2, 23,
    45n6, 56n46, 62–63, 65, 68, 71,
    75, 127, 130–131
demerast, *dêmerastês*, demerastic,
    44, 68, 130–132
democracy, 2, 11–20, 32–36, 38, 49,
    54, 56n49, 60–61, 63, 67–69,
    72–73, 76–78, 80–82, 93–94, 100,
    104–105, 108–109; dissolution
    of, 73–74, 77–78, 93
demophile, demophilia, 20, 44, 46–
    51, 53–54, 55, 59, 67–68
Demos son of Pyrilampes, 129
dêmos, 2, 10, 16, 19, 20, 24, 33–34, 36,
    38n62, 40, 41, 42, 43–44, 45–46,
    47–51, 52–54, 55, 59, 60–65,
    67–69, 71, 74, 77, 82, 87, 98,
    108–109, 129, 131–132, 139, 142.
    See also assembly
Demosthenes, 49;
    Third Olynthiac (speech 3), 51,
    55; *On the Chersonese* (speech 8),
    55; *On the Crown* (speech 18), 48;
    Against Meidias (speech 21), 93;
    Against Aristocrates (speech 23),
    49; *Against Timocrates* (speech
    24), 78; *Against Aristogeiton* 1
    (speech 25), 48n19; *Funeral
    Oration* (speech 60), 26–27;
    Eroticus (speech 61), 24n14;
    Exordia 53, 47, 66
dêmotikos, 49, 77

Derrida, J. 8–9, 113
desire, 2, 9–15, 17–20, 22–23, 28,
    39–42, 45n6, 47, 49–50, 66–67,
    107, 118, 124, 132, 141. *See also*
    epithumia; *erôs*; *himeros*
Diallagê, *see* reconciliation
dialogue, dialogical, 4–9, 10, 15,
    18–19, 20, 34, 83–86, 109, 112,
    114n14, 116, 117–119, 120, 124,
    127–128, 131, 133–135, 145–146
Dionysius *Demosthenes*, 24; *Isocrates*,
    24n15; *Thucydides*, 48, 64n80
Dionysus, Dionysian, 69, 115n19,
    120, 122–124
Diphilus, 137
direct discourse, 48. *See also*
    reported speech
discord, 1, 5n18; civic, *see* stasis
discourse community,
    see speech-community
dissonance, 1, 4–5, 9, 19, 20, 22, 31,
    38, 39, 42, 67, 78–79, 100. *See
    also concordia discors*
distinctions, logic of, 114n11
disturbance, 63, 99
dithyramb, 26–27
Dostoevsky, 5
Dover, J. K., 43–44, 81n43
dunamis, *dunasthai*, 14, 30, 38, 40–41

E

ecstasy, *ekastasis*, 18, 26, 122–123
Edmunds, L., 7n28
egalitarian, egalitarianism, 34–35,
    76–78, 94
ekklêsia, *see* assembly
ekphrôn, 122. *See also* ecstasy
elpis, 66
Empedocles, 1, 15–16

empire, Athenian, 32, 59, 61–62, 68, 72, 84, 89, 91, 100–101, 107–108
entheos, enthousiasmaos, 119, 121–123
epideictic oratory, 23–29, 31
epideixis, 27. *See also* epideictic oratory
epistêmê, 124
Episthenes, 41–42
epitaphios, see funeral oration
epithumia, 10n39, 24n11, 29, 30, 41, 46n11, 65, 139n102
eranos, 39
eristic, 140
erôs, Eros, 2, 4, 9–18, 19, 20, 22–25, 28–31, 37, 38–42, 43n2, 44, 45, 47, 51, 53n35, 54, 56–58, 62, 63, 65–66, 67–68, 90–91, 94, 96n96, 111–112, 116, 117n24–25, 118, 119–122, 124–126, 129–132, 134, 139, 141, 143n110, 144; communal, 11, 15–17, 39, 91; self-assertive, 11, 13–15, 41
erôs-vocabulary, 22–25, 28, 45n6
ethics, 20, 66, 128, 145
eu poiein, 52–53
eunous, eunoia, 46, 48n19, 49–50, 52–54, 87. *See also* goodwill
Euripides *Bacchae,* 107, 123; *Iphigenia at Aulis,* 29; *Medea,* 90; *Suppliants,* 34, 56, 76
evaluation, 7–8, 10–11, 13, 79, 84, 120, 127, 145
evaluative accent, 7–8, 11

F

fish, 96
flattery, 20, 44, 51n32, 54–61, 64–70, 74n16, 131, 136

forgetting, 72, 81–82, 88–89, 91, 99, 105, 108. *See also* amnesty; Lethe
fortune, 126
Foucault, M., 54n41, 66
Frangeskou, V., 26n21
friends, friendship, 44, 46, 49–50, 57, 81, 91, 111, 128, 131, 136, 138–139; help friends harm enemies, 57, 128. *See also philia*
frontloading, 133
funeral oration, 19, 21–22, 25, 26–28, 29, 37, 42, 62n70

G

gender, 1, 97, 99, 109. *See also* men; women
Gestalt, 114
goodwill, 20, 38n64, 46, 49, 53, 79, 84, 87
Gorgias, 25; *Funeral Oration* (fr. 6 D-K), 25, 26, 29; *Palamedes* (fr. 11a D-K), 23, 25; *Helen* (fr. 11 D-K), 25, 26, 29, 127
Gramsci, A., 7
greed, *pleonexia,* 14–15, 24n11, 30–31, 60n62, 65–66, 71n3, 76, 78, 90–91, 94, 98
gynaecocracy, 71, 75, 77, 79–80, 90–91, 94, 96n96, 97–98, 100–102, 105

H

Hall, E., 5
Halperin, D., 13, 54, 93–94
handshake, 6, 84–85
Harmodius, *see* Tyrannicides
harmonia, Harmonia, 15, 17, 74n17, 78, 90. *See also* harmony

harmony, 1, 3–4, 15–17, 31, 72, 90, 91, 104, 109, 115, 146. *See also harmonia*

Helen, 29–30

Heliastic oath, 78

Henderson, J., 44, 53n37, 53n40, 61n67

Hera, 62n74, 144

Hermagoreans, 49n24

herms, 4n14, 93–94

Hesiod *Theogony*, 15

Hesk, J., 49n24, 62n72

hetaira, Hetärentum, 57, 60n62, 74–75, 96, 99, 105, 106, 137n93, 138, 141. *See also* prostitution

hetaireia, 75. *See also* conspiracy

heteroglossia, 5

himeros, 9, 26

Hipparchus, 11n43, 12. *See also* Tyrannicides

hippeis, see knights

Hippias, 11n43, 86. *See also* Tyrannicides

Hippocratic Corpus, 10n39

Holquist, M., 85

Homer, 37; *Iliad*, 26, 63, 65

homonoia, 16–18, 20, 66n89, 72n9, 73–74, 81, 90–91, 104–105. *See also* concord

hope, 66

hoplites, hoplite class, 32, 97n103

Horace, 1

house, 83, 89–90, 92–94

hubris, 4, 20, 72, 76, 86, 93, 98n105, 102, 106, 107n124, 116–117

hunting, 69, 138–139

huperbolê, 27

Hyperbolus, 75

Hyperides *Against Athenogenes* (speech 3), 28; *Funeral Oration* (speech 4), 27

I

ideology, 1, 3, 4–5, 7–9, 10–11, 18n75, 19, 30n33, 31, 32n40, 34, 51, 54, 61, 65, 72, 76, 78, 79, 82, 84, 88, 89, 97, 128–130, 132, 145–146; ideological chain, 7–8, 10, 84, 88, 130, 145–146

imaginary, 3, 10–11

incest, 13

indirect discourse, 48. *See also* reported speech

individualism, 2, 12, 14–15, 17, 19, 41, 90, 146

intention, intentionalist, 6, 8, 124, 130

interpellation, 3

intertextuality, 4n15

irony, 112, 115, 128–129

isêgoria, freedom of speech (political right), 12, 15, 17–19, 73, 92, 98, 109, 104–105. *See also parrhêsia*

Isocrates, 23–25, 30, 40; *Panegyricus* (speech 4), 72, 78–79; *On the Peace* (speech 8), 47–48; *Helen* (speech 10), 29–30; *Antidosis* (speech 15), 24, 30; *Against Lochites* (speech 20), 93n82

isonomia, 14

iunx, 88–89, 96n97

J

jouissance, 56

judicial oratory, 20, 22–24, 25n16, 28, 44, 50n50, 76

jury pay, 54, 59, 61–62, 67

K

Kadish, G., 107 n125
kalos k'agathos, 52, 61, 62n73, 65,
    133–134, 135, 144
kasalbades, 106
kasalbas, 106. *See also* prostitution
Katapugosunê, 64n74
kêdesthai, kêdos, 45–46, 48n16
kharis, kharizesthai, pros kharin
    dêmêgorein, 51n32, 55n43, 56.
    See also flattery
khrôma, 49n24. *See also* spin
kinaidos, kinaidia, 60, 131, 134.
    See also passivity, sexual
knights, 32, 63, 65
kolax, kolakeia, 44, 54–58, 65, 66, 68,
    131, 134. *See also* flattery
Konstan, D., 1, 3, 61

L

Lacan, J., 10, 56n50
Landfester, M., 43n2, 44n5, 51n33,
    53n40, 55n42, 60, 62n72, 68n91
Lear, A., 51n33
Lenaea vases, 123
Lethe, 81, 99
logocentrism, 8
logos, 21–22, 37, 38, 40, 42, 68, 69, 89,
    91–92, 98n107, 99, 100, 116, 117
Loraux, N., 28
love, affection, fondness, 1, 15–17,
    20, 36–39, 43–54, 58, 66, 73n11,
    91, 111, 130–131, 141.
    See also erôs; kêdesthai; philia
lust, *see* desire; *erôs; himeros*
Lycurgus Orator, 29n29

Lysias, 23n5, 24, 46–47;
    Funeral Oration (speech 2), 18,
    26n21, ; *Against Agoratus*
    (speech 13), 50

M

madness, 9–10, 18, 28, 30, 39, 112,
    120–122, 126. *See also mania*
maenads, maenadism, 119–127
magic, 69, 96, 138–140, 144
mania, 120, 122. *See also* madness
manifestation, 85–86, 134, 136
marriage, 7n28, 17, 39, 50n27, 77n28,
    83n49, 89, 91
Marsyas, 116
masks, 112, 117, 120, 123–126, 129,
    135, 137, 140
mastropos, mastropeia, 137, 141–143.
    See also pimp
matchmaker, matchmaking, 121n38,
    138
McGlew, J., 28n26, 33, 38, 42n78,
    62n72, 97n102
medicine, medical, 23
Medvedev, P., 7
memory, 73–74, 80–82, 87–89, 99.
    See also amnesty; forgetting;
    mnêsikakein
men (gender associations *et sim.*),
    11, 12, 13, 15, 20, 28, 53, 58, 59,
    60n62, 61, 63, 71, 73–74, 79–80,
    83n51, 83–89, 92–102, 109, 124,
    125, 127, 133–134, 137. *See also*
    passivity, sexual; pederasty
Menander *Dyscolus*, 56–57
mesos politês, 12, 32
metacommunicative messages, 85
metaphor, 10, 13, 38, 67, 87, 96
metaphysics of presence, 8–9
middling citizen, *see mesos politês*

misogyny, 79, 102, 109
mnêsikakein, 80, 87–88, 102
monologue, 6n22, 8, 34, 117
monsters, 112, 118
mutilation of herms, *see* herms
Myronides, 76
Mysteries, profaning of, 93
Mytilenian debate, 44n5, 66

N

neikos, 16
Neuman, Y., 85n58, 130
Nicias, 4, 18
noble simplicity, 64–65, 69–70

O

Ober, J., 18, 33, 37, 61, 77n29, 101,
    111n2, 127n65
Oedipal dream, 13
oikos, see house
Old Oligarch, *see* Pseudo-Xenophon
Oligarchy of the Thirty, 50, 77, 82,
    93n82, 105n117
oligarchy, 2n5, 12n49, 14, 36n57, 65,
    69, 74, 75n19, 75n22, 76–78, 80,
    92n79, 108, 143n112
Oppian *Haleutica*, 95n91
orators/oratory, Attic, 22–24, 28–29,
    45–46, 49n24, 55, 68. *See also*
    epideictic oratory; judicial
    oratory; political oratory

P

paidia, see play
Panathenaia, 100
parrhêsia, frank speech, 131, 136, 141.
    See also isêgoria

passivity, sexual, 20, 43n3, 44, 53, 56,
    58–61, 64, 94, 117, 131, 134, 137
patriotism, patriotic, 19, 23, 24n11,
    27–28, 46–47, 49, 67
Pausanias, 90
pedagogy, 12, 20, 116–117, 119–121,
    123–127, 130–131, 138–141
pederasty, 11–12, 15–16, 28, 38, 42,
    43–44, 51–54, 56, 58, 64, 116–117,
    130–131, 138n97, 141–143
peithô, Peitho, 16–17, 38n60, 53, 69,
    84, 86, 90, 95n89, 96, 98
Pericles, 2n5, 14, 19, 21–22, 27, 31–33,
    35, 41, 47–48, 62n74, 69n95, 91,
    139, 142, 144
philia, philos/philê, philein, 15–16,
    38–39, 45–54, 55n45, 57–58,
    65–66, 73, 91, 111, 130–131, 136,
    139
philodêmos, 55
philopolis, to philopoli, 38n60, 47–48.
    See also patriotism
philosophy, *philosophia*, 113, 119,
    127, 129, 132–134; Isocratean, 31
Phrynichus *Capture of Miletus*, 80
pimp, pimping, 112, 135, 137–144
plague, 42, 62, 73
Plato, 111n1; 128n66; *Apology*, 45,
    47; *First Alcibiades*, 111, 130–131,
    135; *Gorgias*, 10–11, 127–135,
    136; *Hipparchus*, 12; *Ion*, 122;
    Phaedrus, 58, 112–113, 135, 139;
    Republic, 14, 58; *Symposium*, 16,
    20, 58, 111, 115–118, 135
play, playfulness, 112, 135–136, 143
playing the other, 124, 134, 135, 137
pleonexia, see greed

Plutarch *Alcibiades*, 58, 93; *Caesar*, 13; *De fraterno amore*, 81; *De laude ipsius*, 48; *Praecepta reipublicae gerendae*, 80–81; *Quaestiones convivales*, 81, 136; *Theseus*, 90

Pnyx, 64n83, 84n53, 94, 97

polis, 3, 11–20, 21–28, 32, 38–40, 46, 69, 83, 89–91, 93, 108, 128, 131

political oratory, 10, 23–24, 25n16, 33, 40, 44, 45, 55, 68, 73–74, 94, 96, 98n107, 99

polupragmôn, polupragmosunê, 63, 66. *See also* disturbance

polyphony, 4–5, 91

ponêros, 63n76, 75

pornos/pornê, porneia, 53n35, 60, 105–106, 138n98. *See also* prostitution

Poseidon, 29, 101; quarrel with Athena, 81, 99–100, 102

possession, 120, 122–123. *See also entheos*

poverty, 19n78, 32, 61, 67–68, 71, 72, 77–78, 136

power, 2, 9, 11, 13–15, 17, 19, 21–22, 25, 30, 34, 37–39, 41, 44, 45, 58n55, 61, 62n72, 63, 66, 67, 80, 83, 95n89, 104, 108, 121, 123–124, 127, 146. *See also dunamis*

prepon, 24

proagôgos, 137. *See also* pimp

prostitution, 20, 41, 53, 58–60, 74–75, 96n93, 99, 105–106, 137–139, 141n107, 143. *See also hetaira; kasalbas; pornos*

Protagoras, 140

prothumia, 49n12

Pseudo-Demades, 23

Pseudo-Xenophon, 32, 61–62, 77

public funeral, 21, 26, 33, 40. *See also* funeral oration

puknotês, 64

Pythagoras, 91

Q

quietism, 63, 74

quilting point, 10

quotation, *see* direct discourse; indirect discourse; reported speech

R

rape, 106

re-accentuation, 8

reason, rationalism 4, 21–22, 25, 27, 30–31, 37, 38, 40, 42, 100, 111–112, 122, 124, 126. *See also logos*

reconciliation, Reconciliation, 80, 82, 88, 108

redistribution, 76–78, 107

reported speech, 50–51. *See also* direct discourse; indirect discourse

revalorization, 31, 22, 28–31, 44, 64–65

rhetoric, 2, 9, 10, 25n16, 31, 34n48, 37, 45–46, 62n72, 64, 68, 94, 96, 113, 121n38, 127–129, 131n79, 132, 134; of *stasis*, 64

Rothwell, K., 95n89, 96n96–97, 97n102

S

Sacred Band, *see* Theban Band

salvation, safety, 16, 71, 94, 107n130

Sappho, 100

satyrs, 20, 115–118
Seneca the Elder, 49n24
sense, *sens*, 127, 130–131, 136, 139
sex, sexuality, 9–10, 11–13, 15, 17,
  22–23, 28–29, 42, 43–44, 52–54,
  58n59, 66–67, 77, 80, 83, 87–89,
  92, 95n89, 96, 106–107, 115,
  117, 137, 139–141, 143. *See also*
  desire; *erôs*; *himeros*; passivity,
  sexual; pederasty
shaking hands, *see* handshake
ship of state, 96
Shotter, J., 82
Sicilian Debate, 18, 40, 42, 108
Sicilian expedition, Sicilian debate,
  4n14, 18, 40–41, 42, 83, 87, 108
silens, *see* satyrs
simulacrum, 124–125, 132
slaves, slavery, literal, 13, 56n48, 58,
  65, 92; metaphoric (erotic, etc.),
  2n4, 58, 131, 132, 133
social reality, 9, 143
sociality of language, 6–7, 72, 79, 84,
  130, 145
Socrates, 10–11, 12, 14, 20, 26n21,
  27–28, 58, 81n43, 92n79, 111–144;
  impiety trial, 81n43, 126
Socratic literature, 111
Solon, 142
sophists, sophistic, 27, 45, 107n126,
  113, 126–129, 131n79, 134,
  139–141
Sophocles *Antigone*, 28, 39, 65;
  Oedipus at Colonus, 90
Sosicrates, 16
sôtêria, 16, 71, 73. *See also* salvation
Sparta, Spartan, 16, 28n26, 31–32,
  41, 62, 73, 76n26, 77, 142
speech genre, 24, 40
speech-act, 6n22, 7, 34, 50–51, 84

speech-community, discourse
  community, 7, 20, 22, 31, 40, 79,
  94, 97
Spencer-Brown, G., 114n11
spin, 2, 8–9, 30, 34, 49, 53–54, 64, 68,
  79, 113n8, 125n59, 130, 138, 140
Stadter, P., 27
Stalinism, 145
stasis, 2, 14–15, 17, 20, 29n31, 32, 33,
  40, 44, 62–67, 72, 72–74, 76n26,
  78–79, 80–82, 86–87, 88, 91,
  102–104, 107, 108, 143
state, *see polis*
Stilpo, 117–118
Stoics, 117n28
stuprum, 13
Suetonius *Julius*, 13
sunômosia, 75. *See also* conspiracy
sussitia, 77
sycophancy, 73
symptomatic reading, 3–4
synoecism, 89–91

T

teaching, *see* pedagogy
tekhnê, 121–122, 132
Theban Band, 16
theia moira, 121–122
Themistocles, 121, 124–125, 139, 142
Theodote, 138–139
Theognis, 63
Thirty Tyrants, *see* Oligarchy of the
  Thirty
thôpeia, *thôpeuein*, 54, 55n42–44, 56,
  57, 59, 89. *See also* flattery
Thucydides, 4, 14, 18, 21–22, 25,
  27n24, 32–42, 45, 63–65, 66, 67,
  93, 102–103, 108
tragedy, tragic, 5, 92, 123, 126

tukhê, see fortune
Typhon, 112–113, 118
Tyrannicides, 11–13, 15–16, 29n29
tyranny, 2n4, 12, 13–14, 38, 58, 59,
    61, 62n74, 69n94–95, 74, 86, 92,
    108, 109

U

utopia, utopian, 62n70, 69, 91–92,
    100

V

virtue, *aretê*, 35, 119, 121n38, 125,
    142–143
Vlastos, G., 115, 118
Vološinov, V., 6–8, 10, 31, 50–51,
    84–85, 115, 130, 143n111, 146

W

weaving, 87, 92
Weber, M., 91
wedding, *see* marriage
Winkler, J., 93
Wohl, V., 4, 10, 33–34, 39, 44n5,
    45n6, 93n84
women (gender associations *et sim.*),
    13, 20, 28, 41, 71, 73, 78–80,
    83–89, 90–91, 94–99, 109, 124.
    See also gynaecocracy
women's rule, *see* gynaecocracy
words versus deeds, 35, 48

X

Xenophon, 20, 111n1; *Anabasis*, 41–42;
    Apology, 121n36; *Cyropaedia*,
    139, 142, 143; *Hellenica*, 108;
    Memorabilia, 126, 138–142;
    On Hunting with Dogs, 139 ;
    Symposium, 111, 115, 135–144.
    See also Pseudo-Xenophon

Y

Yunis, H., 56n46

Z

Zeitlin, F., 17, 124n57
Zeno of Citium, 16
Zeus, 14, 26, 29, 62n74, 69n95; Zeus
    sôtêr, 71n1